PROBLEM OF THE SELF
Consciousness, Subjectivity and the Other

Edited by
Manidipa Sen

AAKAR

Problem of the Self: Consciousness, Subjectivity and the Other
Edited by Manidipa Sen

First Published 2019

ISBN 978-93-5002-567-3

Published by
AAKAR BOOKS
28 E Pocket IV, Mayur Vihar Phase I
Delhi 110 091 India
aakarbooks@gmail.com

Laser Typeset at
Arpit Printographers, Delhi 110 032

Printed at
D.K. Fine Art Press, Delhi 110 052

Contents

Preface

The present volume is the outcome of an international conference on "Problem of the Self: Debates in Consciousness, Subjectivity and Otherness", held in the Centre for Philosophy, School of Social Sciences, Jawaharlal Nehru University, New Delhi, on 23-25 January, 2013. Most of the essays (except for the ones by Nishad Patnaik and Ajay Verma) included in the volume were part of the conference.

I would like to, at the outset, take this opportunity to thank the contributors of this volume who patiently bore with me during the long delay in bringing out the book. I am truly grateful to them for their scholarly contributions—which, I am sure, will be of interest to many researchers working in this field. There are many others who participated in the conference but could not contribute to this volume for some reason or the other. They are: Dan Zahavi, Nivedita Gangopadhyaya, Madhucchanda Sen, Maushumi Guha, Prasenjit Biswas, Bhagat Oinam, Rasmus Jensen, Albert Newen, and Kranti Saran. I am certain their contributions would have considerably enriched this volume. Nonetheless, I would like to take this opportunity to express my gratitude towards them for their participation in the conference.

The idea of holding a conference on the above theme was, however, conceived a couple of years before it actually took place when I visited the Centre for Subjectivity Research at the University of Copenhagen in Denmark. There I came across a vibrant and dynamic group of philosophers engaged in questions of self and subjectivity from a truly interdisciplinary perspective. I was certain that philosophy community in India would greatly benefit from an interaction with at least some of the philosophers working in the Centre. Thus my interaction with them, in particular with Nivedita Gangopadhyaya and Dan Zahavi, culminated in holding of the conference. I would like to express my sincere thanks to both of them for helping me formulate my thoughts on the theme of the conference as well as putting me in touch with many of the international scholars who participated in the conference.

I am deeply grateful to the colleagues at the Centre for Philosophy who readily accepted my proposal for organising a conference on the above theme. I am especially thankful to my colleagues Bhagat Oinam, who was also the coordinator of the conference, and Bhaskarjit Neog, who enthusiastically assisted me in organizational matters. The research students of the Centre for Philosophy were another source of support in making the conference possible and I cannot but express my deep appreciation for the work they put together in making the conference a success. During the course of the conference several colleagues both from JNU and from other Universities chaired the different sessions and enriched the event by their intellectual interventions. They are, Vibha Chaturvedi (Delhi University), V. Sanil (IIT-Delhi), Rakesh Chandra (Lucknow University), Ashby Burton (Metropolitan State University, Denver, USA), and Gurpreet Mahajan and Franson Manjali (both from JNU). The then Chairman of Indian Council of Philosophical Research, Mrinal Miri delivered the inaugural address, while my senior colleague Late Satya P. Gautam summed up the proceedings of the conference in his valedictory address. I sincerely appreciate their participation in the conference. I cannot but feel extremely saddened by the fact that Satya P. Gautam is no more with us to see the published proceedings of the conference.

I am indebted to Jawaharlal Nehru University University for financially supporting the conference. I am grateful in particular to the then Vice-Chancellor, Rector, and the Dean of the School of Social Sciences, S.K. Sopory, Sudha Pai, and Mridula Mukherjee respectively, for providing us with a vibrant intellectual environment for pursuing our research activities which we sorely miss at this point of time!

Last but not the least, my sincere thanks to Mr. K.K. Saxena of Aakar Books for the prompt and efficient manner in which he brought out volume, and the effort he and his team made in publishing it.

This conference was the third in a series of international conferences on various debates in contemporary philosophy of mind that were organized in the Centre for Philosophy between 2007 and 2013. We were fortunate enough to be able to have a large number of scholars of national and international repute participating in these events. We were generously funded by the University to organize these academic events. This intellectual journey has helped me personally to enhance and further my research and teaching in the domain of self and consciousness. I am thus happy that this anthology of scholarly essays brings together varied but interrelated debates centering round the nature of the self and its relation to consciousness, subjectivity and the role of the other in its understanding, from diverse philosophical perspectives such as, phenomenology, analytic philosophy of mind and classical Indian philosophy.

JNU, New Delhi **Manidipa Sen**

Introduction

Our experience of the world and thought about the same, presupposes a subject of experience or thought, a self who is the experiencer or the thinker. What is the nature of the self? Does the self exist over and above the body? If it does exist independent of the body, where does it really exist? These are questions that have bothered philosophy from its very inception. In fact, one can say that scepticism regarding the nature of the self and questions regarding its ontological status, are as old as philosophy itself. However, in recent debates centering round the nature of the self, a more closer investigation has been made concerning issues of consciousness, subjectivity and the role of the other in the understanding of the self. The insight behind this may be that the nature of the self can be understood and unravelled only by a closer look into the way consciousness enters into the very articulation of the nature of the self. Do all coherent conceptions of the self necessarily imply understanding the self as a subject of world-involving experiences? Do intentional or content-directed mental states, such as perception or thought, which are about the world, reveal the most fundamental form of self-awareness? Or is self-awareness a form of consciousness revealed in its uniqueness when purged of any robust experiential content about the world? Moreover, can we conceive of the notion of a self without there being self-consciousness or self-reflexivity? What features of consciousness best captures the notion of self—is it intentional or phenomenal or do we need to reconcile between these two features of consciousness?

All these questions indicate that the notions of consciousness and subjectivity may themselves be as problematic as the notion of self itself. Understanding the very idea of our being conscious often is intimately connected with the idea of having a first-person perspective on ourselves, or by noticing that human beings (and may be other animals as well) would not have been able to cope with the world unless they saw things from their own points of view, that is, in terms of the "I" who is encountering the world. It is this being an "I" or experiencing oneself from a first-person perspective, that seems to constitute the very nature of consciousness. The important point to highlight is that "I'-thoughts seem to convey an additional meaning than thoughts about the world or other human beings, though it may not necessarily presuppose an entity over and above an embodied human being. What is it about our "I"-thoughts that provide this additional meaning? What is it that makes a thought to the effect that I am in pain distinct from a thought that Manidipa is in pain? One can say that it is the subjectivity of experience ('what-it-is-like' character of experience) that provides uniqueness to "I"-thoughts. But on the other hand, it has also been pointed out that the uniqueness of "I"-thoughts can be appreciated only when we are able to position the "I" in relation to "you" or 's/he". Thus, our subjectivity is meaningful or contentfull only in relation to not only other human beings, but in relation to the rest of the world. Recent debates in the Philosophy of Mind and Phenomenology concerning the relationship between consciousness and selfhood have focused on these debates which need further investigation.

The proposed book is a collection of scholarly articles written by philosophers looking into the debates centering round the self both from contemporary Western philosophical perspectives as well as classical Indian philosophy. Thus contributions in the book investigate in detail the relation between the notion of the self and the notion of subjectivity or the subjective character of conscious states as well as the relationship between the self and the other. Is it at all possible to think of a pure subjectivity without taking into consideration the intersubjective dimensions of our conscious experience? How does the notion of the other help conceptualize the notion of the self? If intersubjectivity is to elucidate the notion of the self, do we need to think of the other in terms of a radically foreign otherness, capable of highlighting who the self is by a stark contrast to who it is not? Or does the otherness of the other highlight who the self itself is by revealing the self's similarity to another subject of experience? What is the relationship between the question of intersubjectivity and the question of otherness? Can this relationship be understood merely ontologically, or more importantly through considerations which are primarily ethical? Important and critical perspectives can emerge regarding the above questions as well as the answers to them through a dialogue between classical Indian philosophies and contemporary Western philosophies.

The first few papers in this volume, therefore, look at the difficulties that surround in an understanding of the concept of self itself. What is it that constitutes the self? How are we to get a grip on the notion of "I" that is so intimately connected with the self, since learning the use of the pronoun "I" seems to be the first and the most intimate way of being aware of the self? We thus start with the paper entitled "I and Me: The Ambigous Self". In this paper, Bijoy Boruah deals with the paradox that surrounds the very notion of the self. Self's awareness of itself, that is self-awareness, makes the self the object of awareness. But how can the subject itself, the knower, become the object of awareness, that is, the object known? It is paradoxical precisely because in our self-awareness or I-consciousness, we can never be aware of the self as the subject of experience. If the subject of experience, in the awareness of it, can be presented only as the object of that awareness, then we can never be aware of ourselves as the subject that we are. In order to make a headway into this paradox, Boruah makes a distinction between I-ness versus Me-ness, the former capturing the idea of subject-self, while the latter capturing the object-self. According to the author the incompatibility and thereby ambiguity between these two aspects of the self, makes the very notion of the self elusive for us. How are we to overcome this paradox and make sense of the notion of self? Boruah suggests that the paradox is a result of a particular way of understanding self-awareness—an understanding which takes self-awareness to be a cognitive or an epistemic state. If we are able to rid ourselves of this particular model of self-awareness we will, according to the author, be able to integrate the I-self with the Me-self. The paper argues for such an integration.

Connected with the above concerns is the question: How are we to place the self in the larger world? Is it an object like any other object in the world? Answering these questions in the negative, R.C. Pradhan, in his contribution to this volume, argues for a metaphysical self—a self who has to be transcendentally present in order for self-awareness as well as awareness of the world be possible. As the author points out, his aim in this paper is two-fold. He not only wants to show that conscious first-person experience requires a metaphysical subject who is the bearer of those experiences, but he further wants to argue, unlike many phenomenologists, that this metaphysical self is constituted by these first person experiences. Taking clues from Kant, Husserl, and Wittgenstein, Pradhan wants to maintain that the metaphysical self is also the transcendental self—without which our experience, language, normativity and the world itself cannot be understood. It is the self that provides us with the very possibility of understanding and thus is the subject presupposed, rather than encountered, in any understanding.

As opposed to a metaphysically essentialist account of the self, many philosophers, belonging to distinct philosophical traditions, have tried to argue for an impermanent and transient self. The most important among them have been the Budhhist philosophers. Christian Coseru, in his contribution to this volume, called "Presence of Mind: Consciousness and the Sense of Self", takes up a challenge for this Buddhist philosophical stance of rejecting a permanent self. Coseru relates the debate concerning the transient notion of the self with our understanding of the phenomenal character of conscious experience. Phenomenal character of conscious experience, as David Chalmers observes, "characterizes aspects of what it is like to be a subject (what it is like to be me right now, for example, or what it is like to be a bat), or what it is like to be in a mental state (what it is like to see a certain shade of green, for example, or what it is like to feel a certain sharp pain)." (See his article "The Representational Character of Experience" in http://consc.net/papers/representation.html). This kind of phenomenal character or properties of conscious experience, according to Coseru, comes with a sense of first-person ownership, a sense that these properties are mine. However, the transient notion of the self precludes the possibility of such 'mineness' of experience, and thus the ownership of experience. Along with this difficulty that needs to be addressed by the Buddhist account of self, there is a further problem in this account as highlighted by the author. Since the Buddhists reject the very notion of a permenanet self, questions concerning personal identity (for example, how is it that I seem to be the same person over a period of time?) can be answered only by an appeal to experiential or phenomenological grounds. But, as Coseru points out, this phenomenological ground brings in the sense of ownership implicit in first-person experience. Based on this problematization, Coseru explores what constitutes the sense of self, and what sort of notion of self-consciousness can be supported on phenomenological grounds.

The notion of the self is closely connected with that of self-knowledge. In fact, one can say that the epistemological question concerning how I know myself in a way determines a certain ontological account of the self. In traditional philosophical understanding of self-knowledge, it has been considered distinct from knowledge of the world that surrounds us and knowledge of other minds, due to the special features of immediacy and infallibility. My knowledge of my own mental states is transparent to me in a way that it precludes the possibility of doubt. Hence I can never be mistaken about it. C.A. Tomy, in his paper "Minimal Self and Infallibilty of Self-Knowledge" deals with the connection between the epistemic and the ontological questions that arise with regard to the notion of the self. According to the author, there are at least three different and even contesting notions of the self, which he terms "self as given", "self as constructed" and "self as posited". Self as given can also be regarded as a "minimal self", and these minimal selves are transient. But it is with respect to this minimal self, according to the author, that we can claim infallible knowledge. So, infallibilty is not a feature of any and every form of self-knowledge, it is, in fact, a feature of knowledge of a very distinctive kind of self.

As we have noted earlier, Buddhists reject self as the owner of experience. They also, alongside this, reject the idea of a self as the agent of actions (and action here includes thinking of thoughts as well). The question that arises then is, if Buddhist philosophers deny the existence of a self as an experiencer or as a thinker, how can any cognition ever be possible? In his essay, "Core Selves and Dynamical Attention Centering: Between Buddhaghosa and Brian O'Shaughnessy", Jonardon Ganeri deals with this question by considering the suggestion of replacing the notion of self as agent of action and owner of experience with that of "self as an attention centering", clearly an epistemological notion. This idea is available in the Therāvādin Buddhist philosopher, Buddhoghosa and in a contemporoary philosopher of mind, Brian O'Shaunessy. Philosophers who do not accept a permanent and enduring self, have very often identified self with a stream of consciousness, a stream of continuous but ever-changing experiences, one succeeding the other. O'Shaunessy claims that attention consists in nothing but systemetacity or structuring of the stream of consciousness. So, for O'Shaunessy, as Ganeri observes, attention is necessary for consciousness, rather than consciousness being necessary for attention. This idea of the "attention centering" nature of the self fits well with the Buddhist idea of *citta*. How can *citta*, being devoid of any metaphysical underpinnings, be understood in terms of the idea of attention centering ground for cognition? That is the main question that Ganeri addresses in the paper.

Amita Chatterjee in her article "The Testimony of Ananyā: Ramchandra Gandhi's Reconstruction of Self and Subjectivity" critically evaluates a particular interpretation of the Buddhist theory of no-self provided by Ramchandra Gandhi. Gandhi, in his book *Sita's Kitchen: A Testimony of Faith and Enquiry* (State University of New York Press, New York, 1992), draws a parallel between the Buddhist no-self theory with the Upanisadic theory of one supreme self. Can the Buddhist notion of the no-self, which culminates in their idea of emptiness be compared to the non-dualist truth of the Upanisads? This is the question that is at the center of the discussion in this paper. By engaging with this original work of a contemporary Indian philosopher, Chatterjee tries to show that identification of the Upanisadic monism and Buddhist theory of emptiness defeats the point that Gandhi wants to argue for in his book. Hence this set of papers deal mainly with distinct epistemic concerns that centers around self and its knowledge. Ajay Verma's contribution to the volume is also a detailed exposition of the subject-object relation and/or dichotomy in an account of knowledge in Nyāya, Buddhism and Advaita Vedānta. Though the main question is an epistemological one, Verma gives it a phenomenological turn by conceiving of the 'object' of knowledge as the 'other' of the subject/knower/experiencer. Through a close reading of these three most important schools of thoughts in Indian Philosophy the author brings out the distinct notions of the 'Other" in them.

Intimately connected with questions concerning nature and knowledge of the self, is the notion of subjectivity that characterizes and constitutes the subject of experience. The next few papers try to unravel the complex web of connection between notions of experientiality, subjectivity, interiority and self-reflexivity. Therefore, in the paper entitled, "Reflexive Self-Awareness and Subjectivity: Revisting a Dialogue", Tal Correm wants to explore what kind of subjectivity is entailed by the very act of being aware of ourselves reflexively. As the author mentions in the very first footnote of the essay, "I use 'subjectivity' and 'self' alternately", her essay is not merely about subjectivity that characterizes the self, but about subjectivity as being identified with the self. She opens up a dialogue between two most important philosophers from two traditons, Edmund Husserl from the phenomenological tradition and Dinnāga from the Buddhist philosophical tradition in order to show the connection between reflexive self-awareness and subjectivity/ self. The contrast between Husserl and Dinnāga lies in the point that Dinnāga's notion of reflexive self-awareness does not involve a self as such, while Husserl's seems to do so. However, the main aim of the paper is to argue, contrary to what may initially seem, that the notion of subjectivity in Husserl is weaker than the one rejected by Dinnāga. But if we do not think of subjectivity as a prerequisite to experience, and hence distinct from it, how are we to account for the 'mineness' of our experience? That is, how are we to take an experience as mine, as opposed to yours? These questions lead to the next paper in this anthology by Matthew Mackenzie.

In his paper, "Reflexivity, Subjectivity and the Enacted Self", Mackenzie makes a case for anātmavāda (no-self thesis) inspired by another Buddhist philosopher, Sāntarakshita. He begins his paper by raising three questions, to put it in his own words, "First, does consciousness necessarily involve subjectivity? Second, what is the connection, if any, between self-consciousness and subjectivity? And, third, does consciousness necessarily involve an ego or self?" His answer to the first question is in the affirmative, while to the third one is negative. The relationship between self-consciousness and subjectivity is understood in terms of reflexivity or self-luminosity of consciousness. It is this relationship that is worked out in detail in the paper. The idea of self as an emergent and enacted subjectivity is what the author argues for in this paper, as opposed to a substantive notion of the self.

Though the subject is constituted by its subjectivity this subjectivity is not closed within the subject as such but it is constituted and affected by something outside of it—by those other subjectivities that it has to encounter and negotiate with and by the larger world around her. Hence the next few papers are concerned with the question of how and in what sense such subjectivity is affected by something outside of it. Siby George's contribution to the volume "The Affected Subject and the Case of Individuating Pain" looks precisely into this aspect of selfhood. After considering the different ways (in particular, by Martin Heidegger, Edmund Husserl and Immanuel Levinas) in which affected subjectivity has been understood in 20th century continental philosophy, the author goes on to discuss how individuation of pain takes place. The experience of pain poses a particularly difficult challenge for philosophers who accept the exteriority of subjectivity precisely because pain seems to be the most intimate, unshareable, personal and inexpressible of all subjective experiences. The main aim of the paper is to argue that the interiority of the experience of pain and the exteriority of subjectivity need not and in fact, cannot be considered as antithetical to each other. The very notion of subjectivity and experientiality of pain brings with it the affectation that comes from outside the privacy of the subject.

The problematic of the other, the exterior, the outside of the self, cannot be comprehensively dealt with unless and until we relook at the dynamic relationship between the self and the body or that which seems to be the immediate outside/other of the self. In his paper "Facing the Other: Merleau-Ponty and the Ethical", T.V. Madhu reflects upon Merleau-Ponty's concept of "body subject", a subject who is essentially embodied and embedded. But then does not the body remain interior since wherein lies the other in this embodied subjectivity? Comparing the views of Levinas and Merleau-Ponty the author tries to locate the ethical in the complex relationship between the self, the other and the body.

David Carr's contribution to the volume, "Subjectivity and History", as the very name suggests, explains the connection between the notion of subjectivity and that of time. Our subjectivity, though constituted by the present experiences, this present in our experience is founded on its relationship with the past as well the future. Thus there is a continuity of subjectivity in time and through time. Drawing upon the phenomenological tradition, Carr further points out that this temporality of subjectivity is 'historical'. Because of the intentionality of consciousness, our experience is directed outwards—it relates to something beyond itself. But this outside is a world of individuals and groups of individuals, events involving others, their suffering and actions, the world of artifacts and of human creations—that is, a world replete with meaning. Hence what we experience as and what constitutes our subjectivity is not only, as the author suggests, the experience of the social world, but experience as occurring socially. These two notions of temporality (of the past, present and future) and that of the social world is woven together by the author to argue for a kind of intersubjectivity where the "I" is replaced by the "we". Nishad Patnaik takes the idea of historicity of subjectivity forward in his article "Science and the Promise of Objective Knowledge: Husserl's Intersubjective Renewal". Husserl's phenomenological enterprise is an attempt to question both psychologism as well as naturalism. This leads to a critique of the positivist notion of science, a critique of the so-called objective world and the immediacy of experience that accompanies knowledge of such a world. Following upon Husserl's idea that our life-world, of which natural science is a part, is historically mediated, suggests that there is no way of returning to a pre-given immediacy of the objective world, since what is objective is always already temporal and intersubjective in nature. The paper aims to argue whether one can make sense of the "renewal of the 'originally' *constituted* sense of 'objectivity' prior to its positivistic reduction" of the idea of the objective and whether that can be grafted into Husserl's idea of the historically constituted intersubjectivity.

Another aspect of the subject's encounter with the world and the other, an aspect which is also ethical in nature is that of the subject's freedom. Two contributions in this anthology by Wenjing Cai and Hans Feger deal with the question of freedom with respect to the subject's encountering of the world. As Cai points out, by a close reading of Heidegger's account of freedom, the subject is necessarily connected with the world of objects, not in any epistemic sense of the term but in a more primordial ethical sense. The question that she further undertakes to answer in this essay is concerning the relationship between self-understanding and world-understanding. The author argues that the very notion of self-understanding involves my letting the world be "in being obligated by them." More importantly, the precise question that the article tries to answer is: If we accept Heidegger's point that the relationship between the self and the world is such that we let ourselves be bound by things, that is, we, in a way let ourselves surrender to the world around us, then how is self-legislation, which is at the core of the freedom, possible? The author, in trying to answer this question delves into the similarities and differences between Kant's and Heidegger's idea of freedom, as well as the idea of the self in Heidegger that emerges once self embraces the world along with its freedom and that of others. Feger's article, "The Chain of Freedom: Moral Autonomy with Cosmopolitan Intent", directly takes up questions of freedom and autonomy in Kant's ethical and political philosophy. How is self's autonomy realized through freedom? How does freedom operate when we act morally? How does individual freedom position itself vis a vis the modern communitarian and cosmopolitan lives of individuals? These are some of the important queries that are addressed by a close reading of Kant. The author highlights the idea of the "chain of freedom", that is nothing but the possibility of "self-creation", and explains the contours of this very notion.

Thus we can legitimately say that the fifteen contributions to this volume bring out the multitude of concerns centering around the notion of the self. But they go further in connecting these puzzles with larger issues in metaphysics, epistemology and ethics—from self's being an ontological entity, to its rootedness in the unique way we comprehend ourselves as subjects of experience, to its further encounter as its temporal, intersubjective and ethical being.

1

I and Me: The Ambiguous Self

Bijoy H. Boruah

***I-am*-ness**

I am a person and therefore I am someone. My *personal being*, my existence as a person, allows the following existential generalization: 'There is someone insofar as there is (exists) this person.' This also means that I gratuitously enjoy the status of being someone by virtue of being a person. One might then say that the property of *being someone* that I possess in virtue of being a person is existentially gratuitous. What is existentially gratuitous about this statement is that no information is conveyed in stating that there is someone *beyond* the information contained in the statement that there is a (or this) person. This statement is quite analogous to, and structurally isomorphic with, the following statement: 'There is something (in reality) insofar as there is (exists) this elementary particle.'

All this is obvious and trivial as far as it goes. However, this person, who is someone, is not *just* someone, just *a* person, in the way, say, this post box in the city is just a post box amongst many other similar post boxes. There is the *further* fact about this person—a fact which is other than the existentially gratuitous fact of being someone—namely, the fact that *I* am that someone. One might say that this person's being someone is very special in that the person, unlike the post box, is one that has the peculiarity of being *oneself*. This special and peculiar way of being someone is an ontological peculiarity—a peculiar mode of being-in-the-world not true of a post box's being a post box in the world.

It is true, of course, that just as a person has the property of being *oneself*, so also a post box has the property of being *itself*. Why can't we therefore say, in the same vein, of the post box, that it also has the ontological peculiarity of being *itself*? After all, this particular post box, being a particular entity, *has* to be itself—i.e. has to have the self-referential ontological property of 'being *itself*'—rather than anything *other* than itself. Is it not a point about *being* and therefore of ontology, even if the ontological point is non-descriptive?

Perhaps being itself is a non-descriptive, self-referential ontological property of being something, or anything, including being a person. In fact, 'being itself' is not just a property of being or ontology; it is also a formal logical property insofar as the logic of identity holds of every entity: 'everything is identical with itself'. It can therefore be said that 'being itself' is a logico-ontological property which is true of being anything whatsoever, e.g. elementary particles, post boxes, persons, numbers and so on.

Now, this logico-ontological property *being-itself* can be given an existentialist twist, with reverence to Jean Paul Sartre, to yield two distinct properties which are both ontological in character: namely, being-*in*-itself and being-*for*-itself. These two properties are meant clearly to mark out the difference in the nature of being some*thing*, say a post box, and being some*one*, a human person.

Being a post box is not just being itself, being the thing that it is; it is also a being *in-itself* in the sense that it exists in the non-relational, self-contained mode of being. The post box's existence is 'in itself' rather than 'in relation to' (or essentially dependent on) something else, nor does it exist in relation to itself. In contrast, the being of a human person is essentially relational in the sense that the existence of a person is inescapably *apparent* to the person herself. Being a person is ontologically self-revealing, which implies that the person inevitably exists in the self-relational mode of being. This is precisely because consciousness is a constitutive dimension of being a person. Unlike being a post box, being a person is being conscious of being a person. Self-awareness is what accounts for a person's being *for* itself.

It is part of the meaning of being-for-itself—of being someone—that the being in question is aware of being the person one is. This awareness of being oneself is expressed in the act of self-acknowledgement: *I am* (this or that someone). One might say that I-am-ness, which is the content of (explicit or tacit) self-acknowledgement, is the core of personal being, and the very sense of being a person. Personhood is reflexive and the reflexivity consists in this core sense of being the person one is.

For any person to say, or just to have the implicit awareness, that *I am this person* is not to entertain a predicative thought, namely the thought that the predicate 'this person' is true of me. Nor is this thought one of asserting the identity between me and this person. Rather, the existential self-awareness expressed in the dictum *I am* is the ontic mode in which this entity has the reflexive identity of being a person. Thus, the thought *I am this person* is not really propositional or judgemental, but more of an existential gesture of self-acknowledgement—the acknowledgement of being oneself. One might like to construe this as the inner ontic principle of personal existence, of personal selfhood, that must be countenanced as a core idea of what could be described as the *phenomenological ontology of personhood*.

The above sense of 'self' as consisting in the feeling as well as conviction of I-am-ness is applicable to a person understood diachronically, as persisting over time. But at any stage in the life of a person, howsoever small the person-stage might be, *I-am-ness* is true of the person *for* the person at that stage. Whether we talk about the whole person or of particular person-stages in the whole life of a person, what underlies the idea of being an *I* or self is essentially the concept of being a *subject* of awareness, whether awareness of feeling, thought or action that constitute the mental life of a person. Indeed, this is the most fundamental sense of what it is to be a self, that is, its essential subjectivity or subjecthood.

Subjecthood, or the sense of I-ness, is metaphysically significant inasmuch as it introduces, and thereby necessitates, the concept of a 'perspectival being'—a being that has a 'point of view' on the world and a first-personal sense of *its* being in the world. In other words, a human being is a person basically in virtue of the first-person perspective or I-consciousness. There is obviously someone in the world when a person exists in it, and this is an impersonal objective fact about the world. But, of everyone who is a person in the world, there is a subjective fact that corresponds to the first-personal thought or assertion, 'I am in the world' uttered or tacitly acknowledged by the person. Personal existence—a person's own existence—is ontologically perspectival in that it is, as it were, existence in the eye of I-consciousness. Being a person is thus a first-person-centered phenomenon in the realm of being.

I-ness *versus* Me-ness

Given that personal existence is existence in the eye of I-consciousness, what precisely is the nature of I-consciousness? The awareness of being oneself is, of course, a basic awareness that is at the core of being a person, an awareness which constitutes a condition for the possibility of being a person. Being aware of oneself *as* oneself is the self-intimating character of personhood, and another name for I-consciousness or self-awareness. Self-intimation implies that there is a subject or I to which the experience of intimation is attributed. The presence of a subject or I is thus an explanatory requirement for the grasp of the phenomenology of self-intimation. However, the nature of attribution of the experience of self-intimation is far from clear.

One would naturally infer that a subject to which any experience is attributed is distinct from the experience. This inference is understandable because, just as the dancer is distinct from the dance, so is the experiencer distinct from the experience. But the analogy is false; the experiencer is *in* the experience in the way the dancer is not in the dance. The dancer can or would exist even when she discontinues her dance, but it would be meaningless to talk about the experiencer existing without experiencing anything at all. The subject of experience is an inherent feature of the structure of experience. It therefore is immanent in experience, or in the experiential stream of consciousness. Equating the subject of experience with the self, Dan Zahavi argues that the subject 'is not something that stands opposed to the stream of consciousness, but is, rather, immersed in conscious life; it is an integral part of its structure' (Zahavi 2005: 125).

The fundamental point about experiences, and our conscious life in general, is what Zahavi calls their 'first-personal givenness' that makes them *subjective*, and that 'entails a built-in self-reference, a primitive experiential self-referentiality' or 'mineness' (Zahavi 2005: 122). That experiences are characterized by first-personal giveness just means that they are immediately revealed as one's own, as *mine* or as having the for-me-ness quality. What is at the root of first-personal givenness or intrinsically self-specific presence of experience is the reflexivity of consciousness. Experiential awareness is immanently self-aware. So the so-called subject-self is a structural feature of the immanent reflexivity of consciousness.

It is the subjecthood of the self inherent in experiential states that has become a controversial issue in the analysis of self-awareness or self-consciousness. Can the subject of experience really be aware of itself *qua* the subject of experiential awareness? In other words, does reflexive self-awareness of experience imply that one is aware of the subject of experience *as it is in the original state* of its subjecthood? Galen Strawson has recently revived this issue that is said to have ancient roots (Strawson 2011).

Apparently the question is baffling: how can the subject of experience be aware of itself as a *subject* of experience? How can I-consciousness, which is consciousness in the first-person perspective, turn itself around in full circle and thereby, as it were, withdraw into itself so as to realize what it is like to be the locus of the first-person perspective? Since the subject is the 'locus' or 'origin' of the first-person perspective, it is not within the purview or focus of awareness, any more than the eye is within the purview of its own sight, or the finger tip is amenable to touch by itself.

Of course ordinary locutions on self-awareness tell a different story of its possibility. Locutions like 'I know myself when I do that' or 'I am aware of myself brushing my teeth' or 'I was conscious of myself trying not to look like a nervous person' are all instances of self-awareness. But there is a clear distinction in all these instances between 'I' and 'me'. The self that is *my*-self in these examples is not the self that is *I*, because the *I* here is the subject-self, who is aware of *me*, which is not the subject-self but the object-self of this awareness. Anything that I am aware of is *eo ipso* an object of awareness from the viewpoint of the subject that I am. So the I-consciousness of the subject-self is the first-person perspective of consciousness, and what I am conscious *of* from that perspective must be something other than the I itself. If it is none other than *me* that I am conscious of, then this 'me' is an object of I-consciousness. It is my self-image, an image of personal subjectivity, which is reflected in, and comes under the purview of, I-consciousness. *I* do not appear to I-consciousness inasmuch as the *I* is the conscious point of view from which anything appears. What of course appears is *me*—an image of my own subjectivity which is exclusively represented in I-consciousness as an *object* of consciousness. The subject of consciousness is the unrepresented and invisible perspectival source of the representation of all objects including what is *myself*.

William James is quite clear on this distinction between the self-as-subject and the self-as-object, between *I* and *Me*. He elaborates this distinction in the following passage:

> Whatever I may be thinking of, I am always at the same time more or less aware of *myself*, of my *personal existence*. At the same time it is *I* who am aware; so that the total self of *me*, being as it were duplex, partly known and partly knower, partly object and partly subject, must have two aspects discriminated in it, of which for shortness we may call one the *Me* and the other the *I* (James 1892: 176).

James is not unaware that 'the identity of *I* with *me*, even in the very act of their discrimination, is perhaps the most ineradicable dictum of common sense.' He therefore reiterates that this is discrimination in terms of *aspects* of the self, and not an ontological discrimination. Nevertheless, this discrimination in regard to aspects of the self is sharp enough to articulate a significant ambiguity in the notion of self. The metaphysical import of this ambiguity is that being a self in the subject dimension is ontically incompatible with being a self in the object dimension, even though there is no ontological self-division corresponding to this incompatibility.

The ontic incompatibility of the *I*-self conceived under the subject-aspect with the *Me*-self conceived under the object-aspect—the incompatibility of *I*-ness and *me*-ness—renders the concept of self, to use Gilbert Ryle's memorable phrase, 'systematically elusive'. It is elusive insofar as the performance of any I-thought or self-concerned thought is concerned. For this self-concerned, self-directed performance (e.g. self-commentary or self-admonition) is, in Ryle's words, 'not dealt with in the operation which it itself is. [He would know that] he has failed to catch more than the flying coat-tails of that which he was pursuing. His quarry was the hunter' (Ryle 1963: 188-89). The implication is that the inner pursuit of the subject of awareness by that very subject—the pursuit of self-awareness in short—is as doomed to failure as the pursuit of the hunter somehow deluded into conceiving of himself as the quarry.

If the object of self-pursuit is supposed to be the subject-self which is ontically precluded from being an *object* of awareness at all, the pursuit is clearly a self-defeating one. So the self under the subject-aspect, the *I*-self, resists undistorted capture of itself in the purported act of self-awareness, because the execution of any such act would amount to adopting the inevitably objectifying gaze of consciousness. As soon as the self is caught in the objectifying gaze of consciousness, the result is a radical aspectual change from I-dimensional subjectivity to objective me-dimensional selfhood. The intended self of self-awareness eludes forever.

Lived-Experiential I-Awareness

What is clear by now is that any attempt for an undistorted capture of the *I*-self is doomed to failure so long as self-awareness is conceived as a matter of experiential self-encounter between the subject of awareness and itself. The frustrating phenomenological scenario is that of a subject of experience attempting to represent what it is like to be this very subject. Whatever phenomenal representation is formed in that way is tantamount to the emergence of a *new* subject of experience instead of capturing the original subject of experience. The entire effort is, to quote Ryle's eloquent phrase, 'logically condemned to eternal penultimacy' (1963: 186), forever one step away from grasping what it is like to be the original subject-self.

It might therefore be argued that the systematic elusiveness of self-awareness is a consequence of applying a mistaken model, which is the standard *epistemic* model, to the understanding of the possibility of I-dimensional self-awareness. According to this model, any epistemic situation consists of a cognizing subject and that which is cognized. There is thus a methodological gulf between the cognizer and the cognized, and true cognition is a successful relation between the two. So the scenario of self-awareness is set up in a paradoxical way, with the subject of experience as cognizer *vis-a-vis* the same subject of experience posed as what is to be cognized. But this methodological principle of epistemic dichotomy can hardly be applicable in this case, since the requirement is the impossible requirement of a single subject of experience mysteriously splitting into two, so that the first-person perspective—which is the perspective of being a subject—is to come under arrest in an experience emanating from that perspective itself.

The standard epistemic model is therefore inapplicable if we believe that self-awareness is possible. That it is inapplicable was clear to some philosophers long ago. Samuel Alexander had understood this quite well. According to Alexander, I am aware of myself while being aware of an object, 'not in the sense that I contemplate myself, for I do not do so, but in the sense that *I live through this experience of myself*' (quoted in Strawson 2011: 289, emphasis added). As a subject of experience I have a 'lived-experiential' awareness of being a subject of experience or *I*-self. There is no curious phenomenological situation of the subject-self having to capture, as an isolated datum of consciousness, *what it is like to be the locus of the first-person perspective* just as one occupies that very locus of consciousness.

There is no mysterious hiatus in the phenomenological flow of consciousness for an encounter between the original I-self and a shadowy replica of it. Instead, there occurs a direct self-apprehension inasmuch as my being a subject of experience is 'alive' *in* the experience I have of something. The first-person perspective, or the perspective of being a subject-dimensional self, is both immanent and has its quasi-phenomenal presence in the episode or stream of experience.

In Strawson's precise terminology, who favours what I have called the 'lived-experiential' interpretation of self-awareness, 'all awareness on the part of any subject at any moment comports awareness, at that moment, on the part of the same subject, of that very awareness at that very moment' (2011: 283). In short, 'all awareness comports awareness of itself'. Strawson's 'present-moment self-awareness' thesis (PSA) takes recourse to Russellian 'knowledge by acquaintance' as a way of defusing the power of Ryle's claim that 'my today's self perpetually slips out of any hold of it that I try to take' (1969: 187). The present moment of any awareness is such that the subject has direct acquaintance with itself as the subject of that moment's experience. The moment is an occurrent experience precisely because the subject of experience is alive in the experiential episode or stream. It is a moment of self-cognition by direct acquaintance with the subject-dimensional self immanent in the experience.

The direct-acquaintance view that explains PSA seems to me to be on the right track for yielding a viable theory of I-dimensional self-awareness. But I think we must realize that there is a simple, though insightful, ontic twist in the formulation of this approach. The subject of awareness in the present moment is directly acquainted with itself, in its I-dimensional subjectivity, in virtue of *being* the subject of experience it actually is. Given this ontic feature of the phenomenon, it is clear that self-awareness is not a relational form of awareness that characterizes all awareness in the standard epistemic or cognitive scenarios. Rather, it is unique in being *non-relational* awareness, and the uniqueness is accounted for by the fact that I am aware of myself as a subject of a present-moment experience simply because that present-moment subject of experience is what I *am*. My being *aware* of being this subject of experience is a direct and spontaneous cognitive manifestation of my *being* this subject.

I think that it is only when the non-relational structure of I-dimnesional self-awareness is brought to light that its seemingly paradoxical character can be dissolved. The paradox of the first-person perspective of consciousness becoming conscious of that very perspective of consciousness—i.e. becoming aware of what it is like to be an occupant of the first-person perspective—arises only if the model of explanation is such that I-consciousness is required to turn its attention upon itself.

The lived-experiential model of explanation has the simplicity of keeping the first-person perspective of I-consciousness as it is, with no requirement of engaging it to attend to itself by a kind of reversal of the focus of consciousness. In being first-personally conscious of the world, my world-bound experience is also infused with a background feeling of the *I*-self as the source of the first-person perspective that characterizes the experience of world.

Self-Awareness and First-Personal 'Take' on the Flow of Information

If the subject of experience is aware of itself as it is in the present moment of awareness merely *in virtue of* being that subject, then I-dimensional self-awareness is, as it were, available to the subject as an unsolicited datum or content of experience. There is a cognitive or quasi-cognitive self-experience in the present-moment experiential episode, and this self-experience is not the result of the I-self trying to represent itself as the locus of the experiential episode. The subject is quasi-cognitively aware of what it is like to be the subject of experience of that moment. Now, there must be a structurally important difference between the fact of being aware of something (object-awareness) on the one hand, and the fact of being aware of that awareness of something (self-awareness) on the other, given that both these facts are experientially anchored in one and the same subject taken as the locus of the first-person perspective.

In being aware of something, in object-awareness, the subject of the awareness surely has a first-person perspective on something, that is, on the intentional object of awareness. The content of the experience is presented to the first-person perspective (i.e. the first-personal givenness of the experience), and this is what it means to be a subject of experience. But when the present-moment object-awareness comports 'unsolicited' reflexive awareness of what it is like to have the present-moment awareness, what exactly is the nature of the content of the reflexive awareness? Surely the content of reflexive self-awareness will be the subject of experience, the I-consciousness or *I*-self. The operation of I-consciousness in having object-awareness implies awareness of what it is like to occupy the first-person perspective on the world. It is in this sense that the I-conscious act of intentional awareness is self-reflexive. It therefore means that the content of reflexive self-awareness is provided by the spontaneous quasi-cognitive intimation of what it is like to be an embodiment of the first-person perspective of intentional consciousness.

Zahavi has stressed that experiences are always presented to the subject with the *for-me-ness* structure, and that is a structural consequence of the first-personal *givenness* of experience. While it is true to talk in the 'passive voice' about first-personal *givenness* of experience (of the world) as a structural feature of the subjectivity of experience, it is perhaps more fundamental to adopt the 'active voice' stance in elucidating the meaning of the first-person perspective of consciousness. Granted that experiences occur to the conscious subject, it does not mean, however, that the subject is therefore passive with regard to the occurrence of an experiential episode. Consciousness can also be construed as engaged in an act, and this act can be described as consciousness's first-personal experiential 'take' on the world.

Seen from the 'active' angle, the idea of being a subject of experience can very well be understood in functional terms. I-consciousness can plausibly be regarded as a functional notion, its function being the act of 'registering' the flow of information in the first-personal mode of awareness. The first-personally registered flow of information then turns into a stream of experience. (The flow of information is of course 'converted' into a steam of intelligible experience because of the cognitive resources with which human consciousness is supposed to be well equipped.)

Conscious internalization of informational flow involves a two-dimensional awareness complex: intentional and reflexive. While any episode of experience is experience *of* something and therefore awareness with intentional content, the experience is also characterized by reflexive transparency. The reflexive transparency of the experience—the awareness of the experience as an occurrent mental state—may be called 'self-experience' or 'self-awareness' characterized by a peculiar inwardness. This inwardness is the inner 'sense' of experiencing the intentional object, the feeling of being the subject of the intentional state. Self-experience is built into the awareness of the intentional object.

Self-experience is not just an awareness that underlies awareness of the intentional object. This underlying self-awareness also vitally accounts for the phenomenological salience of first-person-centered awareness of the intentional object. Intentional awareness does not present itself as something floating anonymously in centerless consciousness. It rather presents itself as anchored in centered consciousness, and the center is the locus of the first-person perspective.

What is implied in saying that consciousness is intentional or object-directed is the fact that consciousness is open to the flow of objective information. The inevitable impingement of the world of information upon consciousness is causally responsible for lending content to consciousness. Consciousness becomes contentful as soon as it forms content-bearing representational states, which occur to it through its first-personal take on the flow of information.

Granted that the first-person perspective is a truth about the structure of consciousness, this truth presupposes the availability of the flow of worldly information *on* which consciousness has its first-personal take. This flow of information from the world is the objective correlate of states of subjective experience. Indeed, there would have been no such thing as consciousness with its first-personal perspectival orientation, were there no objective correlate of subjective consciousness to be first-personally oriented towards.

Now, consider an effort to conceive of I-consciousness with its first-person perspective, but a consciousness which suspends its disposition for first-personal take on the world. It is as though I-consciousness has managed to remain unaffected by the flow of information with which the objective world normally impinges on it. Would consciousness still be structured by the first-person perspective even when I-consciousness is not actually engaged in the act of first-personally registering any flow of information?

Two answers are possible to this question. The first answer would be to say that consciousness would then become devoid of *I*-ness, because the *raison d'être* of I-consciousness or *I*-self is its first-person point of view on the world. And if consciousness somehow becomes insular enough to overcome its natural disposition for first-personal take on the world, it is as good as saying that this is consciousness *without* a subject-self. The second answer, on the other hand, is to insist that the *I*-self remains as the locus or source of the first-person perspective, but its disposition for acquiring content for consciousness through its first-personal take on the world is held in abeyance. It is as though I-consciousness is rendered functionally idle, so that the *I*-self maintains aloofness with regard to the flow of objective information.

The first-personal content-bearing take on the world—which is the natural functional tendency of I-consciousness—is of course a presupposition of the intentionality of consciousness. To say that consciousness is intentional or object-directed is to imply that, by virtue of its intentional act, consciousness is inevitably loaded with world-bearing content. And the intentional act of consciousness, the act of being conscious *of* something in the world, is basically traceable to, and grounded in, I-consciousness's first-personal take on the flow of information of the objective world.

In my reckoning, the second of the two answers deserves

more attention, because the answer opens up for a deeper consideration of the possibility of I-consciousness without any intentional content. Why is this possibility worthy of deeper attention? I think it is worthy of serious consideration because of the metaphysical nature of the notion of the *I*-self.

If the first-person perspective is what basically defines consciousness and the *I* is the undefined 'point' at which this perspectival orientation originates, then we have a notion of 'pure' I-consciousness which is yet innocent of intentionality. In this 'pure' sense, I-consciousness is non-intentional and therefore without any world-bearing content. However, it is surely characterized by what might be called a *permanent possibility* of transition to intentional consciousness in the midst of continuous flow of information due to the impingement of the world.

From *I*-self to *Me*-self: Construction and De-construction

The *I*-self that consists of pre-intentional I-consciousness is of course a nascent self. In being wholly constituted of the perspectival orientation of consciousness, this self is conceptually not yet a self-in-the-world. For the self-in-the-world is the world-bound I-consciousness, which cannot resist its disposition to view the world as centered in its first-person point of view. In fact, the nascent self is immediately transformed into the self-in-the-world as soon as I-consciousness starts representing the world and assumes ownership of those representational states as their subject. These subjectively owned representations have the form 'I think/believe/know that something is the case', 'I am happy/dejected/surprised that she did that', 'I hope/desire/ or intend that this be the case' and so on.

The point about I-centric representations is not really about ego-centricity; rather it is about how the innocent pre-intentional, contentless, nascent I-consciousness becomes an individual self constituted of contentful states which confer on it some sort of substantive subjective identity. This is the identity of a *Me*-self that is 'constructed' by I-consciousness through its first-personal perspectival take on the world.

Individuality is a property of the *Me*-self but not of the nascent *I*-self. Merely as the 'embodiment' of the first-person perspective, I-consciousness cannot strictly be said to be an individual self, since a perspective by itself is not a basis for individuation. A perspective of consciousness is not a content of consciousness, but rather the way in which the content of consciousness is acquired and given a particular mental shape.

When world-bearing experiential states occur to I-consciousness as it is relentlessly impinged upon by the flow of information, it has the sense of being the owner-subject of these states. These informationally contentful states are predicated of this subject, and it means that the subject acquires an individual identity which is constructed by the ensemble of predicates. There is a third-personal objective recognition of this individual identity as the identity of a person, a particular person amongst others in the class of persons. This is the *He*-identity or *She*-identity of the person counted as an object in the world.

The ensemble of predicates that lends a substantive identity to the person is also self-intimating to the owner-subject, the *I*-self. What is self-intimating is of course self-recognized by the subject of the intimation as owning the individual identity. What is so recognized through self-intimation is the self-image that I-consciousness is exclusively acquainted with. It is this first-personal self-recognition of the individual personal identity that constitutes the *Me*-self *vis-a-vis* the *I*-self.

The identity of the *Me*-self is obviously a subjectively constituted personal self-image which the I-self identifies itself with, either happily or unhappily. Either way, the identification remains undeniably intact: I am happy that this *me* of desirable substantive identity is what I am identical with; alternatively, I am unhappy that it is this *me* of unpleasant substantive identity that I am ontologically identical with. Even when I am assailed by a sense of self-alienation because of the most reprehensible self-identity and self-image that is glaringly apparent to (my) I-consciousness, the pain of self-alienation presupposes my (*I*-self) inescapable sense of ontological identity with the substantive *Me*-self.

What is important to note from this fact of inescapable and

undeniable sense of identification of the *I*-self with the resultant *Me*-self is the asymmetry of the relation between the two aspects of a total self. Within the unified subjective space of a single person, there is the duality of the *I* and the *Me,* but the relation between these two aspects is, respectively, the relation of the subject-self to the object-self. Although the entire space of this inner subjective space is clearly first-personal, the *me*-aspect is objectified as a subjectively constructed self in the eye of the *I*-self, which is also the agent of construction in its involvement with the world. So the subject-object duality in this case is not the duality of the self and the external world, but a duality within the complex space of the same self.

Now, to attribute agency to the *I*-self is to say more about its nature than the embodiment of the first-person perspective of consciousness. Surely the pre-intentional, contentless pure *I* does not seem to qualify for agency. There must be an element of desire and will and as an ingredient of the *I*-self to motivate it into substantive self-construction. What is the explanation of the formation of *I*-self that triggers desire and will necessary for agency? This is a complex question which I cannot afford to answer here, because it would require an extensive exploration which is beyond the scope of this paper.

It must also be added that the agency alluded to in the above is of two kinds. In one kind, it is *engaged* agency which is involved in the more or less spontaneous development of a personal self driven by natural desires and other pro-attitudes. Such a personal self is the relatively uncritical growth of a *me*-self, and it is one with which the *I*-self identifies itself with no significant sense of conflict or alienation. The other kind of agency is essentially characterized by the self-critical attitude; it is *disengaged* agency in that the *I*-self is steadily prone to disengage itself from the already formed *me*-identity in order to subject this self-image to critical review in the light of certain norms and ideals. What such a critical self-evaluation aims at is the modification of substantive self-identity, so that there evolves the rightly modified *me,* which is what *I* truly want to evolve into.

Disengaged agency can have a much more radical role in

the reconstitution of the self. Instead of substantive self-modification through critical review, disengaged agentive exercise may attempt to reverse the process of *me*-construction. It would then be a *de*-constructive process of disengaging the *I*-self from the *Me*-self altogether, that is, the attempt to be a self that is purged of the tantalizing temptation of *being me*. It is perhaps such an attempt of disengaged agency to realize *I*-ness without *me*-ness that constitutes the essence of spirituality.

REFERENCES

James, William. *Psychology: Briefer Course* (New York: Holton & Company, 1892).

Ryle, Gilbert. *The Concept of Mind* (Harmondsworth: Penguin Books, 1963).

Strawson, Galen. 'Radical Self-Awareness', in Siderits, M., Thompson, E. and Zahavi, D. (eds.), *Self, No Self? Perspectives from Analytical, Phenomenological and Indian Traditions* (New York: Oxford University Press, 2011), pp. 274-307.

Zahavi, Dan. *Subjectivity and Selfhood: Investigating the First-Person Perspective* (Cambridge; Mass.: MIT Press, 2005).

2

Self, Consciousness and the World: On How to Situate the Self

Ramesh Chandra Pradhan

This paper addresses the problem regarding the self and its location *vis-a-vis* the world. The problem of the self and its relation with the world arises because the self is the locus of our consciousness and yet it does not belong to the world as one of its items. That is, the self is always at odds with the world. It is in the world and yet it is not of the world.[1] So far as consciousness is concerned, it needs a location where it can be situated. It is necessarily the self which is the locus of consciousness.

This paper has two main arguments regarding the self: (1) the argument from the need of a metaphysical subject of conscious experience; (2) the argument from the insufficiency of the first-person experience or the phenomenal experience to constitute the metaphysical self. The first argument shows that the metaphysical subject is the bedrock of our consciousness and so must be situated as distinguished from the objects and the facts in the world, while the second argument shows that our phenomenal experience does not constitute the self but admits it as its locus. My main contention is that we need a metaphysical concept of self in order to do justice to the concept of consciousness and especially to the concept of the first-person consciousness. Besides, the idea of moral agency itself requires a metaphysical self as the source of normativity.

1. Self and the World: How to Make Sense of the Metaphysical Self

Wittgenstein while introducing the concept of self in his *Tractatus* makes the following remark:

> Thus there really is a sense in which philosophy can talk about the self in a non-psychological way.
>
> What brings the self into philosophy is the fact that 'the world is my world'.
>
> The philosophical self is not the human being, not the human body, or the human soul, with which psychology deals, *but rather the metaphysical subject, the limit of the world—not part of it* [2] (italics added).

What is said here is of paramount importance for any reflection on the concept of self, since it captures the dilemma in philosophy as to whether the self can be discussed about only in psychological terms or whether we can talk about it in a philosophical way that brings in the non-psychological and metaphysical sense of the self. It is at this point that Wittgenstein talks about the metaphysical subject or the self to resolve the above dilemma.

Wittgenstein makes a distinction between the psychological self and the metaphysical self. The psychological self is the one psychology deals with as mind or soul and as the subject of consciousness. Under this rubric, one can include all the conceptions of self normally associated with consciousness, self-consciousness and the first-person experiences in philosophy of mind.[3] The metaphysical or the philosophical self is different from the psychological self because it is the limit of the psychological description of the self. While the psychological or the empirical self belongs to the world as an item in the world, the metaphysical self is the limit of the world and so not a part of the world. Wittgenstein reiterates this point again in the *Tractatus* when he says:

> The metaphysical subject does not belong to the world: rather, it is a limit of the world.
>
> Where in the world is a metaphysical subject to be found?[4]

This goes to show that the world cannot be the location of the metaphysical self because any description of the world presupposes it. For Wittgenstein, the world being "my world", that is, the world which I describe in language, the metaphysical self is already presupposed.

Wittgenstein's notion of a metaphysical self can be retrieved for the present purpose by emphasizing that we can always make a distinction between the self as belonging to the world and the one which does not belong to the world, that is, the self which is an object in the world to be empirically discovered and the self that is not a thing in the world.[5] The self as a thing in the world is either a physical entity like the body or a psychological entity like the soul or mind. Both the senses of the self can capture only an empirical self, and not the self *per se* or the metaphysical self. That only indicates that we must make a distinction between the self-as-an-item-in-the-world and self-as-outside-the-world. The latter can be called the metaphysical self.

Now the question is, how can the metaphysical self be referred to at all, if not by the "I" the first-person pronoun? If the "I" also stands for the empirical self, the embodied self to be precise, how can we distinguish the metaphysical "I" from the empirical "I"? This dilemma occurs because we have one first-person pronoun to do the job for both. But there is a difference. The "I" in its metaphysical use cannot stand for the embodied self or the self in the world precisely because the "I" is not a name of anybody, not even the speaker who uses the "I". Wittgenstein makes it clear thus:

> The word "I" does not mean the same as "L'W" even if I am L.W, nor does it mean the same as the expression "the person who is now speaking". But that doesn't mean: that "L.W" and "I" mean different things. All that it means is that these words are different instruments in our language.[6]

Being different instruments in language, "I" and "L.W." mean different things in language. While "L.W." means the human being, the embodied being, "I" means the self. It is this self that is called the metaphysical self. This is of course the implication which one can derive from the use of the "I", even if Wittgenstein does not so characterize it. This is what he indicated when he said in the *Notebooks:* "The I is not an object. I objectively confronts every object. But not the I"[7]. "L.W." indicates an embodied object in the world, while the "I" does not.

II. Self and Embodiment

Now the crux of the problem is, how do we associate the "I" with the person "L.W.", if the self is different from "L.W."? One possible answer is that the metaphysical self is embodied or incarnated in the person "L.W". The latter is the human being in the world who has a definite life-history, since he was born and was located in a certain time and space. The self has none of these because neither birth nor spatio-temporal location is applicable to the self. Thomas Nagel calls this self the objective self[8] which is different from the human being with whom it is associated. The human being, according to him, is located in the world, while the objective self is not part of the world, though it is associated with the person concerned. Nagel writes:

> The objective self that I find viewing the world through TN is not unique: each of you has one. Or perhaps I should say each of you is one, for the objective self is not a distinct entity. Each of us, then, in addition to being an ordinary person, is a particular objective self, the subject of a perspectiveless conception of reality.[9]

Here the person TN is in the world and has a perspective of the world. But the objective self has no perspective of its own and hence has a view of the world as centerless. This self has a location in TN through whose perspective it has a subjective view of the universe. Thus in TN the objective self has an incarnation, that is, an embodiment.

Nagel's objective self needs a location in the world. The objective self enters the world through the human being which Nagel calls TN. Nagel's problem is not "how a particular person, TN, can be me, but how I can be anything so specific as a particular person at all (TN as it happens)."[10] It is rather puzzling that I become a particular person, since for all practical purposes this relation is accidental and arbitrary. It is contingent, because I could have been any person than this particular "publicly identifiable person" such as TN. Nagel explains this puzzle in the following passage:

> To arrive at this idea I begin by considering the world as a whole, as if from nowhere, and in those oceans of space and time TN is just one person among countless others. Taking up that impersonal standpoint produces in me a sense of complete detachment from TN, who is reduced to a momentary blip on the cosmic TV screen. How can I, who am thinking about the entire, centerless universe, be anything so specific as *this:* this measly, gratuitous creature existing in a tiny morsel of space-time, with a definite and by no means universal mental and physical organization? How can I be so *small* and *concrete* and *specific*?[11]

This puzzle regarding the I becoming TN is the crux of how the objective self becomes the particular person historically situated in the universe. At one level, it means the objective self is located in the space-time world and at another it means the objective self is none other than the particular human being. It is the case that, metaphysically speaking, the self cannot be the particular person, but, practically speaking, it is publicly presented as the particular person. The latter is the embodied self or the self that is incarnated in a particular publicly identifiable living body. The lived body is the self in the world, as Merleau-Ponty[12] suggests, because this self is the seat of consciousness and is structured through intentional cognitive states.

Nagel, like Wittgenstein, does not consider the metphysical self to be identical with the embodied self for the reason that in that case the gap between the metaphysical self and the embodied or the enworlded self would be abolished. The enworlded self, as Merleau-Ponty envisages, becomes the only self without a metaphysical residue and thus paves the way for the de-transcendentalization of the self. The Husserlian self which is the Transcendental Ego merges into the Sartrean (and in a sense, the Merleau-Pontyan) empirical and embodied self.[13] But the argument provided by Nagel and Wittgenstein confronts this non-transcendental point of view by suggesting that the self faces its own devaluation and reduction by shedding its own metaphysical status. To think of an objective self is to engage in a metaphysical approach to self which rules out all forms of reductionism.

III. Irreducibility of the Self

The self in the metaphysical sense cannot be reduced to the embodied self for the obvious reason that for reduction to be possible, one has to presuppose the metaphysical self itself. The self is so fundamental that it cannot be reduced to the body which embodies it or to the mind which is attributed to it. In that sense, self remains the only reality to which both body and mind belong, as P.F. Strawson[14] has suggested. (of course, Strawson calls this the person rather than the metaphysical self). What remains as irreducible is the subject of consciousness itself, that is, that which owns both body and mind. The subject of consciousness is the metaphysical self, but it cannot be the same as embodied self owning consciousness. Bas C. van Frassen's following observations on the metaphysical self are apt in this context:

> I exist, but I am not a thing among things. I am neither a physical object nor a mental substance or abstract entity, nor a compound thereof. I am not an animal, mineral, or vegetable. Nor am I a thing constituted by or composed of that taken together. I am not some piece of furniture of the universe.
>
> Certainly I have a body and I have thoughts as well as feelings. I have a special location as well as a place, however, modest, in history. *But I am not to be identified with any of this. I am in this world*, but *not of this world. I am not a thing among things.*[15] (emphasis added).

Bas C. van Frassen's model of the self is metaphysical to say the least, because it is the one which cannot be reduced to a body or mind and which is not composed of body and mind. It is different from the body and mind though it owns them. The very fact that it is not part of the furniture of the universe shows that the self is metaphysically distanced from the world, though it is empirically in the world. Its being empirically placed in world-history does not detract from its metaphysical status.

Thus van Frassen's argument reveals the category-difference between the things and the self by showing that what we can attribute to the self we cannot attribute to the things. The things have a different ontology from that of the self. While the self can be attributed with consciousness, the things cannot be so attributed. Similarly, we can say that the self is not one of the furnitures of the world, while things are. This difference is a metaphysical difference between things and the self. The self, for van Frassen, is not of the world thereby showing that we cannot make self anything like a physical or mental substance. But from this one can very well argue that self, according to him, must be the metaphysical self and not the embodied self. Now the question is, does van Frassen have the concept of an embodied self or not? If yes, how is it different from the metaphysical self? It seems that van Frassen does not make any distinction between the two kinds of self we have accepted. For him, as for Nagel, the metaphysical self is in the world only as an embodied self to which we can attribute consciousness. Nagel and van Frassen thus retain the metaphysical self while admitting it only as an embodied self in the world. The transcendental character of the self is retained in van Frassen's and Nagel's account.

The irreducibility of the self that we are talking about here is the metaphysical irreducibility because it is this irreducibility which is the crux of the matter. One can even argue that the embodied self itself is irreducible because it is neither a mental nor a physical substance, but a unitary subject of consciousness which is composed of the body and mind. This self is part of the world and is one of the items of the world as a human person. Davidson[16] accepts the irreducibility of this empirical self because he thinks that there is no way we can talk about thought and language without assuming the existence of the speaker who is the embodied self. The self of the speaker is entangled in the web of beliefs and intentions and thus makes claims upon the world from a first-person point of view. The first-person point of view is of the speaker who attributes beliefs and other intentional states to herself.

However, Davidson does not have the notion of a metaphysical self as, for him, the self is always the speaker who calls himself "I" as in "I am in pain" and "I believe that it is raining", etc. For Davidson, the only self that exists is the empirical or the embodied self. But this is not what a metaphysician will be satisfied with. He may demand a much more fine-tuned notion of self that is not reduced to the empirical self. Wittgenstein explains this as follows:

> "But at any rate when you say 'I am in pain', you want to draw the attention of others to a particular person"—The answer might be: No, I want to draw their attention to *myself*.[17]

This shows that the speaker is not the same as the self or "I" because they have two different kinds of grammar and have different kinds of metaphysical implication. The "I" is not the name of an embodied person given in the world. It stands for the self which of course is located in the speaker.

The irreducibility question can happily be resolved only if we make the distinction between the metaphysical "I" or the self and the embodied self. The metaphysical self cannot be reduced to the embodied self just as the embodied self cannot be reduced to the mental or physical substance. The embodied self is as much irreducible as the metaphysical self because both stand for the self in its two aspects. But the search for the metaphysical self is worth our pursuit because, even an embodied self requires the metaphysical self as its source.

IV. Self and the Sources of Normativity

The irreducibility of the self is also linked with the source of the normativity because it is the self which is the source of normativity[18]. Normativity has something to do with values which the self as the moral agent pursues. The structure of the values which human beings pursue is embedded in the moral self or agent. The moral agent cannot but be the normative agent as Bilgrami[19] has argued. This agent cannot be the same as the human being or the embodied self precisely because the moral agent is more than the human being or the embodied self. Bilgrami defines self-knowledge in terms of the normativity of agency by showing that the agent has both authority and transparency[20] regarding his intentional states and thus self-knowledge is a necessary condition of the agent's normative behaviour. Thus the self as the source of normativity appears on the scene as carrying the burden of moral and other normative behaviour. Bigrami writes:

> Encouraged by some ideas in Kant on the subject of freedom and its relation to thought.... the notion of agency and the notion of intentionality are thoroughly normative notions, and that it is these notions so understood, that ground our intuition that self-knowledge has special authority and transparency that no other knowledge possesses.[21]

Thus Bilgrami approaches the problem of self from a normative point of view such that the self is already involved in a network of normative beliefs and other intentional states. He holds that unless we presuppose the normative character of agency we cannot explain how self-knowledge and freedom are possible.

But Bilgarmi nowhere argues for the self as a metaphysical subject because his focus is on normativity and values. But how can there be normativity unless there is a source of it? For Bilgrami leaves the agency web of normativity without explaining how normativity is possible and whether we need a metaphysical grounding for it in what we have called the metaphysical self. Of course, he can argue that his normative self or agent is a metaphysically grounded self which is capable of bearing the moral attributes.

Korsaggard[22] in recent times has argued for the source of normativity in the self because she feels that without the source of it in the human self, there can be no normativity worth the name. For her, like for Kant, the self is the source of all values because the human self itself is valuable. In that sense, there is a source of rationality and other normative attributes in the human self. The self is capable of reflective consciousness which is the source of value-consciousness and so the reflective self-consciousness is the source of normativity. Korsgaard writes:

> As I argued in *The Sources of Normativity*, this same self-consciousness or reflective awareness of our own inner states and activities is the source of free will: precisely because you know that you are inclined to act in a certain way, you are now free to decide whether to act that way or not, and are faced with a question. So it is in this space—the space of reflective distance from our incentives—that the issue of *reasons* arises.[23]

It is indicated here that it is the reflective self which brings in the question of reasons and normativity because only in the reflective consciousness can the self distance itself from the personal desires and inclinations. This reflective self could be called the normative self and hence it is the source of normativity. Besides, freedom itself has its roots in the normative self such that the moral agent is capable of acting according to its own free will. As she writes: "It is because of the reflective character of the mind that we must act, as Kant puts it, under the idea of freedom. He says 'we cannot conceive of reason which consciously responds to a bidding from the outside with respect to its judgment'."[24]

Thus Krosgaard makes the self the seat of moral agency, freedom and normativity and thereby affirms the fact that no ethics is possible in the absence of a full-fledged moral self. That could lead one to argue that the moral self is the same as the metaphysical self because the moral self must be metaphysically grounded.

However, Korsgaard seems to identify the moral and metaphysical self with the human being who has the reflective consciousness. Thus she appeals to the principle of humanity as the metaphysically ultimate principle to explain normativity. She writes:

> To act morally is to act a certain way simply because you are human, to act as one who values her humanity should. Among the many things you are, you are a member of the party of humanity, or a Citizen of the Kingdom of Ends. And this identity like any other carries certain obligations.[25]

Thus, for Korsgaard, the human self as the embodied self is the ultimate source of normativity and obligations. But can this human self be the source of normativity in the absence of a metaphysical self?. The human self as the empirical self in the world cannot bear the burden of moral obligations. For that we need a self that is free from the causal necessities of the world and must be a transcendental self. For that the following reasoning may be helpful:

1. Rationality and normativity are valuational properties which need a subject to be located.
2. This subject cannot be the human being or the embodied self which is itself subject to valuational assessment.

3. So the human self cannot be the subject of the valuational properties.
4. Therefore, the subject of the moral and other normative properties must be different from the human self or the embodied self. It must be the metaphysical self which can act as the moral subject.
5. The metaphysical self is the transcendental self.

The above argument shows the deficiency in the idea of the embodied self's being the moral subject or the agent because the moral properties cannot be ascribed to it for the reason that the latter already presupposes the moral subject which is nothing but the metaphysical subject. In this context, Wittgenstein's following remark is worth noticing:

> God and evil only enter through the subject. And the subject is not part of the world, but a boundary of the world.
>
> It would be possible to say (a la Schopenhauer): It is not the world as Idea that is either good or evil; but the willing subject.
>
> ....
>
> As the subject is not a part of the world but a presupposition of its existence, so good and evil which are predicates of the subject, are not properties in the world.[26]

What Wittgenstein says here fits the present approach according to which the moral agent is not the same as the psychological self embodied in the human person, but the metaphysical subject which is the real source of normativity. In this sense, Bilgrami and Korsgaard can follow Kant and Wittgenstein in seeing that the moral agent or subject cannot be the *human agent* per se but the metaphysical subject. The notion of normative agent is itself closer to Kant's and Wittgenstein's moral self which is what is otherwise known as the metaphysical subject.

V. Looking for the Transcendental "I": Self-Reference, Narrativity and Constitutivity

What we need to locate the self or the "I" is to go beyond the things in the world and also to deny the many versions of the self constructed by the philosophers in their search for the self. One version of the self as the living body or the composite structure of mind and body has already been seen to be inadequate to locate the self. The other version which needs urgent attention is the notion of self as a constructed one that is found in the recent theories of self. It is the narrative model of self which makes the self a matter of logical construction.[27]

The main thrust of the concept of the self which we have seen in Bilgrami and Korsgaard is that the self distances itself from its own first-order desires and belief in search for its evaluative stance. It is this reflective act of the self in search of its normative stance which defines the self and its evaluative activities. As Krosgaard says, "the course of reflection to which this kind of question gives rise leads us to recognize the form of identity which stands behind the others: our identity as human, that is, as reflective animals who need to have practical conceptions of our identity in order to act and live. To treat your human identity as normative, as the source of reasons and obligations, is to have what I have been calling 'moral identity'."[28] This moral identity is something transcendental in the sense that we do not get it in our everyday activities, but only through our morally evaluative activities. The transcendental self is the source of moral identity and not the self as the embodied being which is the subject of our first-order desires.[29] Korsgaard appeals to Kant for this kind of self which is associated with the Kantian notion of Kingdom of Ends. Unless it is the transcendental self, it cannot distance itself from the self as the subject of the first-order desires and intentions.

The transcendental self is not the constituted self in any acceptable sense because the constituted self cannot be the moral self. If the self is constituted by anything external to the self, then the self is already presupposed and hence not constituted at all. The constituted self is either a Humean self that is an illusory self or a self in the sense understood in the Russellian way as logically constructed out of the given sensations or bare experiences.[30] But a constructed self is an illusory self because it does not respond to the moral and other normative evaluations which the subject or agent is known for. From Bilgrami's point of view, such a constructed self cannot be the bearer of the normativity of agency, because such a self cannot be integrated with the value-pursuing self. The self must be metaphysically integrated to give rise to normativity at all. The metaphysically integrated self is what is called the moral self which has 'moral identity'. Korsgaad calls the Kantian model of self as the constitutional model because according to it "it is the person who acts in accordance with the best constitution, the most unified constitution, who is most truly the author of her actions. For Kant as for Plato, integrity is the metaphysical essence of morality."[31] Thus we are required to have a metaphysically integrated self to make moral evaluation possible at all.

But one can argue that neither Bilgrami nor Korsgaard requires a metaphysical subject at all because for them the moral self is all that we require making moral actions and evaluations possible. But the fact that the moral identity of self is grounded in an integrated self requires that morality is dependent on a morally identical self which itself is a metaphysical condition of self. Moral identity requires a metaphysical grounding for its normativity and therefore we cannot say that there is a moral self which is not the metaphysical self. Bilgrami seems to be less enthusiastic about the metaphysical side of the moral agent, but a close reading of his position on agency testifies to the fact that a self-knowing moral agent is as much committed to normativity as to metaphysicality about both agency and values. Like Kant, Bilgrami and Korsgaard are committed to a transcendental self in the above sense where distancing from oneself is a *sine qua non* of morality itself.

The narrative character of the self which has been attributed to the moral agent belies the very possibility of the moral self at all. That is because any narrative self as shown by Galen Strawson[32] presupposes a non-narrative or integrated self that metaphysically grounds the so-called narrative selfhood. The narrative or discourse dependent selves are nothing but the constructed selves which fail to account for morality. Constructed selves are quite episodic to bear the moral identity which is required for the metaphysical self. Therefore on the metaphysical grounds the narraitive selves lack the selfhood which is required for morality to be possible at all.

Thus the question of self-reference, which we started with,

is itself an invitation for the introduction of the metaphysical self. If self-reference can be satisfied by the personal description of the self as so and so situated in space-time location, then there is nothing unique about the "I" or self. It could be dispensed with so as to be taken over by the third-personal description of the person. That will spell doom for the understanding of consciousness and moral agency.

V. Conclusion

The first-person consciousness is in need of a metaphysical rather than a semantic and epistemological account. It is not that the first-person consciousness is itslf sufficient to account for the metaphysical self because it itself presupposes such a self or I. The metaphysical nature of the I is implicit in the use of the self-referring expression "I". Kant, Husserl and Wittgenstein have urged for a transcedental account of the I for the reason that there is no way we can call it the temporal or embodied self. The metaphysical self is the limit of the bodily self and of the world to which the latter belongs. The metaphysical self is transcedental by nature in view of the demands of the world on the embodied self to shed its first-personal perspective on the world. The metaphysical self does not abandon the world but makes its moral and other normative demands on the latter. Therefore there is no causal but normative bond between the metaphysical self and the world.

NOTES AND REFERENCES

1. See Bas C. van Frassen, "Transcendence of the Ego (The Non-Exiştent Knight)" in *The Self?*, ed. Galen Strawson (Blackwell Publishing, Oxford, 2005), pp. 87-110.
2. Wittgenstein, *Tractatus Logico-Philosophicus*, trans. D.F.Pears and B.F. McGuinness (Routledge and Kegan Paul, 1961), 5. 641.
3. See David Chalmers, *The Character of Consciousness* (Oxford University Press, Oxford, 2010).
4. Wittgenstein, *Tractatus Logico-Philosophicus*, 5.632-633.
5. Wittgenstein, *Notebooks 1914-1916*, trans. G.E.M. Anscombe (Basil Blackwell, Oxford, 1961; second edition 1979), p. 80e.
6. Wittgenstein, *The Blue and the Brown Books* (Basil Blackwell, Oxford, 1958, second edition 1969), p. 67.

7. Wittgenstein, *Notebooks 1914-1916*, p. 80e.
8. Thomas Nagel, *The View From Nowhere* (Oxford University Press, New York and Oxford, 1986), Chapter IV.
9. Ibid., pp. 63-64.
10. Ibid., p. 60.
11. Ibid., p. 61.
12. See Maurice Merleau-Ponty, *Phenomenology of Perception*, trans. Collin Smith (Routledge, London and New York, 2002).
13. Cf. Jean-Paul Sartre, *The Transcendence of the Ego: An Existentialist Theory of Consciousness*, ed. and trans. Forrest Williams and Robert Kirkpatrick (Noonday Press, New York, 1957). See also Andrew Brown, trans. *The Transcedence of the Ego: A Sketch for a Phenomenological Descriprion* (Routledge, London and New York, 2004).
14. P.F. Strawson, *Individuals: An Essay in Descriptive Metaphysics* (Methuen, London, 1959).
15. Bas C. van Frassen, "Transcendence of the Ego (The Non-Existent Knight)", p. 87.
16. Donald Davidson, "The Irreducibility of the Concept of Self" in *Subjectivity, Intersubjectivity, Objectivity* (Clarendon Press, Oxford, 2001), pp. 85-91.
17. Wittgenstein, *Philosophical Investigations*, trans. G.E.M.Anscombe (Basil Blackwell, Oxford, 1953), Section 405.
18. See Christine M. Korsgaard, *The Sources of Normativity* (Cambridge University Press, Cambridge, 1996), Chapter 1.
19. Akeel Bilgrami, *Self-Knowledge and Resentment* (Harvard University Press, Cambridge, Mass., and London, England, 2006).
20. Ibid., Chapter 1.
21. Ibid., p. ix.
22. Cf. Korsgaard, *The Sources of Normativity*, Chapter 1.
23. Korsgaard, "Motivation, Metaphysics and the Value of Self: A Reply to Ginsberg, Guyer and Schneewind", *Ethics*, Vol. 109, No. 1 (October 1998), p. 51.
24. Korsgaard, *The Sources of Normativity*, p. 94.
25. Ibid., p. 129.
26. Wittgenstein, *Notebooks 1914-1916*, p. 79e.
27. See G. Strawson, " Against Narrativity" in *The Self*, ed. Galen Strawson, pp. 63-86.
28. Korsgaard, *The Sources of Normativity*, p. 129.
29. Ibid.
30. See B. Russell, *Analysis of Mind* (George Allen and Unwin, London, 1921).

31. Korsgaard, "Self-Constitution in the Ethics of Plato and Kant", *The Journal of Ethics*, Vol. 3, No. 1 (1999), p. 28.
32. See Galen Strawson, "Against Narrativity" in *The Self?*, pp. 63-86. For further discussion on the narrative view of self, see Valerie Gray Hardcastle, *Constructing the Self* (John Benjamins Publishing Company, Amsterdam/ Philadelphia, 2008), Chapter 2.

3

Presence of Mind: Consciousness and the Sense of Self

Christian Coseru

The rejection of a permanent self as the 'thinker of thoughts' and the 'senser of sensations' poses a significant challenge for Buddhist philosophy of mind: if there is no permanent agent (*kartā*), and if actions (*karman*) are merely transient events within a continuum of causally interconnected states, how is the phenomenal character of conscious experience and the sense of ownership implicit in first-person agency to be explained? At the same time, the rejection of a permanent locus for experience offers an opportunity to explore the problem of personal identity on phenomenological rather than metaphysical grounds: answering the question of why self-awareness comes bound up with a sense of self (whether owned or merely occurrent) can thus be pursued independently of metaphysical concerns about what a self is and what are its fundamental attributes. It also allows for an analysis of the structure of awareness without assuming that such a structure reflects an external relation of ownership between consciousness and the self.

Let us note from the outset that there are substantive disagreements among Buddhist philosophers about how the problem of personal identity should be framed, the kind of evidence that is deemed reliable, and the lines of justification that are worth pursuing: it can be (and has been) framed in both epistemological and ontological terms, drawing on both experiential accounts and metaphysical considerations about what there is, and taking the form of both conceptual analysis and ostensive demonstration. Nonetheless, there is a general consensus that at the most basic level the no-self view is entailed by a reductive analysis of experience. The claim is that phenomenal consciousness is actually a synthesis of five different kinds of activities: bodily, affective, perceptual, dispositional, and self-reflexive.[1] This view of personal identity informs all debates in Indian and Buddhist philosophy of mind and is indispensable to any account of cognition. By replacing the cognizing 'self' or 'I' with a causal chain the outcome of which is momentary cognitive events, Buddhist philosophers treat the cognizing subject as an emergent aspect of the embodied and dynamic functioning of these aggregates. In short, talk of 'self' or 'I' as the agent of experience is just a mistaken, folk-psychological way of using the first person pronoun referentially (that is, as referring to subjects of experience).

But if this Buddhist account of personal identity is built, as it is claimed, on phenomenological (thus descriptive) rather than metaphysical grounds, the obvious question arises: is there such a place or locus for experience? And if there is, does it have the sort of character that is amenable to phenomenological analysis? A positive answer would suggest that experience is such that at a minimum, the 'sense of self' must be an ineliminable structural feature of cognitive awareness. In what follows I want to pursue the question of precisely what conception of self-consciousness can be supported on experiential grounds, and whether such conception is sufficient to account for the ineliminable features of phenomenal consciousness.

I. Defining Consciousness

It is generally agreed that consciousness is a somewhat slippery term. However, more narrowly defined as 'phenomenal consciousness' it captures at least three essential features or aspects: *subjective experience* (the notion that what we are primarily conscious of are experiences), *subjective knowledge* (that feature of our awareness that gives consciousness its distinctive reflexive character), and *phenomenal contrast* (the phenomenality of awareness, absence of which makes consciousness intractable) (cf. Siewert 1998). I will only discuss here the subjective and epistemic aspects of phenomenal consciousness, specifically what I take to be two of its constitutive features: *presence* and *reflexivity*.

Phenomenal consciousness is what makes present, disclosing at once a world and a minimal sense of self. It is also constitutive of the character of experience. That there is something it is like to be conscious means that experience is what it is by virtue of being present to itself: the smell of roses is all that is needed for an experience to be disclosed as an instance of olfactory self-awareness. As such consciousness marks a specific cognitive event as being for someone or as having what phenomenologists call 'for-me-ness' (Kriegel and Zahavi 2015). There is no such thing as a generic experience, as if from nowhere and for no one. We do not experience the world and ourselves as though we were a witness in a Cartesian theatre or a voyeur peeping from behind the scene. Rather, awareness makes manifest, enacts, and transforms the world and ourselves as we move through it. We look on in utter amazement at a world that glances back and makes us blush, for the world in question is the world *as perceived*.

To open up to a world is not to be thrust, as a bystander might, onto a stage and asked to play some unfamiliar part. Rather, it is like taking your turn as the play moves along and the plot unravels. As embodied and minded creatures 'we' are always in character, though, of course, not always in the same character. Consciousness does not begin in reflection, when we pause to remember a line or to ponder an idea. Rather, as a reflection it always finds itself, as the conventions of epic poetry tell us, *in medias res*, in the middle of things. Awareness, and empirical or perceptual awareness in particular, has an intentional character: we always find ourselves in a world, or as Heidegger puts it, in one mood or another, and never simply there, as bare existence.

Phenomenal consciousness is important if we are to understand the world we live in and our place in it. Some argue that the phenomenal character of experience is such that our most basic beliefs, call them perceptual beliefs, are not only immediately justified (Pryor 2000, 2004) but in effect are nothing but judgments about experience (Dennett 2005); others that experience has a seeming character, that there is a way things seem to us that is different from our judgments about them (Carman, 2005, 2007; Huemer 2005, 2007). Furthermore, some claim that we cannot have first-personal knowledge of our own mental states without phenomenal experience (Pitt 2004); others that perceptual experience must be conscious in a phenomenal sense in order for us to have access to demonstrative thoughts (Smithes 2011); and still others that phenomenal experience is what makes our beliefs, perceptual or otherwise, reliable (Chalmers, 2003). Lastly, some argue that the phenomenal character of experience and its phenomenal content are in effect inseparable (Chalmers 2004, Coseru 2012).

Indian and Buddhist philosophers likewise are split on this issue: some, such as the Vaibhāshika and the Sautrāntikas offer reductionist accounts of experience, others (Vedānta and Sānkhya philosophers) argue that an experience should count as such insofar as it is attributable to a self that owns it, and still others (chiefly the Naiyāykas) that such a self might not admit of qualitative experiences or possess anything like determined awareness. At least in the Indian philosophical context, the main disagreement about phenomenal consciousness is between those who take consciousness to be simple and unanalysable, and those who understand consciousness as a property of certain mental states (typically, states of so-called metacognition or metacognitive awareness).[2]

Despite significant contributions in this area, we still lack reliable methods for charting the phenomenology of conscious experience. In recent years, a new proposal about the character of phenomenal consciousness has emerged that challenges the received, orthodox view that perceptual phenomenology is the only phenomenology there is. Proponents of this new view argue that conscious thought too possesses a kind of distinct or proprietary phenomenology. Introduced under the rubric of cognitive phenomenology this proposal is meant to extend, supplement, and even supplant about the range and scope of the phenomenal character of experience (Bayne and Montague

2011). Cognitive phenomenology or the phenomenology of thought extends the role of phenomenal consciousness beyond the domain of the present at hand to include all mentality. In other words, proponents of cognitive phenomenology do not simply state that thought has phenomenal character in virtue of being associated with some sensory or affective state.[3] Rather they claim that thought, much like sensation, has its own proprietary phenomenology or 'what it is like.' My thought "Paris is the capital of France" does not derive its character from association with co-occurrent sensory, affective, or imagistic experiences. That is, there is something it is like to entertain that thought that is not reducible to how I feel about Paris, political geography or French people.

However, while cognitive phenomenology may help extend the boundaries of conscious experience beyond the sensory and affective domains, it does little to augment our still rather rudimentary methodological toolset. Instead of using the language of qualia to capture the character of what it is like to have a certain kind of experience, it uses the language of introspection and self-knowledge to ground the content of thought in an experience of the thought's own determinacy.

I am sympathetic to the project of cognitive phenomenology, but, just as with the phenomenology of sense perception, I find it problematic that we are trying to justify the epistemic relevance of phenomenal consciousness rather than explore its structural features. If consciousness is what makes present then arguably it is constitutive of experience. Coming to terms with phenomenal consciousness, then, means resisting the many ways in which it can be substituted for more concrete phenomena like the so-called datum of experience or to judgments about it.

II. Presence and Reflexivity

Let us begin then with experience. Imagine you are travelling to a distant place, perhaps to attend a conference, and upon arrival you step out of the airport only to find yourself immersed in a strange and unfamiliar world. You look around for clues about how to proceed: directions to a taxi stand, an airport shuttle or the information desk. Before long, and with some luck, you are on your way to your hotel. As airport ramps give way to freeways and freeways to avenues and narrow streets a whole new urban fabric unravels before your eyes. Everywhere, a seething mass of people is going about their daily affairs. You are drawn in, you attend to every gesture and detail of this vast quivering tapestry. As the scene moves along, you find yourself adjusting your gaze to get a better grip. Perhaps you are riding in a shuttle or sharing a taxi with a colleague. Your colleague has been here before, and she knows the place very well. She is a gifted and gregarious storyteller, and on your way into the city you get your first guided tour, punctuated with anecdotes and solicitous advice. You are intrigued, fascinated, but also slightly apprehensive. You wonder what lies ahead for you.

As you zoom past imposing landmarks and through crowded thoroughfares, reaching deeper into the heart of the city, it slowly begins to sink in. Like Mary the colour scientist who, upon being released from her black and white room, has her first experience of colour, you are experiencing a world you have only indirectly known about. This is the world *made present*. What kind of presence is this? On reflection, one might say that it is a subjective one, a transformation of self-awareness by immersion into an unfamiliar environment. But this horizon of experience where you now find yourself has not come about solely as a result of what the new surroundings afford.

What do scenarios like the one just described tell us about the phenomenal character of consciousness? Herein lies the problem: unlike the typical thought experiment, there is no setup; no argument about what could conceivably be the case. Inferential relations, though part of the structure of awareness, are not constitutive of it. Small infants are aware, and so are many animals, despite lacking the complex conceptual schema of metacognitive awareness. To proponents of belief based theories of perception this scenario might seem contrived, even impossible, given assumptions about what empirical awareness can and does deliver. But it should not be. And here is why.

In perceiving we do not simply register objects within our field of experience. Neither do we stand over against these objects in a type of representational relation. Rather, the perceiving act itself makes present its object, say a red apple, as an event that has duration and takes place within a horizon of experience that is pre-reflectively given. On this account of perception, suited to capture its enactive and sensorimotor contingencies, *presence*, that is, the sense we have of enduring objects, states, and events, and *reflexivity*, the notion that our cognitive awareness has a for-me-ness structure, are intrinsic features of experience rather than concepts that frame our thinking about the character of experience.

Critics of sensorimotor accounts of perception (e.g. Clark 2006) claim that perception cannot apprehend past and/or future events, and thus that presence and temporality are not within the purview of perception. Proponents of the view that perception has a horizon structure and is reflexively constituted (Kelly 2008, Noë 2012) argue that what I perceive seems to include not only those elements that are immediately present to awareness but also those that are only intuitively available. The sensorimotor account of perception, thus, advances the phenomenally plausible view that in perception we apprehend whole objects (and events), not merely their perceptible parts, and apprehend them actively as occasioning different types of experience (the red apple affords such experiences as seeing red, picking or tossing).

While many agree that this debate about the nature of perception cannot be settled on phenomenologically neutral grounds, few doubt that framing it as an account of the structure of phenomenal consciousness can extend it in a profitable direction. Such a framing, not surprisingly, is also at work in Buddhist Abhidharma accounts: Vasubandhu, for instance, understands presence (*smīti*) as the capacity to "not allow to be carried off" (*ālambana-asampramoca*): that is, the capacity to retain the present moment.[4] My claim is that a solution to the problem of how best to account for the elements of existence and/or experience (*dharmas*), much like contemporary attempts to frame perceptual awareness in terms of its enactive and sensorimotor contingencies, cannot satisfactorily be offered without coming to terms with the reflexivity of phenomenal consciousness.

Let us briefly consider the Buddhist analysis of experience. First, the Buddhist rejects the notion of a permanent self as the agent of sensory activity. But this rejection, of course, poses a significant challenge. Indeed, as we noted above, if there is no agent, and if actions are merely transient events arising within a continuum of causally interconnected states, we are confronted with an explanatory gap: how is the efficacy of causal or, in Buddhist terms, kārmic processes to be explained? That is, why is it that some causal chains give rise to the emergent phenomenon of conscious awareness and its implicit sense of self and others do not? It is not surprising therefore that early interpreters of the no-self doctrine in the West (much like Brahmanical critics of the Buddhist no-self view in India) have argued that the denial of self in Buddhism should be understood as targeting common views such as those that associate the self with the psychophysical aggregates, and not the metaphysical notion of self (Bhattacharya 1973: 64).

Can Abhidharma reductionism, with its account of primitive atom-like 'qualitons' of experience, and its various accounts of consciousness in terms of life continuum (*citta-santana*) and repository consciousness (*ālaya-vijñāna*)) provide an adequate conceptual basis for advancing the thesis that mental states have a self-presentational character? That is, does the phenomenal mineness implicit, for instance, in Asaṅga and Vasubandhu's notion that I-thoughts are occurrent features of afflicted minds (*klicma-manas*) count as a descriptive account of the structure of experience? Or is it just an instance of failure to secure epistemic access to what there is? Ganeri (2012: 156ff) has recently claimed that it does not count, and has built a strong case for regarding the first-person stance by means of which thoughts are individuated in the mental stream as an instance of constitutively owned rather than deluded I-thoughts. Later Buddhist solutions to this conundrum vary considerably, from the Pudgalavādin's proposal that first-personal agency non-reductively supervenes on the aggregates to reflexivist accounts of consciousness as articulated mainly by Dignāga and Dharmakīrti and their successors. It is the reflexivist's proposal that interests us here for the promising way in which it accounts for the character of mental states in terms of features that form an integral part of their structure (such as, for instance, the principle of reflexivity which states that essentially consciousness consists in conscious mental states being implicitly self-aware). Proponents of Buddhist reflexivism claim that consciousness is best understood as a continuum of self-aware experiences that are dissociated both in terms of their phenomenal content and their phenomenal character (Dreyfus 2011: 123; Coseru 2012: ch 8). Additional proposals range from memory-based accounts (Thompson 2011) to enactivist and performative accounts of self-awareness (MacKenzie 2011) that argue for some minimal self as the pre-linguistic structure of lived experience.

III. Mineness without the Self

It is more likely, however, that the early Buddhist tradition is characterized primarily by an attempt to break free both from the speculative notion of an ultimate, immutable and eternal self and, at the same time, from the notion of a concrete psychological or biographical self (Hulin 1978: 43). As I have argued elsewhere (Coseru 2009), the frequent use of indexicals such as 'I' (*ahaṃ*) and 'mine' (*mama*) should not be taken as indicative of the view that the Buddha accepts the conventional reality of persons. Indeed, later Buddhist traditions develop specific notions, such as that of mind-stream, life-continuum mind, and repository consciousness (*citta-santāna, bhavaṅga-citta,* and *ālaya-vijñāna*, respectively) precisely in order to avoid not only the trappings of metaphysical notions of the self but also the view that such notions might have a fixed referent.[5] The denial of a permanent self, as well as the refusal to treat persons as referring to anything real and permanent, does not, however, extend to consciousness, whose temporal and horizon structures make possible reflective or introspective thought.

The centrality of the no-self doctrine in Buddhist thought is explained on the basis of its pragmatic role in guiding the adept on the path to enlightenment. Furthermore, the no-self doctrine provides a justification for treating endurance, independence, and self-subsistence as neither desirable nor attainable, but rather as what they are: mistaken notions resulting from the habitual tendency to construct a substantive identity from a stream of psychophysical phenomena. Now, how exactly a person without a self lives a good and meaningful life, and makes progress along the path to awakening is, of course, deliciously puzzling.

This Buddhist claim that our sense of self is imputed and our attribution of inherent existence to it habitually acquired,[6] is not that different, of course, from Hume's claim that a self is never apprehended in the mental series.[7] The Buddhist, much like Hume, is a bundle theorist, the first such theorist. The routine misapprehension of the discrete phenomena of experience as a self leads to a dualistic perspective: things appear and are categorized as either objective (thus external, but empirically accessible) or as subjective (thus internal, and immediately accessible to consciousness). Puzzled by this dualistic outlook, we cope by constructing a conception of the self as the permanent locus of experience.

What we are left with, then, is the picture of a constantly changing world of sensory phenomena in which there are no independent entities, only textures or clusters of sensory impressions that constitute the content of conscious awareness. In this fluctuating world of minimally sensory awareness entities exist only as aggregated phenomena of experience. But the phenomenality is not simply the experiential counterpart of corresponding physical objects and functions, for what lies outside the sphere of perception is always already constituted by the dynamic structures of our cognitive architecture.[8] The world *as perceived* is brought into existence through the activity of the senses and goes out of existence with the cessation of sensory activity. This phenomenal realm is not an objective world that exists over and above its intersubjective apprehension, for such a world, devoid of any reference to subjects of experience, is not within the purview of empirical awareness.

Now, Buddhist Abhidharma philosophers do not deny the reality of the constitutive elements of existence and/or experience (*dharmas*). Rather, the suggestion is simply that we cannot properly discern between the phenomenal character and content of experience if consciousness is not taken to have a specific kind of structure. That structure or schema is most apparent in the dual nature of empirical awareness: indeed, the body, as an instrument (*karaṇa*) of perceptual activity, is both the medium of contact with the world *and* the world with which it comes in contact.

As I have argued elsewhere (Coseru 2012: ch. 3), such a view finds an interesting parallel in Husserl's account of the paradoxical nature of the body as revealed through phenomenological reduction. For Husserl, phenomenological reduction (*epoché*)—essentially a method of bracketing ontological assumptions about the natural world in order to examine the intentional structures of consciousness—reveals the two-fold appearance of the body, first as a biological entity (*Körper*) connected to the continuum of life, and second as a medium for the expression of life (*Leib*). The body is thus the locus of lived experience and, as such, has the capacity for both exploration and receptivity. This intuition about the dual nature of embodied awareness (as locus of lived experience) discloses a world of lived experience whose boundaries are not fixed but constantly shifting in relation to the desires, actions, and attitudes of an agent (Husserl 1970: Part III: A). The world or, better still, the environment that I inhabit is not just a structured domain of causally nested objects and relations but also a meaningful world of experience. The question that both Buddhist philosophers and contemporary philosophers interested in phenomenal consciousness must address is whether intentional experiences—of the sort that disclose a world as pre-reflectively but meaningfully given—presuppose that consciousness itself, as the disclosing medium, is a knowable object. My claim is that we cannot answer this question in the affirmative: consciousness is not diachronically (or inferentially) known by a subsequent instance of cognitive awareness but rather is inherently self-aware, even if only minimally so. Though we may intend a previous moment of conscious awareness in introspection, this retrospective apprehension of consciousness as an object cannot be its essential feature.

Presence and *reflexivity* capture at the most basic level what it is like to be in a world whose boundaries are not fixed but constantly changing as the stream of consciousness follows its course. As one of the earliest proponents of what has come to be known as the active perception theory, Merleau-Ponty writes, "I cannot understand the function of living body,—except by enacting it myself" for "my body appears to me as an attitude with a view to a certain actual or possible task" (Merleau-Ponty 2002: 87, 114). What is the best or most effective way of merging this phenomenological account of temporality and disclosure with the subject of experience, the elusive domain where experience presumably takes place?

In a recent take on the debate over whether presence is basic and effortless, a kind of readiness-to-hand, or, on the contrary, something that has to be achieved, making explicit what was hitherto unthought and thus absent, Alva Noë (2012: 10) writes: "... presence does not come for free. We achieve presence. We act it out... [T]his does not mean that our attitude is that of a stranger in a strange land, and that we must always strive to bring the world into focus." Noë faults existential phenomenologists like Heidegger, Merleau-Ponty, and Hubert Dreyfus for presenting us with a distorted picture of presence. According to one version of this picture, presence stands for deliberate and effortful engagement with the world, and thus for thoughtful as opposed to unthinking attunement. Against the prevailing legacies of intellectualism and empiricism, what is sought is not thematized thought but the unthematized, absorbed coping of the readiness-to-hand of the door knob, the remote control or any other piece of equipment. Noë thinks something has gone amiss here: the problem is not that absence better captures the implicit character of our habitual practices but rather that the ways of presence have not been properly explored.

Now, if experience is a kind of presenting, the contents of which become available for interpretation and understanding only on a subsequent move, then Noë is not entirely right that presence does not come for free. If, on the other hand, conscious experience is the product of a long and complex process of skill acquisition that opens up to a domain of objects, situations, and events (rather than, say, to a world simpliciter), then there is no pristine encounter and our attitude can never be that "of a stranger in a strange land."

Recall the early account I gave of what it might be like to be a traveller to an unfamiliar destination. First of all, no destination, no matter how faraway and exotic, is upon arrival entirely unfamiliar. It cannot be, for the journey itself is an opening toward, and getting accustomed to, the unexpected. Journeying to a distant land is a lot like dwelling in anticipation for the arrival of an unknown guest: it alters the perception of one's surroundings and it invites circumspection. We are strangers in a strange land every time we let this body that is better informed, indeed, than we are about its dispositions and its surroundings fill us in about what is going on. One must choose one's examples carefully if one wants to get presence right.

Noë uses the phenomenon of reading to make his case that presence is a kind of achievement. We don't pay attention to words and letters when we read. Rather, what makes reading possible is the possession of a complicated set of skills, including but not limited to, such as the capacity to recognize symbols, to interpret, remember and anticipate. Reading takes place in a language the cultural and communicational norms of which affect how and what one reads, and what for. And while the phenomenon of reading provides a good illustration of how Noë wants us to think of presence, it does little to advance the case that we can never be strangers in a strange land, and that experience can never disclose a wholly unfamiliar world. But travelling is not like reading, unless one takes travelling to be a slow progression through the book of life. At most it is like reading in a foreign language one is yet to master fully. There are always blocks and slippages, half-meanings and guesses. Even in one's native tongue reading is not like reading in this high achieving sort of way that Noë has in mind. Ask any poet.

IV. Conclusion: Co-constitutive Emergence

Can Buddhist reductionism about persons be reconciled with an analysis of the phenomenal character of consciousness? From a philosophical standpoint, the progressive move towards an analysis of consciousness in terms of its ineliminable phenomenological features championed by thinkers like Dignāga, Dharmakīrti and their successors, can be conceivably claimed as an effort at effecting precisely such reconciliation. That we must and should identify those irreducible elements of experience (sensations, volitions, dispositions, patterns of habituation, etc) that any analysis of phenomenal consciousness can reveal does not mean, however, that there could be unintended consequences to this process of reductive analysis. Although we may debate whether or not the Buddhist phenomenological project is informed by certain metaphysical assumptions about the nature of reality, specifically the assumption that the entities that populate our world do not endure for any length of time, there is no denying that momentariness is taken not only as a principle of the nature of reality, but also (and more significantly) of cognitive awareness itself. The awareness that arises in conjunction with the activity of a given perception, thought or desire is itself impermanent and momentary: visual awareness and visual object, for instance, are both events within a mental stream of continuing relations. The question that Buddhist philosophers confront is precisely what accounts for the sense of presence that accompanies these cognitive series. In other words, if discrete, episodic cognitive events are all that constitutes the mental domain, how does appropriation and grasping, for instance, occur? I have in mind here specifically the basic mode of givenness of our experience.

Some causal account is on offer. But the causal account, it seems, gives only an incomplete picture of the mental, for even as the Sanskrit term for cognitive awareness, *vijñāna*, conveys the sense of differentiation and discernment, it is not exactly clear how such discernment also sorts between the pre-reflective and reflective aspects of experience. Indeed, consciousness is not merely a faculty for discerning and sorting through the constitutive elements of experience, but is itself an event in a series of interdependent causal and conditional factors. Thus, while the generic Buddhist viewpoint is that there is no such thing as a self as the agent of experience, for at least one group of Buddhists, generally associated with the logico-epistemological school of Dignāga and Dharmakīrti, an adequate account of phenomenal consciousness cannot dispense with a minimal sense of presence.

These Buddhist epistemologists are concerned, much like Brentano, Husserl, and many contemporary philosophers working on phenomenal consciousness, not with how things, including mental states, are judged to be (without any reference to their mode of presentation) but with how things show up to us, with the phenomena of experience just as they appear to us before we set out to reflect and theorize about them. The picture they present roughly corresponds to what some have termed non-reductive "one-level theories of consciousness": that is, theories which propose that consciousness is essentially a matter of having or being an awareness of a world that does not require a prior (representational) awareness of our own mental states.[9]

If experience is perspectivally given, it has both phenomenal salience and epistemological grounding. Reflexivism, thus, serves as a grounding principle, enabling the intentional and subjective aspects of experience to emerge co-constitutively and simultaneously. Can such a priniciple provide enough metaphysical support for I-thoughts of the sort "I am in pain," given the requirement of a criterion for individuating such thoughts in the mental stream? Do such self-ascriptions require independent criteria for individuating streams of subjectivity or can they occur solely on the basis of features that are intrinsic to each mental state?

If reflexivity has a distinctive character, a specific givenness or for-me-ness, then mis-ascriptions are unintelligible if we assume that thought is transparent with regard to its occurrent for-me-ness. This first-personal givenness of experience is unmistaken. Indeed, mental states do not just arise in a mental stream: rather, they arise as having a distinctive intentional content and phenomenal character. Reflexivism then becomes a statement about the self-presentational character of mental states: there are simply no such generic experiences of seeing or judging a particular state of affairs. Rather, there is experiential or reflexive awareness of occurrent perceptual or conceptual mental states. To postulate a basis for reflexivity outside the structure of experience is to mistakenly assume that experience is an emergent property of something that, while not itself experiential, has the functional organization to support such experiential self-ascriptions.

We do strive to bring the world into focus and we do ourselves show up in an effortful way: by walking, turning, and adjusting our posture and gaze. But it is this implicit and non-reflective awareness that lets new elements effortlessly enter our horizon while others fade away. It may seem natural to think of experience in representational terms or in terms of relations of logical entailment. However, all to often such accounts of experience obscure the fact that the operations of representation and logical entailment are not primitive. Experience is not about representing facts or establishing logical and metaphysical truths, but about acquiring, perfecting, and transmitting practical knowledge and skills.

NOTES

1. These are the so-called five *skandhas*, known as the aggregates of existence and/or experience. For details, see Coseru (2012 ch. 3).
2. Extensive discussions of these classical debates are found in Williams (1998), Garfield (2006), Dreyfus (2007), MacKenzie (2007), Kellner (2010, 2011), Chadha (2011), Arnold (2010), Coseru (2012), and Ganeri (2012).
3. This is a claim principally made by Prinz (2011).
4. For Vasubandhu's discussion of *smiti* see the *Abhidharmakośabhācya* II 24.5 (in Shastri 1970: 187). See also Jaini (2001) and Gethin (1998, 2011) for detailed discussions of the phenomenology of *smiti.*
5. Extensive critiques of the attempt to find support in the canonical literature for the existence of a higher self, perhaps equated with consciousness, are found in Warder (1970), Collins (1982), Kalupahana (1987), Harvey (1995), and De Silva (2005). Vasubandhu's *Pudgala-praticedha-prakaraṇa* ("Treatise on the Negation of the Person") provides one of most detailed Buddhist critiques of the personalist view.

6. Cf. Saṃyutta Nikāya IV, 102 (Feer 1975-2006); Majjhima Nikāya I, 130 (Chalmers 1994).
7. The parallelism between the Buddhist and Humean reductive analyses of the self is explored at some length in Giles (1993), Tillemans (1996), and Kapstein (2001).
8. It is this analysis of the content of experience that leads the ābhidharmikas to the notion of 'cognitive aspects' (*ākāra*), which represent the particular mode of presentation of the contents of one's experience. For an account of the aspectual nature of cognition, specifically of perception, in the Abhidharma literature, see Dhammajoti (2007).
9. See Thomasson (2008). One level-theories of consciousness oppose higher order thought theories, which postulate that conscious of phenomenal states are essentially those states of which we are immediately aware.

REFERENCES

Arnold, D. 2010. "Self-Awareness (*Svasaṃvitti*) and Related Doctrines of Buddhists Following Dinnāga: Philosophical Characterizations of Some of the Main Issues." *Journal of Indian Philosophy* 38: 3.

Bayne, T. and Montague, M. 2011. "Cognitive Phenomenology: An Introduction," in *Cognitive Phenomenology*, edited by T. Bayne and M. Montague. Oxford: Oxford University Press.

Bhattacharya, K. 1973. *L'ātman-Brahman dans le bouddhisme ancien*. Paris: îcole FranÁaise d'ExtrÍme Orient.

Carman, T. 2005. "On the Inescapability of Phenomenology." In Smith, D.W. and Thomasson, A.L. (eds.), *Phenomenology and Philosophy of Mind*, Oxford: Oxford University of Press, 67–89.

———. 2007. "Dennett on Seeming," *Phenomenology and the Cognitive Sciences* 6: 99–106.

Chadha, Monima. 2011. "Self-awareness: Eliminating the Myth of the 'Invisible Subject'," *Philosophy East and West* 61 (3): 453–467.

Chalmers, David J. 2003. "The Content and Epistemology of Phenomenal Belief". In *Consciousness: New Philosophical Perspectives*. Oxford University Press.

Chalmers, Robert. 1994. *The Majjhima-Nikaya*. Oxford: Pali Text Society.

Clark, A. 2006. "That Lonesome Whistle: A Puzzle for the Sensorimotor Model of Perceptual Experience," *Analysis* 66(1): 22-25.

———. 2004. "The Representational Character of Experience". In *The Future for Philosophy*, edited by Brian Leiter. 153–181.

Collins, Steven. 1982. *Selfless Persons: Imagery and Thought in Theravāda Buddhism*. Cambridge: Cambridge University Press.

Coseru, C. 2009. "Mind in Indian Buddhist Philosophy," *The Stanford Encyclopedia of Philosophy* (Winter 2009 Edition), edited by Edward N. Zalta. http://plato.stanford.edu/entries/mind-indian-buddhism/.

_______ C. 2012. *Perceiving Reality: Consciousness, Intentionality, and Cognition in Buddhist Philosophy*. New York: Oxford University Press.

Dennett, D. 2005. "What Do You Believe Is True Even Though You Cannot Yet Prove It?," *Edge World Question Center*, ed. by John Brockman.

De Silva, Padmasiri. 2005. *An Introduction to Buddhist Psychology*. 4th ed. London: Palgrave Macmillan.

Dreyfus, Georges. 2011. "Self and Subjectivity: A Middle Way Approach." In Mark Siderits, Evan Thompson, and Dan Zahavi, *Self, No-Self? Perspectives from Analytical, Phenomenological, and Indian Traditions*. Oxford: Oxford University Press, 114–156.

Dhammajoti, K.L. 2007. "*ākāra* and Direct Perception." *Pacific World Journal* 3 (9): 245–272.

Feer, L. 1975–2006. *SaCyutta Nikaya*. Pali Text Society, London: Oxford University Press.

Ganeri, Jonardon. 2012. *The Self: Consciousness, Intentionality, and the First-Person Stance*. Oxford: Oxford University Press.

— 2006. "The Conventional Status of Reflexive Awareness: What's at Stake in a Tibetan Debate?" *Philosophy East and West* 56 (2): 201–228.

Giles, J. 1993. "The No-Self Theory: Hume, Buddhism and Personal Identity." *Philosophy East and West* 43 (2): 175–200.

Harvey, Peter. 1995. *The Selfless Mind: Personality, Consciousness and Nirvāṇa in Early Buddhism*. Richmond, Surrey: Curzon Press.

Huemer, Michael. 2005. *Ethical Intuitionism*. Palgrave Macmillian.

Hulin, M. 1978. *Le Principe de l'ego dans la pens.e indienne classique: La Notion d'ahaṃkāra*. Publication de l'Institut de Civilisation Indienne. Paris: Diffusion E. de Boccard.

Husserl, E. 1970. *The Crisis of European Sciences and Transcendental Phenomenology*. Translated by David Carr. Evanston, Ill.: Northwestern University Press.

Jaini, Padmanabh S. 2001. "*Smiti* in the Abhidharma Literature and the Development of Buddhist Accounts of Memory of the Past." In *In the Mirror of Memory*, edited by Janet Gyatso, 47–60. Albany: SUNY.

Kalupahana, D. 1987. *The Principles of Buddhist Psychology*. Albany, New York: State University of New York Press.

Kapstein, Matthew. 2001. *Reason's Traces: Identity and Interpretation in Indian and Tibetan Buddhist Thought*. Somerville, Mass.: Wisdom.

Kellner, Birgit. 2010. "Self-Awareness (*Svasanvedana*) in Dinnāga' *Pramaṇsamuccaya* and *–v[tti*: A Close Reading." *Journal of Indian Philosophy* 38: 203–231.

_______2011. "Self-awareness (*SvaṣaCvedana*) and Infinite Regresses: A Comparison of Arguments by Dinnāga and Dharmakirti." *Journal of Indian Philosophy* 39 (4 5): 411–426.

Kelly, S.D. 2008. "Content and Constancy: Phenomenology, Psychology, and the Content of Perception." *Philosophy and Phenomenological Research*, 76 (3): 682-690.

MacKenzie, M. 2011. "Enacting the Self: Buddhist and Enactivist Approaches to the Emergence of the Self." In Mark Siderits, Evan Thompson, and Dan Zahavi, *Self, No-Self? Perspectives from Analytical, Phenomenological, and Indian Traditions*. Oxford: Oxford University Press, 239–273.

Merleau-Ponty, M. 1962. *Phenomenology of Perception*, (tr.) C. Smith. London: Routledge.

Noë, A. 2012. *Varieties of Experience*. Cambridge, MA: Harvard University Press.

Pitt, David. 2004. "The Phenomenology of Cognition, or, What is It Like to Think That P?" *Philosophy and Phenomenological Research* 69: 1–36.

Pryor, James. 2000. "The Skeptic and the Dogmatist". *Noûs*, 34:4, 517–549.

———. 2004. "What's Wrong with Moore's Argument?" *Philosophical Issues* 14: 349–378.

Siewert, C. 1998. *The Significance of Consciousness*, Princeton, NJ: Princeton University Press.

Smithies, Declan, 2011. "What is the Role of Consciousness in Demonstrative Thought?" *The Journal of Philosophy*, 108.1: 5-34, 2011.

Thomasson, Amie. L. 2008. "Phenomenal Consciousness and the Phenomenal World." *The Monist*, 91 (2): 191–214.

Tillemans, T. 1996. "What Would It Be Like to be Selfless? Hīnayānist Versions, Mahāyānist Versions and Derek Parfit." *ìtudes Asiatiques / Asiatische Studien* 50 (4): 835–852.

Williams, P. 1998. *The Reflexive Nature of Awareness*. London: Curzon Press.

Zahavi, Dan and Uriah Kriegel. 2015. *Philosophy of Mind and Phenomenology: Conceptual and Empirical Approaches*, edited by D.O. Dahlstrom, A. Elpidorou and W. Hopp. London: Routledge, forthcoming.

4

Minimal Self and Infallibility of Self-Knowledge

C.A. Tomy

One of the reasons why philosophical discussions on self becomes difficult is that philosophers have used the term 'self' in different senses. In this paper, I identify three ways in which the term is used: *self as given*, *self as constructed* and *self as posited*. Failure to appreciate these different senses in which the term is used leads to unnecessary controversies regarding the existence, nature and knowledge of the self. Such debates and controversies can be weeded out if we succeed in clarifying the way we employ the term while we talk of self. Of the three senses, the concept of self as given, I believe, is philosophically more challenging and interesting. Therefore, a substantial part of my discussion is devoted to explicating the notion of self as given. After elucidating the three notions of self, I shall delineate the implications of this discussion for the issue of infallibility of self-knowledge.

1. Self as Given

There seems to be a general agreement that the notion of the self originates from experience. Hence, a way in which one can start making sense of the nature of the self is to begin with an analysis of the notion of experience that we have. By experience, we understand a conscious mental episode, having three features: intentionality, phenomenality and self-awareness. The burden of the current paper is to understand the feature of self-awareness exhibited in our experience.

An important characteristic of conscious experience is that it does not occur without someone's being aware of it. By self-awareness, we understand this feature. There are no free-floating experiences; it is not possible to conceive of them without a subject to whom they belong. As Searle observes, the mental states like "[b]eliefs, desires, etc., are always somebody's beliefs and desires" (Searle, 1992, p. 17) or, as Evan Thompson points out, "[m]ental events do not occur in vacuum; they are lived by someone"(Thomson, 2007, p. 16). This someone to whom experiences belong we call self.

The truth that experience always occurs for someone is unique in the sense that it is both empirical and conceptual. It is an experiential fact that experience occurs as belonging to someone who feels it as "my experience". At the same time, it is also some sort of conceptual truth that experience necessarily involves a subject because, by the very fact of being an experience, it is always for someone. By 'self as given,' I mean that notion of the self which is both empirically given and conceptually related to episodes of experience.

The self as given is an invariable feature present in each experience. It may be called the I-revealing feature of our experience. However, we should not, allow the expression 'I-revealing' to mislead us into thinking that there exists a self or an 'I' distinct from the experience. By the I-revealing feature of an experience, I mean that feature of a conscious experience by which its occurrence is revealed to itself. It is the awareness that each experience has of itself. An episode of experience by its very nature can access itself because there is a constitutive relation/connection between conscious experience and its accessibility. This access is a reflexive access in the sense that it is turned towards itself, or reveals itself; therefore, I shall call this feature of experience reflexivity. In my view, the reflexivity that a conscious experience exhibits is the same as the sense of 'I' given in an experience. It plays a significant role in imparting a first-person perspective to one's experiences and the feeling of 'mineness' associated with them. An experience that one cannot claim as one's own cannot be an experience for that person.

We have a plurality of conscious experiences and the feature of reflexivity accompanies each one of them. Given two such experiences, say A and B, the feature of reflexivity that accompanies A cannot be differentiated from the feature of reflexivity that B exhibits. So, an experience cannot be differentiated from another experience on the basis of the feature of reflexivity alone. Reflexivity, therefore, does not figure in the identity conditions of one's experiences. What contributes prominently to the identity conditions of experiential events is their intentionality. If two experiential events have different representational content, then they are two distinct experiences. Given that there is plurality of experiences with distinct intentional contents, it follows that the feature of reflexivity or the sense of 'I' given in an experience is not that of someone who continues to exist despite the occurrences of differing experiences. The self-revealing feature that accompanies an experience is dependent on that particular experience and nothing else. Being a dependent feature of an experience, reflexivity is present only as long as the experience persists. This means that the self as given cannot be understood as an abiding substantive principle that acts as a bearer of one's experiences; self as given, on the other hand, is a non-substantive, transient one. Because the self as given is not a substantive self that persists across various time segments, I shall call this a minimalist sense of self. An important consequence of this view is that there are as many minimal selves as there are experiences. Minimal selves form a discrete plurality because none of them are numerically identical with another.

The two features under consideration, namely intentionality and self-awareness, may thus be considered as two inseparable features of one and the same experience. So, a conscious experience is a self-revealing-intentional episode. This self-revealing feature of our experience arises not only when one is conscious of external objects, but also when one is aware of one's own experiences as experiences. Since each experience can manifest itself subjectively, it makes no sense to speak of unconscious experience unless we talk of it as a possible experience, i.e. a mental state that can come to conscious level *a la* Searle. If an experience is not something available to consciousness, then it would belong to the class of theoretical entities. But something that manifests itself cannot be considered as theoretical entity. Hence, there cannot be an unconscious experience.[1]

One cannot be a self without being reflexively aware of oneself. Hence, it could be said that the defining feature of self as given in experience is its self-awareness. To put it differently, the self as given cannot exist without being aware of itself. Echoing Berkeley's famous dictum, we may say that for self as given, *to be is to be self-aware*, and conversely, *to be self-aware is to be*. Being aware of oneself constitutes the very being of self. That is to say, self as given is both a mode of being and a mode of knowing. Husserl articulates the indistinguishability of being and knowing that constitutes a subject as follows: "To be a subject is to be in the mode of being aware of oneself."[2] Since the essence of self as given is to be self-aware, and to be self-aware is to be, we may say that in the case of self as given, existence and essence are identical.

Self as given that manifests itself is an invariant dimension of each experience. Each experience is such that it occurs for itself. This sense of 'I' or self as given in experience is primitive in the sense that it is pre-theoretical. Without reflexive access that each experience has of itself, there cannot be consciousness, subjectivity, or self.

2. Self as Constructed

The thesis that self is a construct is articulated as a reaction to the view that the self is a simple substantive entity that remains unchangeable. Constructivists do not buy the idea that the self is either simple or unchanging. A construct, we know, is a complex entity built out of some basic elements. The process of construction takes place in accordance with a set of principles. While the principles at work in the production of a given type of construct may remain the same, it is not necessary that elements or the material that go into the making of the construct should remain the same. So when one says that the self is a construct, what he/she means is that the self is not a unitary entity but a complex produced in accordance with a set of principles. The constructivists do not subscribe to the view of the self as an unchanging entity; they are of the opinion that the components that go into the making of the self undergo constant change and, therefore, the phenomenon we call self is in a state of flux.

The notion of a construct is closely related to the idea of reduction. The constructs and the elements out of which they are produced belong to different ontological levels or spheres. The constructed objects are higher-level objects that can be analysed into a set of basic elements and the relations that hold among them. Therefore, our talk of the constructed object is translatable into our talk of its components and the relations that obtain among them.

Constructivists believe what we call self is analysable into its component entities and the relations permitted by the principles employed for its construction. David Hume champions a classic example of the constructivist account of self. Within his framework, the self is a bundle of interconnected perceptions furnished by the senses either external (sensation) or internal (reflection). The sensory perceptions, which form the bundle, are distinct and discrete. Since they are transient in nature, Hume rejects the notion of an abiding self. Hume emphasizes that there is no self, who acts as the substratum for the discrete short-lived perceptions.

In the absence of a substratum that unites various perceptions, it is necessary to specify how various perceptions are bound together to form self. For Hume, the principles responsible for binding the perceptions together are relations of similarity and causality. These relations are available to us because of memory. The relation of resemblance holding among a group of succeeding perceptions is responsible for the notion of continuity. Apart from providing the notion of continuance of perceptions, memory also familiarizes us with the extent or range of the succeeding of perceptions we have had. The extent of perceptions and their resemblances help us identify some sort of regularity among the perceptions, which according to Hume, is the relation of cause and effect. Though the relation of cause and effect originates from memory, once it is available it helps us extend the causal chain beyond the records of memory, think of the past perceptions, and anticipate the future ones. In short, for Hume, the self is a set of perceptions structured by the relations of similarity and cause-effect in addition to the temporal relations of simultaneity and succession.

This does not, however, mean that Hume denies that we have the sense of a self or feeling of self-identity. There is indeed the appearance of a self that is unified and self-identical. But a systematic scrutiny of this appearance shows that such a self is not real. The appearance of self as something unified and self-identical (in the sense of numerical identity) and abiding arises because of the relations of resemblance and causality that obtain among various passing perceptions.

Memory retains some of our past perceptions; it enables the mind to see that some of those perceptions are similar to the current ones. The relation of similarity helps the mind to move from one perception to another with ease. The frequent occurrence of resembling perceptions conveys notions of continuance and identity to the imagination. The relation of causation too contributes its share to the notion of self-identity and continued existence. Cause-effect relation enables one to think of the past perceptions and to anticipate the future ones, thereby suggesting to the faculty of imagination the notion of continued existence of self. Thus, our notion of self-identity results from "the smooth and uninterrupted"(Hume, 1960, p. 260) transition from one set of perceptions to another because of the relations of resemblance and causation that they hold among them (Hume, 1960, p. 260-61).

Self as constructed and self as given need not be conceived as two mutually opposing concepts of self. They could be considered as complementary provided empirically given minimal selves are taken as building blocks for the construction of the self.

3. Self as Posited

There are philosophers who view the self only as a posit and nothing else. The best example is Fichte, who is of the view that "the I posits itself as an I" (see Fichte, 2000, pp. 106-110). A posit is something that we invoke for the explanation of a given phenomenon. The self would be considered a posit if it is postulated in order to account for something. We presuppose that the I exists in order to explain the possibility of our ordinary experience. Such positing is the result of theoretical or philosophical reflection.[3] Though the behaviour of a person can be explained by appealing to various experiences the person has, some of the features of experiences themselves like feelings of self-consciousness, self-knowledge, and ownership associated with experiences and actions, sense of the unity of experiences, and the sense of agency and freedom themselves call for explanation. These features are explained by posting a self that is responsible for their emergence when experiences occur.

Self-consciousness presupposes the existence of someone who has the ability to ascribe experiences to oneself. That is, self-consciousness is possible only if there exists a self who is aware of one's own experiences. Those who understand self as a posit think that in order to have self-knowledge, it is not sufficient that there should be someone who is self-aware; genuine self-knowledge is possible only if there exists a self that does not undergo any radical changes. Thus, the self that is revealed in self-knowledge must be one that remains the same. It is this unchanging someone that is responsible for the feeling of self-identity and abidingness. The notion of ownership associated with one's experiences, and the feeling of the unity of experiences are also accounted for by invoking an abiding self that is the owner and bearer of one's experiences. Thus, we find that self as posited is part of an explanatory device. The posited I is not a given self available to us in experience. It never presents itself immediately. Hence, we are not directly aware of the posited I and we are aware of it only from a philosophical point of view, i.e. from philosophical reflection. So the posited self is not an empirical entity, but a presupposition. Hence, self as posited may be considered transcendental in nature. Like other posits, the posited self too is an object of knowledge, but unlike other posits, it is an object with subjectivity attributed to it. A similarity between the concept of self as a posit and the concept of self as a construct is worth noting. Both concepts are scientific in their orientation and are theory-laden. But there is a major difference between these concepts: philosophers who think of self as a construct believe that self is a phenomenon to be explained, whereas those who invoke self for the explanation of some of the features of experiences conceive self as part of their explanatory apparatus.

4. Is Self-Knowledge Infallible?

If we approach the controversy regarding the infallibility of self-knowledge in the light of the distinction that we have drawn above, it can easily be seen that one's response to the issue of the infallibility of self-knowledge depends on the concept of self one has in mind. If by 'self one means self as given, he/she would be committed to the infallibility of self-knowledge. On the other hand, those who consider self to be either a construct or a posit would think that it is possible that we may go wrong with regard to the knowledge of the self.

We have already seen that, in the case of self as given, being and knowing cannot be separated because to be a self is to be self-aware. Hence, in knowing the self, there cannot be a dichotomy between the subject and the object of knowledge. In the absence of a distinction between knower and the known, it is not possible to distinguish between self as it is in itself and the self as it appears. In other words, self as it appears is identical with self as it is. Thus self-knowledge is unique in that it is both subjective and objective.

Our discussion of self as given has unveiled three important aspects. They are:

(1) To be and to be self-aware are identical.

(2) In knowing self as given, there is no real distinction between the subject and the object of knowledge.

(3) Self as given does not allow any appearance-reality distinction.

These features together imply that one cannot make mistakes in knowing oneself. In the case of ordinary empirical knowledge, errors are possible because the knower and the known differ in nature and are distinct. For example, we might go wrong in perceiving an object because the object as it is in itself may differ from how it appears. Since the knower and the known are distinct in ordinary epistemic situations, the relation that obtains between subject and object would be a contingent one, which allows for the possibility of a mismatch between the representational states of the knower and the states of the object claimed to be known. The situation in self-knowledge is different in that both the subject and object of knowledge are identical. And identity being a necessary relation, there cannot be a distinction between being of the self and knowing of the self. This rules out the possibility of error. From this it follows that the knowledge of self as given is infallible.

There is another reason why knowledge of self can be considered infallible. It can be understood by contrasting the way one comes to know one's own existence and the way one comes to know the existence of physical objects and their properties. We come to know of physical objects through either observation or some sort of mediate inference. On the other hand, we come to know of the existence and nature of the self by being in a first personal mode of existence; philosophers often characterize it as some sort of acquaintance. That self-knowledge is acquired though acquaintance does not mean that there is some sort of entity by coming into direct contact with which one comes to have self-knowledge. What is meant by acquaintance here is the constitutive relation between the being of the self and self-awareness. Acquaintance understood in this way does not allow one to go wrong in knowing that one is. The knowledge that I am is not mediated knowledge based either on observation or inference but an immediate knowledge that cannot be erroneous.

Self as given, we have said, must be understood as minimal self. On similar lines, it could be maintained that the knowledge of self as given must also be minimal. The content of minimal self-knowledge is the proposition that I am or that I am self-aware. Since being of self and self-awareness cannot be distinct, the statements'I am and 'I am self-aware' convey the same proposition. We cannot conceive of a situation where 'I am' is true while 'I am self-aware' is false or vice versa. Thus, what is considered infallible is the minimal knowledge that I am or I am self-aware.

It is quite unfashionable these days to talk about the infallibility of self-knowledge, and it is not uncommon to encounter arguments for the fallibility of self-knowledge. I do not claim that all these arguments are wrong. The strength or weakness of the arguments depends on the concept of self-knowledge at issue. It cannot be maintained that the whole of what we consider self-knowledge results from self-acquaintance. One attributes to oneself a number of things based on observation or inference. Such attributions could be taken as part of self-knowledge understood in a broad sense. Such self-attributions are fallible. A second reason why we consider self-knowledge fallible is the fact we sometimes go wrong in describing our own experiences. But in such situations what we have is not fallibility of self-knowledge but error of description.

Though we cannot go wrong with regard to the knowledge of the self as given, it is possible that we are mistaken with regard to our knowledge of self as a construct or self as a posit. With regard to the constructed self, we may go wrong in identifying components that go into the making of the self or in discovering the principles and processes involved in construction. Similarly, knowledge claims about the posited self cannot have immunity from error.

Self as a posit is a theoretical entity possessing those properties that the theory in question specifies. It is possible that the posited self with the kind of properties attributed to it may not be there at all. Or, alternatively our inquiry into the nature of the phenomenon to be explained may show that in order to provide an adequate explanation, the properties attributed to posited self needs to be revised. This is a case of our theoretical knowledge going astray. Such errors are not possible in the case of minimal self-knowledge because our notion of self as given is pre-theoretical in nature.

Conclusion

The use of the concept of self in philosophical literature is not uniform. Sometimes philosophers understand it as signifying something given. Other philosophers might consider self a phenomenon that needs explanation or conceive of it as a theoretical entity for the explanation of certain aspects of our experiences. Keeping in mind the kind of distinctions outlined here, I have been arguing how the self as given must be understood. Self as given is the reflexive accessibility of one's experiences. Such a self is a minimal self whose existence and nature is known to us infallibly. If we go beyond the scope of this minimal knowledge and start attributing properties to self, it is possible that one could be mistaken about the resultant knowledge claims. However, the minimal knowledge claim that I am or I am self-aware would always remain infallible.

NOTES

1. There have been attempts to grant status of theoretical entities to phenomenal features of experience. For example, Shoemaker is of the view that qualia must be considered as theoretical entities (See Shoemaker, 1991). In accordance with the position defended in this paper, self-awareness, intentionality and phenomenality are inseparable features of our experience. For details, see Tomy (2003). The view that these features are separable is the result of abstraction, an abstraction of the kind we have when we think of colour without extension.
2. Husserl, *Zur Phanomenologie der Intersubjektivitat* II. (Husserliana 14/151). Quoted in Zahavi (2005, p. 11).
3. Ramchandra Gandhi, for whom too self is a posit, argues that it is wrong to think that the one comes to know the self inwardly. In his view, the nature of the self is known only through philosophical analysis. See Gandhi (1976, pp. 19-21).

REFERENCES

Descartes, Rene (1985). *The Philosophical Writings of Descartes*, Vol. I. Translated by John Cottingham, Robert Stoothoff, and Dugald Murdoch. New York: Cambridge University Press.

Fichte, Johann Gottlieb (2000). *Foundations of Natural Rights*. Edited and introduced by Frederick Neuhouser and translated by Curtis Bowman. Cambridge: Cambridge University Press.

Gandhi, Ramchandra (1976). *The Availability of Religious Ideas*. London: The Macmillan Press.

Hume, David (1960). *A Treatise of Human Nature*. Edited, with an Analytical Index, by L. A. Selby-Bigge. London, Oxford: Clarendon Press.

Kant, Immanuel (1998/2000). *Critique of Pure Reason*. Translated and edited by Paul Guyer and Allen W. Wood. UK, USA: Cambridge University Press.

Searle, John Rogers (1984). "Intentionality and Its Place in Nature," *Synthese* 61, 3-16.

Searle, John Rogers (1992). *The Rediscovery of Mind*. Cambridge: Bradford Books, The MIT Press.

Shoemaker, Sidney (1991). "Qualia and Consciousness," *Mind* 100, 507-24. Thompson, Evan (2007). *Mind in Life: Biology, Phenomenology and the Sciences of Mind*. USA: Harvard University Press.

Tomy, C.A. (2001). "On What It is Like to Be a Human Being: Towards an Alternative to Ramchandra Gandhi's Model of Self-Awareness," *Journal of Indian Council of Philosophical Research* 18/3, 226 241.

Tomy C.A. (2003). "An Argument for the Unity of Consciousness." In Amita Chatterjee (ed.), *Perspectives on Consciousness* (154 173). New Delhi: Jadavpur University in collaboration with Munshiram Manoharlal.

Zahavi, Dan (2005). *Subjectivity and Selfhood: Investigating the First Person Perspective*. Cambridge Mass.: MIT Press.

5

Core Selves and Dynamic Attention Centering: Between Buddhaghosa and Brian O'Shaughnessy

Jonardon Ganeri

The Buddhist philosophy of mind is fascinating because it denies that there is a self in either of the two ways that have traditionally seemed best able to make sense of that idea: the idea that the self is the owner of experience, and the idea that the self is the agent of actions including the thinking of thoughts. It is in one or both of these senses that experience might be said to have a subject. In Buddhaghosa's philosophy of mind neither agency nor ownership is permitted any role; what does the explanatory work is instead attention. Attention replaces self in the explanation of cognition's grounding in perception and action; attention replaces self in the knowledge we have of our own minds and the awareness we have of the minds of others. Buddhaghosa is emphatic that there is no self as normally conceived: "The self of the sectarians does not intrinsically (*sabhāvato*) exist" (Vibh-a. 77). Again, "[the Wheel of Existence] is devoid of any self as an experiencer of pleasure and pain conceived as 'this self or mind which speaks and feels' (M.i.8). This is how it should be understood to be without any maker or experiencer" (Vibh-a. 190); and "For this is said with reference to such feel as is accompanied by clear comprehension of [the question]: 'Who feels? Whose feel it is? For what reason do these feels come to be?' Herein, who feels? No being or person feels. Whose feel is it? Not the feel of any being or person." (Vibh-a.

263). Instead of self there is only the "minded body" (*nāma-rūpa*):

In many hundred *suttas* it is only minded body that is illustrated, not a being (*satta*), not a person (*puggala*). Therefore, just as when the component parts such as axles, wheels, frame poles, etc., are arranged in a certain way, there comes to be the mere term of common usage 'chariot', yet in the ultimate sense when each part is examined there is no chariot—and just as when the component parts of a house such as wattles, etc., are placed so that they enclose a space in a certain way, there comes to be the mere term of common usage 'house', yet in the ultimate sense there is no house—[similarly for 'fist', 'city', 'tree' etc]—so too, when there are the five aggregates [as objects] of clinging, there comes to be the mere term of common usage 'a being', 'a person', yet in the ultimate sense, when each component is examined, there is no being as a basis for the assumption 'I am' or 'I'; in the ultimate sense there is only minded body (Vism. 593–4 [xviii.28]).

The self being denied here is "'[the self] that speaks, that experiences' and so on again are modes of firm adherence to the eternalist view itself. There it is the speaker (*vado*) because it speaks. It is said that it is the doer of verbal action. It is the experiencer (*vedeyyo*) because it experiences: it is said that it becomes aware of and experiences" (Ps 71; Jayawickrama 2009, para. 35). The argument from grammar is swiftly refuted: "It was also asked: 'Since there is no experiencer of it, whose is that fruit?' Herein: 'For mere arising of the fruit/The common term 'experiencer' is used,/ Just as one says 'It fruits'/when a fruit arises on a tree.' For just as it is simply owing to the arising of tree fruits which are one part of the states called a tree, that it is said that 'the tree fruits' or 'has fruited', so it is simply owing to the arising of the fruit consisting of the pleasure and pain called experience, which is one part of the aggregates called 'deities' and 'humans', that it is said that 'a deity or a human being experiences or feels pleasure or pain.' There is therefore no need at all for another [i.e. separate] experiencer" (Vibh-a. 164; Vism. 555 [xvii.171–2]). "[The words] 'I feel' are merely a conventional expression [used] with regard to the occurrence of that feeling. In this way it should be understood that 'he knows: I feel a pleasant feeling' while discerning thus that 'it is feeling that feels by making the basis its object'." (Vibh-a. 264). The basic idea here is that a sentence containing a non-agentive active verb (as in "The door was banging in the wind") replaces a sentence with an agent ("The postman banged the door") (for discussion, see Ganeri 2012, Chapter 15).

What concept of self is rejected when self is rejected? We should understand this to be a rejection of any concept of personal or psychological identity based on agency or ownership: there is no "doer", as an agent of speech; and there is no "owner", a possessor of feelings and experiences. The "self of the sectarians" is a self that owns experience and that performs actions. Although the only actions mentioned here explicitly are speech and bodily movement, presumably they stand in for the standard Buddhist triplet of words, deed, and thought: the self denied is neither a speaker of words, nor an agent of acts, nor a thinker of thoughts. Buddhaghosa does not clarify how these two dimensions in the concept of self—agency and ownership—are related to one another. Can one have an owner of experience that is not an agent of actions, or an agent of actions that is not an owner of experience? Is the analysis of that self which we call a "being" (*satta*) or a "person" intended to be a conjunction or a disjunction of the two defining features? The first quotation suggests, but only barely, that agency is due to ownership; but the idea is not expanded upon.

Rune Johansson, nevertheless, has proposed that we can see *citta* as a sort of "core self". He says that "*citta*, generally translated 'mind' [is] the core of personality, the center of purposiveness, activity, continuity and emotionality. It is not a 'soul' (*atta*), but it is the empirical, functional self. It is mainly conscious but not restricted to the momentary conscious contents and processes. On the contrary, it includes all the layers of consciousness, even the unconscious: by it the continuity and identity are safeguarded. It has a distinctly individual form" (1969: 30). It "is by nature a center of emotions, desires and moral defilements. It is partly conscious, partly unconscious. It has also intellectual capacities and is capable of being transformed" (ibid., 107). It is "not simply the mind and also not simply personality but something of both: the organizing center, the conscious core of personality, often described as an empirical and functional self (but not *atta*), perhaps ultimately analysable into processes" (ibid., 131). In his earlier 1965 article, *citta* is "a center within personality, a conscious center for activity, purposiveness, continuity and emotionality" (1965: 179); insofar as it is not "an inner core...very much similar to all individuals" but rather "an individually formed center" (ibid., 174), it "comes very close to the psychological concept of personality" (ibid., 178). Johansson notes that "only once is it explicitly denied that *citta* is the self (S.ii.94), while it is very often denied that *viññāGa* and the other *khandhā* are the self" (ibid., 168).

The concept *citta* is certainly not that of "being" or "person" (*satta*). Is the redescription of *citta* as "core self" consistent with the evident denial of self? It could be, as long as *citta* is neither the owner of feelings and experiences nor the agent of acts of speech, deed, or thought. It does seem right that *citta* does not own the *cetasikas*: they are concomitants, not properties, of *citta*. It seems right too that *citta* is not an agent cause, for although it is a cause, it is itself causally conditioned, so it is not the "uncaused causer" that the idea of an agent cause implies. Its claim on selfhood consists simply in its being a "center". Harvey agrees with much of Johansson's description, but corrects him on two points: neglecting to emphasize that *citta* is "not only active but also acted upon" and suggesting that *citta* is a "basis" for the aggregates, when in fact "it is equivalent to one of those components, namely discernment, in its aspect as deployed, directed and directing in various ways" (1995: 114–5). Yet Johansson does say that *citta* is capable of being transformed, and although it may not be the "basis" of the concomitants, it is nevertheless not itself a concomitant but a part of the "*citta-cetasika*" complex; it is not itself mindedness (*nāma*).

Is it then nothing more than the *cetasikas* "arranged in a certain way", a point of reference in common usage alone? Certainly aware of the chariot metaphor and of general Buddhist rhetoric against self, Johansson must have had more in mind than this in what he surely intended as a provocative claim. What function or aspect of *citta* might one point to as the source of entitlement to describe it as self? It is not Zahavi's "minimal self", because the minimal self experiences and feels, indeed experiences and feels with a sense of "mineness" (Zahavi 2005). Yet is anything even more minimal than the minimal self rightly described as a self? In fact in what Johansson himself describes as the "dynamic psychology of early Buddhism", it is far from clear that there is anything properly described as an "organizing center", as opposed to an ever-evolving organization in which various components exercise various sorts of control. The main justification for this claim seems to be that *citta* is held apart from the concomitants individually, and neither can it simply be identified with the second-order property which is their organizational structure.

The most promising way to understand the idea is by appeal to the idea that attention consists in the systematicity or structuring of the stream of consciousness (O'Shaughnessy 2002; Wazl 2011). Specifically, Wazl says that "consciously attending to something consists in the conscious mental processes of structuring one's stream of consciousness so that some parts of it are more central than others" (2011: 158). The claim that *citta* is a core self might now be rephrased as being that *citta* consists of those parts of one's stream of consciousness (*santāna*) that have been made more central in the course of consciously attending. So then *citta* is not a mere collection, nor is it the mere totality, but rather it is, at any given moment, those specific elements which attention centralizes. We need not endorse Wazl's claim to have identified the essence of attention in order to agree with him that in attention there is a structuring of the stream of consciousness; and insofar as what is distinctive of attentional structuring is that it enables a center/periphery distinction to be drawn in relation to the stream of consciousness, we can use that distinction to explicate the idea that *citta* is a core self. In this case, what is meant by "self" is "those aspects of the structure of the stream of consciousness which dynamically take center stage when there is attention." The core self is the way attention shows up in the organization of the stream of consciousness. So the notion of self as agent of actions and owner of experiences is replaced with a notion of self as attentional centering. This fits nicely with the prominent idea, in early Buddhism, that *citta* can be modified and transformed in the training and cultivation of skills of attention. The reason it is possible to modify *citta* by training one's attention is simply that *citta* consists in the way attention structures the stream of consciousness. And it fits nicely too with the central claim of this book, that attention replaces self in the grounding of cognition. The "core self", *citta*, is a surrogate self, something that performs many of the principal cognitive tasks of the "self of the sectarians" but has none of the metaphysical baggage, and cannot properly be called "self" if it is fundamental to the functional role of that concept that it provides experience with ownership and agency.

Jennings (2012) has argued that many aspects of attention can be unified under the rubric "attention is a process of mental selection that is within the control of the subject", that it is "subject- directed mental selection", where a subject is "that to which we attribute such capacities as consciously experiencing, knowing, thinking, planning, and perceiving" (2012: 537). Let us ignore the possibility that our attribution practices might themselves be what produce the "subject", and take it that she is simply articulating the concept of the "self of the sectarians", the experiencer and the doer. The claim is then that the subject directs the selection processes in attention. This is the heart of the disagreement between the two concepts of "self" in play: one claims that the center/periphery distinction within the structure of the stream of consciousness is directed by a subject external to itself; the other identifies the center with the self. In the second view, attention is itself intentional, not requiring direction from the outside. It contains its goals and plans within itself, as it were. As restricted to the case of selective attention, then, a first element in the claim that attention replaces self in the grounding of cognition is that dynamic attentional centering is sufficient for action-planning, perception, and other cognitive tasks.

Let me turn to reflect on the very important discussion in

O'Shaughnessy's *Consciousness and the World* (O'Shaughnessy 2002). O'Shaughnessy begins by arguing that attention is necessary for consciousness, or, more precisely, that consciousness "necessitates the accessibility of the perceptual attention" (2002: 10). Attention is necessary for consciousness because consciousness has a necessary truth-orientation; it is a "reality-detector", and indeed that is what it means to say that consciousness puts us in contact with reality, that "whereas dreams merely putatively are of Reality, consciousness is 'in touch with' Reality" (ibid., 12). There are already echoes here of two claims Buddhaghosa has made, that engagement (*phassa*) and attention (*manasikāra*) are concomitants (O'Shaughnessy speaks rather of *commitments*) of consciousness. As for the nature of attention, O'Shaughnessy says that a natural and appropriate imagery can easily turn into a myth. The natural imagery is of attention as mental 'life-blood', as "a sort of mental 'space' of awareness present in the mind, which is occupied exclusively by the experiences it enables to exist" (ibid., 285), for "if (say) emotion or thought or perception are to so much as *exist*, attention needs to be available" (277). The point of the imagery is that it captures that sense in which attention is limited ("occupied"), a sense that O'Shaughnessy illustrates with the example of driving a car through a narrow pass, one's attention to the driving precluding one from attending to a difficult conversation at the same time. O'Shaughnessy cautions that this imagery can easily be misunderstood, for it may lead to the impression that the experiences which attention enables to exist are one thing and the "mental space" of awareness is something else:

The myth in question takes the following form. It is of a mental existent (which I shall call S), a particular mental 'space' that is of type awareness (in some sense), which coexists with and is distinct from contemporaneous experiences. Those experiences relate to that awareness-space, not as its objects, but as its occupants, and that property enables them to exist. (285).

Or again,

That to which these various expressions refer ["the

attention", "awareness"] is something that is closely akin to a psychic space. And yet as we have just seen in the recent discussion of the mythical S, it cannot be something that, like the space of a canvas or stage, precedes and outlives its occupants. (288).

Instead of falling into the myth, O'Shaughnessy says that we should realize that "what we have in mind in speaking of 'The Attention'... is nothing less than Experiential Consciousness itself...To repeat, it is what we frequently refer to as 'the stream of consciousness' (of literary fame)" (288).

'Experiential Consciousness' is O'Shaughnessy's term for the stream of consciousness (15). His idea is that to find our attention occupied by a certain given experience is for the experience to partly constitute the attention, much as a single piece does a jigsaw puzzle; what is occupied by experiences is, as he puts it, a *system* of those experiences, the system being the network of interrelationships which experiences need in order to exist (288). He concludes:

Denuded of the above of array of [systemic] properties, they [sc. experiences] would be like so many psychological atoms wandering in a void. Endowed with them, they constitute a continuous ongoing phenomenon which is a sort of circle or center of awareness. This awareness is the Attention. (289–90).

I need hardly add that "the mythical S"—this unspeakable nothing whose possible existence is acknowledged not even in the index of *Consciousness and the World*—is the self. For O'Shaughnessy, as for Buddhaghosa, attention replaces self in the explanation of perception, thought, and emotion. What O'Shaughnessy does brilliantly is to demonstrate how the natural imagery of attention is what itself gives rise to the Myth of Self as Detached from Experience; the "self of the sectarians" is a bad attempt to formulate a good insight about attention. Of course nothing can prevent us, should we so wish, from stipulatively *defining* the word "self" to mean the attention, and this I think is just what the claim that *citta* is "core self" ultimately comes to.

REFERENCES

Ganeri, (Jonardon (2012). *The Self: Naturalism, Consciousness, and the First-Person Stance* (Oxford: Oxford University Press).

Harvey, (Peter (1995). *The Selfless Mind: Personality, Consciousness and Nirvāṇa in Early Buddhism* (London: Routledge Curzon).

Jayawickrama, Na (2009). "The Exegesis of the *Sabbāsava Sutta*,"in K.L. Dhammajoti and Y. Karunadasa eds., *Buddhist and Pali Studies in Honour of Kakkapalliye Anuruddha* (Hong Kong: Centre for Buddhist Studies, University of Hong Kong, pp. 1-42.

Jennings, Carolyn D. (2012). "The Subject of Attention," *Synthese* 189: 535-554.

Johansson, Rune E.A. (1965). "Citta, mano, viññāṇa—A Psychosemantic Investigation," *University of Ceylon Review* 23.1&2: 165–215.

Johansson, Rune E.A. (1969). *The Psychology of Nirvāṇa* (London: George, Allen and Unwin).

Johansson, Rune E.A. (1979). *The Dynamic Psychology of Early Buddhism* (London: Curzon).

Ñāṇamoli, Bhikkhu (1991), transl. *The Path of Puri:ication: Visuddhimagga by Bhadantācariya Buddhaghosa* (Kandy: Buddhist Publication Society, 5th (ed.). [Vism]

Ñāṇamoli, Bhikkhu (1996), transl. *The Dispeller of Delusion (Sammohavinodanī)*, Revised for Publication by L.S. Cousins, Nyanaponika Mahāthera and C.M.M. Shaw (Oxford: Pali Text Society, 2 vols.). [Vibh-a]

O'Shaughnessy, Brian (1980). *The Will: A Dual Aspect Theory* (Cambridge: Cambridge University Press).

Tin, Pe Maung (1920), transl. *The Expositor (Atthasālinī): Buddhaghosa's Commentary on the Dhammasangaṇī, the First Book of the Abhidhamma Pimaka* (Oxford: Pali Text Society, 2 vols.). [As]

Wazl, Sebastian (2011). "Attention as Structuring of the Stream of Consciousness," in Mole, Christopher, Declan Smithies and Wayne Wu eds. (2011). *Attention: Philosophical and Psychological Essays* (New York: Oxford University Press), pp. 145-173.

Zahavi, Dan (2005). *Subjectivity and Selfhood: Investigating the First-Person Perspective* (MIT Press).

6

The Testimony of Ananyā: Ramchandra Gandhi's Reconstruction of Self and Subjectivity

Amita Chatterjee

Self is an entity many-splendoured and multi-dimensional. So a search for self often involves unravelling its different layers, hence the oft-used metaphor of peeling of an onion. After its different layers are taken apart, whether there remains anything which can be identified as the 'core self' is a much-debated issue. Both common men and philosophers are comfortable to pin down the salience of self in its subjectivity and reflexive awareness—as 'a pure identity pole'. Self is supposedly autonomous and shines by its own light. But interestingly, as one separates its different strands, one is bound to encounter its 'other' because self sustains its identity only in opposition to its other, through construction and representation of alterity. Let us consider some important arguments that have been advanced by different schools of Indian philosophy which will render the 'othering' process quite trasparent. I am, however, presenting these arguments without making any reference to the specific philosophical systems.

The self is something individual and biologically it is distinct from the 'other'. This distinction needs to be acknowledged across all life forms, since it is the key to self-preservation. Fundamental to self-preservation is demarcating or defining the identity of the respective organism so that it can distinguish itself from all the 'others' and then devising a mechanism to defend itself from its predators. So *self-recognition* and *resisting self-destruction* constitute the basic biological principle of self-preservation. This brings in the notion of boundary, which is the primary strategy of demarcating 'self' from 'other', 'me' from 'rest of the world'. Here the boundary of self is considered coextensive with the body which it inhabits.

Think of self as the referent of the personal pronoun 'I'. Immediately the single bounded entity will differentiate itself from each and every non-I.

While you posit self to explain a unity of consciousness, the other subjects and objects of consciousness become its other.

If self is defined as the experiencer, as corollary all material objects incapable of having experience become its other.

If you say that our thought, knowledge, etc. imply the existence of a knower or a thinker which is none other than self, then that knower stands apart from the known and the process of knowing.

The self in the traditional scheme is thought of as the agent who has knowledge of the materials and the means for attaining some end. The self also has goals, beliefs and desires and hence is conscious. Again, agency is thought to be the correlate of responsibility. We attribute beliefs, desires, sensations and intentional actions to the self along with responsibility for those actions. Thus, the self is not merely an agent but also a moral agent who is liable to be blamed or praised for his actions. An objection was raised as to why moral responsibility is ascribed to the self when the performer of all our actions is the body. Two common responses to this objection are available in the Indian philosophical literature. The traditional theorists believed that the body could not have beliefs, desires, etc., since it is inert. Moreover, the body is never free. It is bound and often performs actions under biological constrains. Unlike the body, the self has autonomy over what it does. Hence in this sense the body becomes the other of the self.

This process of construction of the other is not confined to the construction of identity (given temporary identity in the process of identity construction is always open to revision) of individual self, but spills over to the social process of categorization and classification. The most general strategies involved in construction of others are as follows. First it is proposed that whatever is other than ourselves is less/ inadequate than ourselves. Consequently we divide between in-groups and out-groups on the basis of some normative expectations. In the process of building solidarity for in-group, we establish certain norms and boundaries and exclude those as deviants who do not meet our expectations. So our concept of the other is always judgmental, always implies a value difference in which our values are considered superior to those of the other. Owing to this, some people, some beings are pushed to the periphery and marginalized. Through adopting such means for the construction of alterity, we also foster prejudice and stereotypes. This marginalized category of 'less than ourselves' and 'less than human' has been historically found to include different sub-categories at different times using as markers gender, race, class, ethnicity, language, sexuality, national origin, culture. religion, etc. Further, by this process of othering, the human race has been alienated from non-human creatures and non-living nature thus perpetuating various disastrous and invidious consequences for the marginalized. The marginalized, in turn, loses autonomy, subject-hood, personhood and agency. The relation between self and others thus becomes absolutely skewed. Under the circumstances, the question of contention is: given that the same process of identifying self is at the root of creating its other, how are we supposed to bridge this gap? Ramchandra Gandhi in *Sita's Kitchen*[1] has attempted to give an answer to this question by reconstructing the notion of selfhood and subjectivity in the light of Ramana Maharshi's teachings.

Let us now look at Ramchandra Gandhi's adaptation of the *Vinaya-pitaka* text 'Bhaddavaggiyavattu'. Literally rendered, it means 'Story of the Rich' or more idiomatically 'Something Noble' or 'A Thing of Class'. The original story runs thus. Once while the Buddha was sitting inside a grove in Uruvela, a large group of young aristocrats, both men and women, approached him and asked whether he had seen a slave girl in the vicinity. These young people were partying in the adjacent forest. They had brought the slave girl with them to act as a harlot for one of the rich young men who had no wife. Engrossed in fun and play, they did not pay any attention to the slave girl who was asked to keep a watch on jewellery and other valuable items that they were carrying with them. Being bored and dejected, the slave girl absconded with all the valuables. When her masters found her missing, the entire party started looking for her to recover their valuables and to punish the thief.

The Buddha persuaded these young men and women not to go in search of the thieving slave but to start searching for their own selves, which according to the Buddha, are ever-elusive, yet that which those of noble birth must seek. The Buddha preached to them, they saw the truth and received the *upasampadā* ordination from the Buddha. Here ends the original story. Ramchandra Gandhi transforms the narrative slightly. In *Sītā's Kitchen*, the slave girl is from a tribal community; her name is Ananyā, meaning, 'no other', i.e. self. Initially the name appears rather ironical though it may be appropriate for the underlying philosophy which shows that self is peerless, the true surplus/ extra in existence, which cannot escape from us but we often escape from it through our acquisitive self-forgetfulness. The identity of Ananyā at the beginning of the story reveals others within others. Ananyā was a woman, a tribal woman and on top of it she was a slave. In a patriarchal urban society, she lacked subjecthood, agency and autonomy and was branded as a perpetual other, a no-one, non-self. As a tribal slave girl, she enjoyed no rights but was a victim of all sorts of injustice. Ananyā took refuge in the Buddha and confessed that she did steal the valuables of her masters. The Buddha received the information calmly, offered water to the thirsty woman and talked to her in a soothing manner so that fear of death and other forms of humiliation were removed from her mind and she felt sufficiently empowered as an individual being.

The Buddha had already convinced the young aristocrats to purify their selves by not taking revenge against an escaping, thieving slave. The converted aristocrats even granted Ananyā freedom from slavery. But the nihilists and the dualists of the then society were unhappy with the outcome of the Buddha's intervention and a symposium was called to debate the issues relating to morality and freedom, self and subjectivity, arising out of the aforementioned incident. In that imaginary symposium, the Buddha, Mahāvīra, Brahmanical philosophers, Paurāṇikas, nihilists, dualists, sceptics, a group of high and low born citizens were all present. Lord Mahāvīra had a silent presence there, and the rest discussed in detail the significance of human life and the future of human civilization. However, there were no representatives of sub-human species or of nature.

In the symposium, the opening statement was made by Ajita Keśakambalin. Ajita was an annihilationist who did not believe that there was any center to anything at all and hence was an opponent of both the Upanishadic monists who admitted the centrality of one transcendental self and of the Buddha who explained the concept of self from within his philosophy of the Middle Path. Ajita insisted that the young aristocrats should not pin their faith and hope on the Buddha's teaching of non-violence. He predicted that very naturally human civilization would come to an end due to internal strife amongst human beings. Such conflicts are unavoidable because of violence built in Nature and ineradicability of the ego. That is the lesson we derive from our epics—the Rāmāyaṇa and the Mahābhārata. According to Ajita, that egotism provokes violence and injustice has been amply exemplified in Rāma's unjust behaviour towards Sitā and Krishna's engineering of the destruction of the entire Kaurava clan. It is, therefore, inevitable that eventually the ego and its counterpart—the material reality, will reduce the entire creation to naught. Ajita here adopted the classic strategy of othering by projecting on to Nature qualities like violence and egotism which we consider 'disvalues'.

The Buddha countered this view by pointing out that neither the material nature nor life is essentially violent, rather these are suffused with self-restraint. The Buddha and Mahāvīra preached the virtue of selflessness and aimed at the eradication of the self-centered ego because this is not only possible but also natural. The Rāmāyaṇa and the Mahābhārata stories actually bear witness to this fact, asserted the Buddha in his speech, contradicting Ajita's reading of the epics. The Rāmāyaṇa story begins with the violation of an ecological principle (killing of one of a pair of copulating birds) followed by other instances of a similar nature, as a result of which Rāma and Sītā were separated. Ramchandra Gandhi, therefore, attributed these prophetic words to the Buddha: 'It is not impossible that future humanity will fall into the *āsuric* temptation of breaking open the secret vaults of matter and robbing it of untamable energy in the service of greed and terror and endanger all life on earth...But do not make human folly unredeemable by grounding it this time in some alleged unrestrained causal fury at the heart of the nature of material process and reality. Causality everywhere is compassionate in its reigned-in-effectuality. It is not *hiṃsā*, but *ahiṃsā*, which is rooted in the nature of life and matter and nothingness.'[2] The Buddha ended his long elaborate speech by declaring that self-restraint or self-limitation is even more dramatically exemplified by nothingness than by life or material reality and thus reminded all present in the assembly the identification between upanishadic self-realization and nirvanic enlightenment.

This move of the Buddha annoyed Ajita and his followers to no end. Ajita chided the Buddha for not disclaimimg the upanishadic grand narrative of self-realization which according to him is the grandest of delusions, which the Buddha himself realized but surprisingly in his present discourse he had dressed up nothingness in such a manner that the nothingness of *nirvāṇa* looked exactly like upanishadic *moksha*. However this move was heartily welcomed by the Pauraṇikas as well as the representatives of the aristocracy. They considered it fortunate that thanks to the compassion of the Tathāgata they could realize that there is no real otherness, each and every other is an image of the self and therefore a mere apparent other.

This view might appear strange to the scholars of Indian philosophy because we all know that the Buddha's theory of no-self is diametrically opposed to the upanishadic theory of one supreme self. So we need to look for some justification of such an apparently inauthentic account. To understand this position, first, we need to contrast the Buddhist ideal of liberation with that of the orthodox philosophical tradition. The aim of both traditions is absolute eradication of pain and suffering. But, according to the Hindu thought, the path to liberation involves 'disentangling' myself from everything external to me, which includes body, sense organs, mind and even intellect. In the liberated state, there remains self alone disembodied and property-less. To the Buddhist, on the other hand, liberation means getting rid of the 'me' conceit. In one's journey from self-centeredness to selflessness, one needs to 'deconstruct' experience thoroughly. This is the significance of the Buddha's 'vision' under the Bodhi Tree, which was of experience-in-itself, abstracted not only from the object of experience, but also from any supposed subject of experience (supposed because in reality, there is no self). Hence, emptiness became the central way of thinking in Buddhism, there being no subjectivity, no objectivity, no substantiality either. This is the unifying thread that runs through the thought-process of different Buddhist sects which Ramchandra names the Buddhist *advaita*. 'Nothingness is not a *thing* in competition with other things. Indeed it is continuous with the heart of each thing which is also a not-thingness, like the selfhood of human personality which is also not a being in competition with other beings and things but the limitless space of not-thingness, emptiness.'[3] The practice of compassion by human beings is a realization of the omnipresence of self or nothingness and also a realization of their identity.

To lend authenticity to this position Ramchandra Gandhi writes, 'The Tathāgata in this text is daring the lost sheep of the upanishadic tradition (who are in danger of becoming predatory wolves in that age of metaphysical and moral bankruptcy) to return to its source, self which is not an entity among entities but non-entitative self-consciousness and self-realization, i.e. emptiness. The rich young aristocrats have not lost their slave-owning status in society, and the Buddha is not asking them to make good a non-existent loss. What they have lost is not status but self, self-realizing self-consciousness; which the Tathāgata compassionately asks them to seek.'[4] The Buddha was wise enough to realize that to get rid of iniquities and violence prevalent in a society it is necessary to change the outlook of its people. Only a change of heart can ensure a radical change in outlook. It is futile to enjoin some laws and hope to bring about a social change, if people do not feel the need and urge for change. The Buddha felt that a hierarchy-less compassionate society will emerge only when members of that society are inspired by the ideal of selflessness. It cannot be imposed from outside.

The narrative works up to a climax when an important member of the aristocracy, Prince Parantapa, requests Ananyā to give her testimony as the concluding speech of the symposium. Parantapa declared, 'our presumptuous ownership and mistreatment of Ananyā was a blasphemous denial of the unenslavability of omnipresent, infinitely many-centered ātman. Ananyā literally means self and we treated her as an other, not-self, distorting, instead of imaging, the truth of ourselves and all things and nothingness in our unethical relationship with her.'[5] Whoever could think of this a week ago that a slave belonging to a marginalized tribal community would receive such a recognition? The miracle nonetheless happened as a result of internalizing the compassionate teaching of the Buddha.

Ananyā having paid her homage to the Buddha and Mahavīra, started speaking confidently. She confessed at the outset that she absconded with jewels and ornaments of her former masters entirely on an impulse. It was not pre-planned. While she was waiting to be called, all of a sudden, it dawned on her that her masters had been unjust not only to her and her community, but also to all non-human life and nature. Her masters really did not have any right to the jewels and ornaments which she was safeguarding. These things belong to the Mother Earth. She heard from her own mother that there is a shrine of the Mother Goddess Sitā in Ayodhya by the river Sarayu. She wanted to make an offering of the jewels and ornaments to Sītā, the archetype of the Mother Earth, at her shrine in Ayodhya, 'which was a field of nourishment of all self-images of self'. Ananyā stole the valuables to make atonement for humanity's violence towards and insensitive plundering of the Mother Earth. Ananyā, however, was conscious that though her ultimate end was good, it did not justify the means she had adopted for attaining that end. She was too conscious of the fact that she herself was a betrayer. She had betrayed the trust of her employers; a betrayal, she understood, cannot atone for betrayal. But she knew that if she were caught she would be summarily executed or else she would once again have to go back to her life of indignity. So she wanted to hand over the ornaments to the Buddha and kill herself by drowning in the river Sarayu after offering worship to Sitā.

The Buddha restrained her from taking any extreme step. That Ananyā stole the jewellery to atone on behalf of humanity and not for her own benefit proved that she had already advanced in the path of selflessness and therefore should not contemplate dying. Besides, Ananyā would soon be released from bondage as the Buddha had been able to convince her masters that no one can ever take away the timeless autonomy of self just as one cannot ever be banished from the boundless expanse of the sky, a symbol of the limitless kingdom of self-realization. The Buddha thus freed Ananyā of all duality, the root cause of all her mortal fear simply by walking compassionately towards her and by providing her asylum. It was surprising that even before Tathāgata uttered a single word, the ignorant and illiterate tribal girl could receive the wisdom that the Buddha wanted to impart to her. She said, 'our walking towards each other abridges the distance of duality and highlights the singularity of selfhood. The circumambient sky which envelops us and all things is self's image of itself, not as a thing among other things, but as limitless inclusiveness.'[6] The Buddha said, 'enslaved and compromised though it is increasingly, aboriginal humanity still matchlessly images self's beginninglessness in its dateless co-habitation with all non-human forms of life on earth. A regenerate modernity would cease to be a past-denying and a future-destroying aberration if it became a trustee of contemporaneity, self's intimate image of itself as ever-presentness, timelessness, unfading freshness, thus acquiring the status not only of civilization but also of recurrent realization.'[7] How could Ananyā grasp the intent of this deep thought?

Ananyā said that after several hours of running she had collapsed in a thicket of bushes and fallen asleep out of sheer exhaustion. She had a dream which prepared her for her blessed meeting with the Lord Buddha. In her dream came an adivasi ascetic who told her of this great meeting and prophesied, '...the Buddha's greatest gift to humanity is his realization and restatement of the non-dualist truth of the upanishadic tradition without recourse to the scriptural authority and vocabulary of that tradition: a simultaneous vindication of independence and inheritance....Self-realization and self-restraint—the heart of advaita and aboriginality would thus become available to all humanity.'[8]

Through this prophecy Ramchandra Gandhi tried to convey to us what he took to be our philosophical inheritance. Before the advent of modernity and city-centered civilization, there were highly ecology-sensitive tribal societies. The motto of the primitive tribal cultures was to live and let live—a form of life which the tribes imbibed from Nature herself. The tribal world-view was holistic where each and every creature has its own place. Every existence is intertwined with its other and because of this interdependence, a being and its other cannot really be separated—here 'otherness' is merely apparent. The chief binding factor in an ecological community is self-restraint—no one encroaches upon the territory of the other without necessity. This brings all components of nature closer to each other; compassion and cooperation reign there, not conflict and competition. Both the Buddha and Mahāvīra in the story have internalized these values but in different ways. The Jaina non-violence (*ahiṃsā*) emphasizes the most rigorous form of self-restraint, while in Buddhism non-violence is the other name of compassion, the Golden Mean. As the tribal communities were the closest to Nature, members of these communities supposedly manifest this inter-relatedness in every walk of their life, the most natural consequence of which is the denial of hierarchy in all forms. That may not be a historical fact; most probably, that is an unreal romantic reading of the primitive communities. However, even if there were no non-hierarchical societies in the past anywhere in the world, establishment of such a non-hierarchical society should be our dream. This vision alone can save humanity from annihilation—'inviting us to live ethically and ecologically sensitively by loving one another and the world as ourselves.'[9] This is the message of the Buddhist *nirvāṇa*, the upanishadic *advaita* and the fertility cults of tribal religions which teach us to replace hierarchy with interdependence and homogeneous inclusion by heterogeneous synthesis.

This also reminds us of the truth of the aboriginal culture which the tribal king Guha told Rāma in the Rāmayaṇa story. Before Rāma with Lakshmaṇa and Sītā entered the forest, Guha narrated to him how the Earth in her role as the Divine Mother nourishes all and takes care of all her creatures that are forms of manifestation of herself, i.e. the Primal Energy. This Primal Energy, however, is characterized by exemplary self-restraint. Even non-material nature does not release the relentless violence that is churning in the bosom of the earth. It gets released only when some ecological principles are violated. Rāma was thus offered the ancient wisdom of interdependence of the whole of nature and was warned of the evil consequences that might result from the violation of ecological principles amounting to violence against one's own self. 'In the animate world this wisdom is disowned by the human species alone, especially if not exclusively by its non-aboriginal societies.'[10] On many occasions, in the Rāmāyaṇa story, this precept was forgotten precipitating calamitous consequences. Not only that, says Professor Gandhi, the modern society too has totally forgotten this message and is continuing its indiscriminate plundering of the earth and its unjust denial of the rights of the forest-people.

Apropos bridging the gulf between self and other, the upanishads and Buddhist texts propose apparently diverse solutions. According to the upanishads, originally there was only one Being. It wished to be many. Out of itself by exercising its power, it created the world. So the entire world with all things and beings in it is nothing but images/objects of imagination/ play of the ultimate reality. The ultimate reality is of the nature of existence, consciousness and bliss. The same real manifests itself differently in different life-forms (*Eko baśi sarvabhutāntarātmā ekam rūpam bahudhā yah karoti, Katha 98/12).* So I and my other, being manifest images of the same self-conscious reality, merge into that one ultimate reality, singular self-consciousness when we attain self-knowledge and the distinction between self and other disappears. Just as a doll made of salt gets dissolved if it is thrown into the sea, similarly both I and my others lose our temporary identities and get united in that transcedent self. The Buddhist tradition, on the other hand, denies the reality of a permanent transcendent self. Both the Buddha and early Buddhists maintain that when realization dawns one realizes that there is neither objectivity nor subjectivity nor substantiality but only experience-in-itself, hence no ego and therefore no distinction between self and other. According to interpreters like T.R.V. Murti, the Buddhist theory of impermanent self or no-self is the flip side of the upanishadic self. Ramchandra Gandhi takes this interpretation seriously and describes the upanishadic moksha and the Buddhist nirvāṇa as complementary to each other. However, in both the schemes the distance between self and other is bridged through homogenization by obliterating the differences among self and others. In the last analysis either there is one thing or there is nothing. These theories highlight the similarity amongst different selves but cannot support pluralism or explain alterity. The aboriginal philosophy, on the other hand, could accommodate alterity in the true sense of the term within its holistic structure. Here, however, Ramchandra Gandhi is rather ambivalent. His narrative right from the beginning has been placed in a dialogical setting. In a well-developed dialogue recognition of alterity is a necessity. It is true that it is expected that different parties participating in a dialogue will be able and willing to revise and change their initial standpoints by taking the position and utterances of others into account and thus divergent voices are expected to converge, yet this convergence does not mean that all differences will be thereby eliminated. In some places in the dialogue we find him talking in this vein. Self as has been pointed out by Parantapa is many-centered—meaning each self sustains its being in relation to others. There is other in me as well as I in others. Each self in relation to multiple others has to situate itself in different I-positions and negotiate its subjectivity and agency vis-a-vis its numerous others. As in this whole, there is no fixed center, each can retain its nature and act accordingly in harmony with others. Besides, the coupling between self and other being constitutive, peeling layers of self also leads to peeling layers of others. Thus if the slave girl attains her freedom and becomes an autonomous agent, her others also cease to be masters; if the person Ananyā is not identified in terms of her gender, her others too lose their gender identity. Each in relation to others maintain the stability of the whole and being endowed with ecological subjectivity leaves the space of negotiations open for all.

But by repeated identification of the upanishadic monism, the Buddhist theory of emptiness and the philosophy of aboriginal holism, Ramchandra Gandhi has shifted from this position. I would like you to consider the following quote where he succinctly identifies all three approaches. 'The apparent otherness of fellow human beings, non-human living beings, non-human matter and nature and environing nothingness melts down in the fire of moksha, revealing self's infinite variety of self-images in an ecstatic dance of ethically and ecologically sensitive interdependence and existential autonomy.'[11] Because of his overwhelming faith in Vedantic monism, Ramchandra Gandhi interpreted the so-called aboriginal philosophy too in an idealistic/monistic way according to which every particular is internally inseparable from every other, because of which even the slightest disturbance in any part of nature is sure to cause upheavals all over the whole—a view which is perfectly compatible with idealistic monism. In the end he simply ignored the fact that the mode of bridging the distance between self and others is not exhausted by finding similarity or homogeneity among different participants, and that it is possible to read our epics and some systems of philosophy in a different way in the model of dialogical self theory where the relation amongst different beings is not internally constituted or a priori given but emerges through dialogues and negotiations. If we had raised this point he would probably have said that simple people rarely get involved in dialogues, rather they have some direct means of understanding others and this mode of communication is markedly spiritual. However, one with a realist and pluralist propensity would still like to bring self and others closer to each other within an overarching dialogical frame without obliterating the alterity of alter-egos and thus upholding the norms of a dynamic pluralistic democratic society.

NOTES AND REFERENCES

1. *Sita's Kitchen: A Testimony of Faith and Enquiry*, Wiley Eastern Limited, New Delhi, 1994.
2. Ibid., p. 44.
3. Ibid., p. 44.
4. Ibid., p. 117.
5. Ibid., p. 66.
6. Ibid., p. 78,
7. Ibid., p. 79,
8. Ibid., p. 74,
9. Ibid., p. 10.
10. Ibid., p. 5.
11. Ibid., p. 66.

7

Perception, Apperception and Understanding of the 'Other': A Phenomenological Appraisal of Nyāya, Buddhist and Advaitin Theory of Knowledge

Ajay Verma

Philosophical problems regarding what constitutes the object of knowledge are predominantly epistemological in nature. From a realist or scientific point of view the question is more ontological in nature than epistemological. In the West, Husserl raises some important questions regarding what should be the starting point of philosophy. This question leads him to consider the question regarding what constitutes the actual object of knowledge. In Indian philosophy such questions are not so well pronounced and remain obfuscated at best. Rejection of any purely formalistic account of knowledge by realist schools of Indian philosophy makes the discussion on these issues even more difficult. This difficulty widens even further if we try to consider these questions in isolation from their metaphysics. The reasons for predilection towards metaphysics specially among orthodox schools of classical Indian philosophy are far from obscure. Emphasis on schools of thought over independent thinking, adherence to the metaphysical tenets or beliefs of the parent system, scriptural authority of words of Vedas and of the living seers, are some of the predominant features of Indian orthodox systems. Indian philosophical texts are replete with debates on epistemological issues but there is a subtle sheath of metaphysics that almost invisibly runs through every dimension of such debate whether it is the *vṛtti-jñana* of Advaita or the notion of *vijñāna* in Buddhist idealism or the theory of 'threefold concourse' in Indian Realism.

In this paper I present an exposition of Nyāya, Buddhist and Śamkara's perspectives on the issues related to the phenomenological constitution of the object of our knowledge. An important question that comes into relief when we consider any question regarding the epistemological status of the object of knowledge is the role of the subject in this process. Does the subject in any way contribute in the generation of knowledge in a given knowing instance? How could one account for unity of apperception without assigning any role to the knower's mind? These are some of the queries that I consider in this paper and juxtapose Nyāya, Buddhist and Śamkara's answers to these questions. As an appendix to my discussion on these various themes, I conclude with a short comment regarding how these different epistemological accounts of subjects and objects of knowledge and the way the two relate in a knowledge instance could have ramifications for how we conceive of and relate to *the Other* in a collectivity.

I

It is generally admitted by all the schools of Indian philosophy that perceptual knowledge results from an instance of sense-object contact which produces a certain idea of the object in the mind. Regarding this idea of the object in mind different philosophers have given different opinions. For Nyāya-Vaiṣeśika which is a realist pluralist school of thought, the idea of the object in our mind which is further encoded in language represents the actual nature of the object concerned without any gap. The Naiyāyikas maintain that language, thought and reality are three different dimensions of the same ontic plurality. The structure of language defines the limits of thought and exhausts completely the universe of discourse such that there is nothing that exists but cannot be expressed or vice-versa. On this account the structure of the outside world is what reflects itself in the structure of our language. As one can clearly notice here, under the Nyāya scheme of things the human subject or knower does not contribute in any proactive way to what constitutes the content of thought or knowledge. Rather it is the locus of knowledge not the maker of it so to speak. The human mind is considered here as just a mirror whose only function is to reflect the structure of the object along with its own properties and its place in relation with other objects. This view of knowledge-knower relationship is not agreeable to Śamkara and the Buddhists where the human mind plays a proactive role in the process of knowledge-formation.

Proposing an entirely different kind of ontology, Buddhist idealists maintain that an actual unique particular object (*svalakṣaṇa*) exists only for a moment. Nonetheless it creates a sense-impression in the subject of knowledge. For Buddhists the actual point of reference on the basis of which we can explain the causal efficacy of the object presented in a case of perception is the sense-impression. The real issue of contention for the Buddhist epistemologist is whether to posit an actual real object going beyond the given sense-impression or to remain content with sense-impression without bothering about its cause. This contentious issue creates a schism in the Buddhist school of thought along this idea. A certain section of Buddhist philosophers believes that the sense-impression is the only given content that we have in an instance of perceptual knowledge but the human mind has a tendency to gloss over the subtle differences (*bhedāgraha*) between point-instants and imagines a continuant (*abheda kalpanā*) in its place. This obfuscates the uniqueness of each sense-impression and propels the mind to view this discreet array of unique particular sense-impressions as a continuous flow of undifferentiated sense-data. Thus according to this view what we perceive as an object existing out there is actually a projection of our own inner *schema* of thought. This point is made through the *reductio ad absurdum* argument in Dinnāga's *Ālambanaparikṣā* as the following:

1. Though atoms serve as causes of the consciousness (*vijñāpti*) of the sense-organs, they are not its actual objects

like sense-organs; because the consciousness does not represent the image of the atoms.

2a The consciousness does not arise from what is represented in it.

2b Because they do not exist in substance just like the double moon. (The double moon is perceived [by a man] on account of the defects of his sense-organs. But [this perception is not produced by the double moon, as] there exists no object like the double moon.)

2c-d Thus both the external things are unfit to be real objects of consciousness.[1]

Buddhists therefore are mostly reluctant to accept existence of an outside world which presents itself to the knower to its fullest extent. A certain significant proactive role is granted here to the knower's mind that contextualizes the object according to its training, reflexes and contingencies of a given situation and constructs a schemata for the object whose truth then depends upon the causal efficacy of the object thus schematized by the subject.

According to Śamkara's Advaita Vedānta on the other hand, reality behind the manifold that appears to exist external to us is non-different from the overarching all inclusive unifying principle called Brahman. Somewhat similar to the Buddhist argument for dismissing the ontological reality of the universal, for Śamkara, appearance of the world as composed of discreet objects characterized by their differences is a mere construct of the human mind. From the higher philosophical point of view (*parmārtha*) Brahman is the only all-inclusive, self-existent whole which is viewed as sheer consciousness beyond all contingencies and enlightens all individual discreet instances of knowing. Somewhat along the Buddhist line of thought, Śamkara's philosophy grants a proactive role to the human mind and explains the cases of individual knowing with their theory of *antaḥkaraṇa-vṛtti*. According to this theory the mind propelled by its inclinations (*vṛtti*) establishes a concourse with the object by flowing out towards and enveloping it in such a way that it takes on the form of the object thus cognized. Though superficially similar to the Buddhist theory of knowledge,

Śamkara's explanation for the knowledge of the object follows a unique independent approach. This approach is neither realistic like Naiyāyikas nor predominantly idealistic like the Buddhists. It rather follows a middle way between the two. Like Naiyāyikas Śamkara presupposes a sense-object contact in a knowing situation and like the Buddhists, he views the mind as playing a constructionist role so far as it is characterized at the practical level by its reflexes and pre-dispositions which have inevitable consequences for the knowledge-generation process.

Now after giving a synoptic view of what according to the Naiyāyikas, Buddhists and Advaitins constitutes an epistemological situation, I proceed to discuss in detail the role played by the mind according to each of these schools of thought.

II

Before we carry the discussion any further, let me offer a brief note on the difference between the object of perception (*artha*) and the subject-matter of perception (*viṣaya*), as it is presupposed in most of the discussions on the epistemological status of the object. *Ālambana* refers to the object as it exists outside and independently of the knower. *Grāhya* on the other hand refers to the same as grasped by the knower's mind. The former is the object as it presents itself and the latter refers to the object as it is presented before our mind. One could also define it as an internal and external object of perception in the same knowledge episode. It does not require much speculation to understand that this distinction has to be pre-supposed and defended tooth and nail for realists like Naiyāyikas and has to be collapsed for any school of idealism.

According to Nyāya philosophers the process of knowledge centers around four main components. They are object of knowledge (*artha*), sense organ (*indriya*) and internal organ (*manas*) and the soul (*atmā*). The process of knowledge generation comprises different types of concourses among these four components. An ordinary, normal case of knowledge through perception takes place in three different stages:

i. Concourse between the object and the sense organ.

ii. Concourse between the sense organ and internal sense organ (*manas*).

iii. Concourse between the internal sense organ and the soul (*ātmā*).

These three stages once complete result in the knowledge of a particular object by the knower. But the question that concerns us here is—what is the relationship between the object as it exists independently outside of us and the object as it is known by us as a result of three stages of perception? Naiyāyikas maintain that this relationship is that of congruence. Knowledge by definition reflects its object as it actually exists. There is no violation of this chronology of concourses in any ordinary case (*laukika*) of perception. Though it could be mentioned here that Nyāya philosophy gives recognition to a certain kind of cases of perception which do not go full circle with this process. These exceptions are discussed by Nyāya philosophers under the head of extraordinary perception (*alaukika pratyakṣa*). Now once the first step in the ladder of perceptual knowledge, namely that of object-sense concourse is completed and the sensory data is delivered to the *manas* or internal sense organ, then the object of knowledge (*artha*) becomes the subject matter or content of knowledge (*viṣaya*). The distinction between the two does not arise before this stage of perception. What is unique about the subject matter of perception is that it bears a reference to some object outside of itself but its composition and belongingness is entirely mental. From the epistemological point of view *viṣaya* provides us much richer contexts for discussions than the actual object or *artha*. The boundaries of *viṣaya* of perception extend beyond sense-object contact. Whereas the atual object (*artha*) is presented to the external sense organs, internal sense organ delivers it to the Self resulting in the awareness of the object in the Self. In so far as it has to be oriented towards the object of knowledge in the epistemological context the internal organ or *manas* is much more of a constructive, creative and potent device than outer sense organs. For example, imagination, pure contemplation, hallucinations and dreams do not involve any role of external sense organs and depend entirely on inner psychological processes for their existence drawing upon past impressions or memory. One could probably say that although not directly present, the outside object, needs to be presupposed as a trigger for these mental perceptual processes but the subject matter of knowledge or *viṣaya* presents itself in definite contexts even in the above mentioned instances. Therefore except for the state of temporary loss of consciousness and dreamless sleep all the given instances of knowledge bear a reference to some particular object but it is not necessary that this object should be outside of us. Nyāya philosophy provides ample space for this view in so far as they allow the possibility of internal perception and recollection even though the latter is not considered knowledge *per se* within their system. But what is even more important to notice at this stage of our discussion is that even if we grant that perception is always of an external object even then as discussed before, the subject-matter or content of knowledge exists within the subject not outside of him or her and known through a second order awareness called *anuvyavsāya*.

Another question that crops up at this juncture is—whether the actual correspondence between *artha* and *viṣaya* of perception is necessary and inevitable for all cases of perception. We could discuss this issue specially in the context of cases of error. When we perceive an oyster-shell as a piece of silver the *viṣaya* of our judgment bears the form of silver but the *artha* has the form of an oyster-shell which induces us to procure the object. Another point to be noticed here is that our behaviour towards the object is propelled by the object as conceived in our judgment and not the *artha*. One of the major difficulties with the Nyāya epistemology is that once we grant equal status in terms of reality to the *artha* and *viṣaya* of perception, we have the onus of explaining the relationship between the two even in a case of error. According to Nyāya, the *artha* of perception is a necessary condition for any external perception to take place. That could be taken to mean that the object of perception through an act of presenting itself to the senses makes itself the cause of the origin of the subject-matter of perception. But if we grant this explanation for the relationship between the *artha* and the *viṣaya* of perception, then how do we account for the cases of error where there occurs a gap between the *viṣaya* and the *artha*. Whatever explanation Naiyāyikas may offer for such cases, they cannot deny the fact that at times the awareness of an object may arise without its object being presented to our senses. An extraordinary type of *jñānalakṣaṇa sannikarṣa*, sense-object contact, is not a sound explanation for it because if at all, it only gives us a theory of how errors occur, not why they should occur when the actual object is lying there right before us. In other words, they only tell us about the 'how' of this gap between the object and its awareness in case of error, not the 'why' of it. Also Naiyāyikas need to explain how an object that is locationally not presented to our senses may trigger certain feelers in us in case of errors. Furthermore, an object may feel warm to somebody but may feel slightly cold to somebody who is running fever. In these cases it is really problematic to determine the locus of these feelings. They are of course *viṣaya*s of perception but it is difficult to account for their objective support. The same object is presented in these cases to one person as endowed with one property and with a different property to somebody else. One also cannot explain away these cases as instances of error. Coldness and hotness though they seem to belong to the object, are actually there in the subject. As a matter of fact for Naiyāyikas feelings are an object of perception not modes of consciousness as Buddhists would maintain. Within such a framework it becomes even more problematic to explain such cases. Thus we could observe from our discussion so far that once this gap between an object and its awareness is opened up and accepted as real then a whole lot of difficulties are thrown into relief for which a realist like Naiyāyika does not seem to have sufficient explanation.

After taking stock of the Naiyāyikas' theory of knowledge and the problems they are posed with, we could examine if the Buddhist theory of knowledge is successful in avoiding these difficulties.

According to the Buddhists there are two modes in which we get related with our sense stimulus. One way of relating to them is to look at each one of these stimuli as a unique particular existing in a zero space and time frame of here and now. Needless to say that such unique particulars cannot instigate us to any activity. Also, if we do not arrange these discreet units together under some larger, more encompassing conceptual schemes, no philosophization or theorization would become possible. Second, the mode of relating to our sense-stimuli is to arrange them together and subsume them under larger conceptual schemes which are guided by our contextual practical interests and yield to us also philosophical narratives which in turn guide our ways of looking at the world and our behaviour towards it. But what the Buddhists view as two different modes of representations of the externality or alterity, are also two different stages of the same linear process. The human mind which is imaginative by nature, guided by past sense-impressions and habituated by them is impelled to view the amorphous sense-impressions in certain definite ways. But definitions which the human mind interpolates between discreet sensations rather belong to us and not to anything outside of us. This way the 'actual' that is available to us is the discreet sense-data called *svalakṣaṇa* by the Buddhists which is both subject matter (*viṣaya*) and the object (*ālambana*) of our perceptions. These *svalakṣaṇa* are further used to build up certain imaginative constructs called *sāmānyalakṣaṇa* which are yielded to us through inferential processing of the discreet particulars. Thus an interesting matrix of two different modes of presentations of content of knowledge and corresponding means of knowledge have to be maintained by the Buddhists in accordance with their metaphysics. This arrangement of two different kinds of contents of knowledge requiring two different kinds of *pramānas* are called *pramāna-vyavasthā*.

What we observe from the above discussion is that the starting point of the Buddhist theory of knowledge is raw unprocessed sensations or the *viśaya* of perception. But the question that naturally and inevitably arises is—what is the source of these raw sensations? It has to have a trigger. The whole process of perception in Buddhist epistemology is subject-centered. Dinnāga's concluding statement in *Ālambanaparikṣa* is—"the interior object [which is not different from consciousness] is endowed with two factors [image and cause] and therefore it is logical to conclude that consciousness [alone] is transformed into [external] object (*viṣaya*)."[2] The second factor affirms this viewpoint further that the external object is only a convenient presupposition which is constructed in our own mind and appears as if it exists outside of us in the natural world. Thus according to the Buddhist view the 'outside of mind' has no contribution in the knowledge-generating process. This view is also in consonance with phenomenological reduction where at the level of transcendental *epoche* even the presupposition about the external world has to finally disappear. Thus strictly speaking, Buddhist epistemology is by and large silent about the source of sensations. In Dignāga's view all instances of knowledge whether perceptual or inferential refer back to the sensations which are the *viṣaya* of perception in both cases. Sensations being themselves the subject of consciousness, the distinction between the knower and the known is collapsed in a certain phenomenological way in Buddhist epistemology.

Tha anatomy of Buddhist epistemology as we have observed above does carry a lot of conviction but is at the same time infested with certain incompletions, reasons for which lie in lack of metaphysical support in their epistemology. Dignāga and other Buddhist epistemologists gloss over the fact that if no sensations are available to consciousness then it can neither exist as a knower (*Pramātṛ*) nor as a known (*prameya*). In other words, the entity of consciousness for its experience either of itself (*svabhāva*) or that of the object (*arthābhāsa*) depends on availability of some sense-data. For sense-data consciousness depends entirely on the sense organs. Further it stands to reason and also to scientific belief that sense organs do not construct their own objects or sense-data. Even hallucinations derive their status as free of *ālambana* incumbencies vịs-a-vis their sublation later on by what we refer to as reality. Thus Buddhist *svalakṣaṇa* are in need of further explanation in terms of a trigger. Buddhists have to agree that being devoid of imaginative construct, consciousness has no role in the production of *svalakṣaṇa* and it depends entirely on sense-organs. But the space from where these sensations come forth and become *viṣaya* of perception for the consciousness is empty in Dignāga's epistemology. Dignāga, the pioneer of Buddhist epistemology and logic is silent on these questions. Probably his silence is not without epistemological significance. Given that limits of direct knowledge cannot extend beyond sensations and direct knowledge only has philosophical and epistemological significance, then questions regarding the source of sensation are already in excess of epistemological space available to us. Notwithstanding, we have to agree that sensations have to have a source and it is a different matter that there are epistemological difficulties in ascertaining its nature. Instead of narrowing our epistemological boundaries further, it would be philosophically more commendable that we create a logically sound metaphysical foundation for a more convincing theory of knowledge.

After examining the pros and cons of Buddhist epistemology, let us now focus our attention on Advaitin epistemology. In Śamkara's non-dualism the word used for the object of perception is not *ālambana* but *Adhiṣṭhān*. If conditionalities, contingencies and situatedness of a given knowledge instance were to be bracketed out, Brahman presents itself as the *Adhiṣṭhān* of all knowledge instances. Let us examine Advaitin epistemology by first viewing the process of perception according to them. Just as *manas* plays the role of messenger between the sense-data input and the self in the Nyāya theory of knowledge, in Advaita Vedānta *antaḥkaraṇa* provides a link between the inner and the outer. *Antaḥkaraṇa* on Śamkara's account is subtle but not atomic like the *manas* as considered by the Naiyāyikas. In Advaita epistemology, *antaḥkaraṇa* is viewed as endowed with such power that it can assume the form of the object of knowledge which is in touch with the sense-organs. *Antahkarana* in this view flows out of the sense organs and envelops the object of knowledge and thus assumes the same form. Sense organs in this scheme of things are the channels or vehicles of *antaḥkaraṇa*. This role of *antaḥkaraṇa* has been explained with the analogy of water assuming the form of the container in which it is poured, similarly *antaḥkaraṇa* assumes the form of the object where it is channelized by the sense organs. *Antaḥkaraṇa* is perceived as a function of the *sattva* element which is the principle of activity. *Sattva* is also of the nature of light. Therefore *antaḥkaraṇa* like light quickly diffuses out from the sense organs and enlightens the object which is thus perceived.

Dharmarāja Adhvarin writes in Vedānta Paribhāsa:

> Just as the water of a tank, going out through a hole and entering fields through channels, comes to have, even like those [fields], a quadrangular or other figure, similarly, the internal organ too, which is of the nature of light, going out through the sense of sight, etc. and reaching the locality of contents like pot, is transformed into the form of contents like pot. This same modification is called a psychosis (*vṛtti*).[3]

Before I go on to discuss the Advaita theory of perception we should remind ourselves here that Advaita is mainly a system of metaphysics which supports absolutism in the guise of Brahman which is of the nature of self-enlightening consciousness extended to its fullest extent with the form (*vṛtti*) of pure infinite existence. Śamkara's epistemology therefore as we would observe is subservient to his metaphysics. Questions regarding *viṣaya* and *ālambana* of perception can be reformulated in Samkara's perspective as follows. What should be considered as the actual cause of the process of perception—is it knowledge (*pramā*) or the source of knowledge (*pramāna*)? Further how do we understand this perceptual process which gives pure existence which is the foundation of all knowledge instances, a characteristic set of particularities? This question becomes particularly important because in Advaita epistemology the word *pratyakśa* is used for both the perceptual knowledge or *pramā* and also for the cause of it.

There are thus two possible ways of looking at these questions:

(i) We could consider the content (*viṣaya*) of perception as the factor that endows consciousness with particularity or distinctness.

(ii) We could consider the generative cause of perception as the factor which endows perceptual knowledge with characteristic particularities.

Both these ways of looking at perceptual knowledge become possible with regard to Samkara's Vedanta because Samkara's theory of perception is rooted in consciousness.

Knowledge in Śamkara's scheme of things whether we consider it as eternal or caused is always a subject matter of perception because it is self-manifest. Śamkara does not admit the Nyāya view that knowledge is apprehended through another act of cognition (*anuvyāvasāya*) because that according to him would lead to infinite regress. Thus in so far as knowledge is rooted in consciousness and is self-enlightening all knowledge is perceptual. In other words in so far as all knowing entails awareness of the knowledge-act also, all knowledge is direct or perceptual. Dharmarāja Adhvarin writes in this context:

> Because of the twofoldness of the witness, there is twofoldness of perceptual cognition. And perceptual nature has been demonstrated both as present in the object cognized and as present in the cognition. Of these, for the perceptuality present in the cognition the general definition is but consciousness; for, even in 'The hill is fiery, etc.' the consciousness qualified *per accidens* by the psychosis having the form of fire, etc. being self-luminous in respect of its own nature [as cognition], is perceptual. In respect, however, of the respective contents, perceptual nature is only as stated above.[4]

But there are two problems that would need to be addressed for defending such a view which collapses the distinction between the knower and the known. Firstly the object of perception which is mostly material in nature cannot ever collapse into a state of non-difference (*abheda*) with the knowing subject, which according to Advaitin is of the nature of pure impartite consciousness. Further, all perceptual knowledge is of the nature of a definite judgment, for instance—I am watching this object X. Such judgments become possible only on the supposition of a distinction between the object X and its knower. In response to these questions, Advaitins point out that non-difference (*abheda*) does not mean identity. Non-difference is only supposed to convey that content of perception which is supposed to refer to an actual object has no existence without the presupposition of a knowing consciousness which claims and arranges the judgment into unity of apperception.

Dharmarāja Adhvarin writes:

> What is called non-difference from the cognizer is not oneness, but rather the non-possession of reality different from the reality of the cognizer.[5]

Connection between the consciousness principle and the real material is explained through the mobile nature of consciousness which is a rather unique stance in philosophy. Since consciousness in Śamkara's view is mobile and flashes out through the senses like light from the lamp therefore according to the Advaitin account it is possible for the knower's consciousness to reach out and connect to the object. In this process the non-difference between the object of perception and the knowing consciousness is explained through the formation of *vṛtti* which envelops the object and therefore is dependent on it and since it has consciousness as its main principle, is the locus of both the perceptual content of object thus perceived and the knowing consciousness (*pramatṛ*). From this Advaitin concludes that consciousness as the ultimate founding principle of all knowing instances is non-different from what it knows. Dharmarāja Adhvarin writes in this context:

> Pot etc. being superimposed on the consciousness defined by themselves, the reality of content [-defined] consciousness is itself the reality of pot etc.; for, reality for the super-imposed over and above the reality of the substrate is not admitted. And since, in the manner aforementioned, the content [-defined] consciousness is but the cognizer [- defined] consciousness alone is the substrate of pot, etc. Hence the reality of the cognizer is itself the reality of pot, etc. not any other; hence the immediacy of pot, etc. is established.[6]

This explanation, though it seems to resolve the difficulty between the outer physical object and the inner perceptual content, is not entirely without difficulties. In a judgment like 'I know the pen in my hand' not only do I know that I know the pen but also that I know in that cognitive act the form (*vṛtti*) of the pen. In answer to that, Advaitin argues that *vṛttis* do not require other *vṛttis* to become *ālambana* of perception. Instead they are themselves *viṣaya*, that is they are themselves also the content and the cognitive act which is directed towards that content. Therefore the characteristic of self-enlightenment is not only a feature of the knowing consciousness but also that of *vṛttis*. Dharmarāja Adhvarin writes in this context:

> For, though for fear of infinite regress a psychosis is not the content of [another] psychosis, being its own content, is admitted; hence, there too the possession of reality non-different from the reality of cognizer [-defined] consciousness, qualified *per accidens* by psychosis having itself for content is possible.[7]

This solution as suggested by Advaitin is cogent in a certain sense and not so in another. This view that *vṛttis* also enlighten themselves holds water in so far as *vṛttis* being modifications of the consciousness which is characterized by self-enlightenment, imbibe the same characteristics in themselves. But the weaker side of the explanation is that since whatever is known lies on the other side of the consciousness as an object however subtle, it has to be viewed as different and distinct from the knowing consciousness. Object known (*prameya*) in the Advaitin epistemological scheme can be almost dispensed with. Śamkara's epistemology in this sense looks somewhat lopsided towards idealism and does not score very far from Buddhist idealism.

Thus from our discussion so far we could probably conclude that in any given instance of cognitive experience, we have to take three elements into consideration, namely the object that stimulates our senses to yield to us a certain experience, the immediate sense data thus yielded which are made available to the cognitive apparatus of the mind and finally the determinating process of mind, namely construction or interpretation that results in categorical judgment whose epistemological value can be tested by judging it against the actual object. But different theories of knowledge that I have attempted to discuss in this paper differ mainly with regard to how these different elements are conceived in their correlation with each other. The points of divergence regarding this correlation marks the principal distinction among the three schools I have discussed in this paper. To put the same thing conversely different activities that yield to us the content of perception along with their correlation has to be considered as an aggregate to arrive at some proper viable theory of knowledge. On this count the Nyāya and Advaita theories of knowledge fare better than the Buddhist theory. But at the same time, one should also not forget that when we consider consciousness or the mind as the only object and departure point of knowledge-formation, then we are also chiefly making a claim that there is no element of knowledge which is completely divorced from inner phenomenological processes. One cannot ignore the fact that knowledge is a psychological process and no theory based completely on Nyāya realism can claim to exhaustively explain the knowledge process. When a realist like Naiyāyika accepts an external object as the object of perception without any proactive role played by the internal organ and the soul then certain other tenets of their system are robbed of proper justification. In this context it is the acceptance of concourse between the internal organ and the soul where Nyāya realism comes under the scanner. If we accept that the soul and the internal organ play an active role in any given instance of knowledge process then we cannot unscrupulously at the same time claim that the object of knowledge bears a complete resemblance or is congruent with the object it represents. The reason that can be adduced in support of the above claim is that there is no way to find out how the internal organ is related to the sense data yielded by the external sense organs, because in the very process of finding that out we use the same processes and pre-suppositions which are to be examined. Furthermore, in any instance of determinate perception the role of memory cannot be ruled out. Sense organs in themselves cannot account for the contribution of memory. Memory being something mental in nature cannot be accounted for with the help of inanimate objects alone. It can only be accounted for with reference to internal organ or the soul. Thus though the Naiyāyikas score a point over Buddhists when they give a proper account for the trigger of the sense-data which an idealist like *Vijñānavādī* Buddhist does not, but they do not go far enough from there in so far as they choose not to consider a more proactive phenomenological contribution of the internal organ or the soul. If we wish to account for both the trigger element for the sense data and the proactive participation of the consciousness to account for phenomenology of perception, then probably Advaitin fares best on both counts. Advaitin agrees that the external object is necessary to account for the modifications of consciousness and gives a proactive role to the consciousness of the knowing subject in so far as consciousness is actually supposed to flow out of the sense organs and envelop the object of perception thereby preserving both the autonomy of the object and a non-passive role of the consciousness. Thus whereas in Nyāya metaphysics and Buddhist epistemology sense organs delimit the domain of consciousness, for Advaitin sense organs are the only channels through which consciousness transcends itself in order to collapse the absolute dichotomy of the subject and the object in the form of *sākśi-jnāna*. One should not fail to notice here that in none of the schools of Indian philosophy except to a certain extent Sāmkhya, mind-body dualism has ever been viewed in terms of absolute dichotomy, not even in the Cārvāka system where consciousness is considered as the property of the body.

Buddhists, on the other hand, have a strong point in so far as they argue that each individual experience is unique (*svalakṣaṇa*). Extending this argument further one could say that when we raise questions like—what is it like to have a certain conscious experience? It inevitably dovetails into questions like —what is it like for the experiencer to have that kind of experience, such that the subjective phenomenological character of the experience is viewed as inexorably related to a particular unique vantage point in terms of its relative time and space framework. But what Buddhist idealists seem to ignore is the fact that the qualitative features of experience possess more structural complexity than they are prepared to accept. The fact that the actual content of our visual experience is extended in a two dimensional space, whereas our judgments are a priori structured in three dimensions could be one such case in view. Advaitin metaphysics where consciousness is viewed as flowing out of senses takes care of such structural complexities of experience in a manner which is much more plausible and parsimonious than the Naiyāyikas who postulate a whole new set of extra-sensory perception which despite being entirely constructed by and located in the subject's mind are supposed to carry an objective validity. Thus on all these counts, Advaitin epistemology is overall much more responsive to the questions regarding phenomenological processes involved in a knowledge instance than his Naiyāyika or Buddhist counterpart.

III

In the concluding section of the paper, I wish to collect and glean some cues from the Nyāya, Buddhist and Advaita theories of knowledge to draw upon issues relating to 'phenomenological constitution of alterity' or 'otherness'. Any debate on these issues would inevitably involve a philosophical analysis and theorization of our view of the 'other'. Sociological and anthropological studies of the 'other' would focus on the construction of the 'otherness' in the arena constituted within the space provided by the traditional and religious specificities. Philosophical analysis of these issues on the other hand should involve digging out the epistemic foundations of the constitutiveness of the 'other' and analysing its accompanying ontological presuppositions and then drawing upon and drawing out their implications on certain socio-political issues. This is what I intend to do in the present section of my paper.

The realist pluralist epistemology of Nyāya points towards a conception of the Other which does not apparently draw its constitutiveness from any source other than its natural self. The Other in this scheme of things is as it is essentially and naturally constituted from within and without. There is actually no gap according to the Naiyāyikas between the two. According to Nyāya epistemology an act of awareness originates through a concourse (*sannikarṣa*) between the sense organs and *manas*, where the subject does not necessarily reach out in order to draw upon the other. The presentativeness (*yathārthatā*) of object is an important factor on this account whereby 'knowing' becomes a dialogical process where an object or the Other presents itself as itself along with all its internal relational schemes and the subject has an awareness of it as it actually is without any mental constructions on its part. In other words only for Naiyāyikas a limited extensionality is required from the self towards the other in the knowing process and its intentionality is even more limited in scope since the object is supposed to present itself in its fullest reducing the phenomenological account of the knowing-mind to the minimum. Further, Nyāya pluralism also results in not only the acceptance but also the endorsement of the Other. It is based on an acceptance of the claims of the otherness of the object and in so doing the self re-essentializes and reifies the identity and the schemas that go into the constitution of the Other.

The conception of the Other implied in the Buddhist idealist theory of knowledge is quite to the contrary of it. Such epistemology is based on human cognition per se as a highly individualistic enterprise. Cognition of the other is viewed here as an individual construction thereby de-essentializing the claim of otherness of the object that the consciousness engages with. In this epistemological model no categorical ontological schematic unity or integrity is granted to the other. To the contrary the constitution of the object (the other) is subsumed under one's own schema which could be propelled by soteriological concerns which are viewed as intrinsic to the consciousness where these schemas are storehoused. Thus my argument here is that though it is not an express theme in idealist Buddhist thought to exclude the Other but the implicit overall ramification of Buddhist idealist thought is that it results in the 'overcoming' or 'subsumption' of the Other rather than an express synthesis with it.

The claims regarding the 'Other' explicated in Advaita philosophy present a synthesis of the above mentioned two approaches. The Advaitin theory of knowledge could be truly called epistemology of 'reaching out'. As I mentioned earlier in this paper, sense organs which are viewed as self-contained and self-limited by the Buddhist idealist are rightly viewed by the Advaitin as the bridge across to the 'other'. The reason I term it as the epistemology of 'reaching out' is that unlike Nyāya where the object also has to carry a certain presentativeness along with itself, the Advaitin model presumes a certain proactiveness on the part of the subject to reach across to the object. Consciousness in a proactive effort channelizes and propels itself to bridge the gap between the self and the other. Furthermore unlike the Sāmkhyan model where *Puruṣa* symbolizing consciousness, goes into oblivion or self-forgetfulness when it is directed towards the other (the *Prakṛti*), in the Advaitin model, the consciousness is viewed as intrinsically endowed with a witness component which preserves the unity of the self on the one hand and acts as an important metaphysical device to explain the process of apperception in the Advaitin theory of knowledge on the other.

NOTES AND REFERENCES

1. Sastri, N. Aiyaswami (trans.), *Ālambanaparikṣā by Dignāga*, The Adyar Library, Madras, 1942, pp. 41-43.
2. Ibid., p. 55.
3. Sastri, S. S. Suryanarayana (trans.), *Vedāntaparibhāṣā by Dharmarāja Adhvarin,* The Adyar Library, 1942, p. 13.
4. Ibid., p. 34.
5. Ibid., p. 21.
6. Ibid., p. 21.
7. Ibid., p. 24.

8

Reflexive Self-Awareness and Subjectivity: Revisiting a Dialogue

Tal Correm

I. Reflexive Self-Awareness and the Question of the Self

The question I pose here is whether a theory of reflexive self-awareness requires a notion of subjectivity. Can we speak about an awareness of consciousness to itself without presupposing some sense of *self*?[1] I will look at two theories that present similar accounts of reflexive self-awareness but have opposing views with regard to the necessity of a notion of subjectivity in that account. The two accounts of *reflexive self-awareness* in which I examine the place of subjectivity are the theory of pre-reflective self-awareness in the phenomenology of Edmund Husserl and the theory of self-awareness (*svasam vedanā*) in the Buddhist epistemology of Dinnāga (c.480–540 CE).[2]

Reflexive self-awareness is a one-level self-awareness that is distinct from higher-order types of awareness such as *reflective self-awareness*, introspection, or inner-perception. According to this account, every experience is aware of itself in an unthematic way while it is simultaneously aware of its object. There is no additional act for an experience to be aware of itself as in the higher-order types of awareness.[3] The reflexive nature of consciousness is characterized as self-luminosity and exemplified by the simile of a lamp: in a similar way that a lamp illuminates itself while it illuminates other objects in the room, consciousness is aware of itself while it is aware of its objects in each of its acts and experiences.[4]

Yet, these philosophers hold contrasting positions with regard to the relation between reflexive self-awareness and subjectivity. The phenomenological account understands subjectivity as indispensable to this form of self-awareness, although, as I elaborate below following Dan Zahavi, subjectivity is not conceived as a substantial entity that is separate from or bears the conscious acts and experiences but it is a structural feature of consciousness. In contrast, according to the Buddhist account, reflexive self-awareness should be understood without any reference to subjectivity. This view is in accordance with the Buddhist doctrine of *anatman* (*'no-self'*) that denounces any notion of self as enduring entity or essential core of conscious life. The fact that similar accounts emerge in two positions that hold contrasting understandings of subjectivity invites exploration into the significance and even the necessity of these understandings and, in the deep level, the presuppositions that underlie them. Both agree that reflexive self-awareness is a certain type of awareness that is not an awareness of a *self* to itself but an awareness of consciousness to it*self*. But is there any sense of self that remains? Another way to formulate the problem is whether reflexivity also entails subjectivity.[5]

In what follows, I will offer, first, a brief delineation of the theories of self-awareness of Husserl and Dinnāga. Then I will examine the status of subjectivity in each theory: I will discuss the sense of subjectivity that the phenomenologist account entails and how the Buddhist account might respond to it, in an attempt to elucidate the status of subjectivity in a theory of reflexive self-awareness.

II. Two Views of Reflexive Self-Awareness

Husserl's conception of pre-reflective self-awareness appears in his account of inner time-consciousness. According to his analysis, this self-awareness is pre-reflective in two senses: first, it is tacit and unthematic. Second, it precedes reflective self-awareness and it is a condition of possibility of it. It is the most fundamental awareness that is present in each conscious act and is the ground for higher-order self-awareness.[6]

The discussion of self-awareness in Buddhist philosophy began in the early schools of Buddhism but became systematic in Dinnāga's work, the *Pramānasamuccaya* ('The Collection of the Writings on the Means of Right Knowledge' c. 540 CE). Dinnāga contributed extensively to the fields of logic, philosophy of language, and philosophy of mind in classical Indian philosophy and developed a doctrine of Buddhist epistemology (the Buddhist *pramāna* theory), a project that was continued by his follower, Dharmakirti (c. 600–660 CE). Dinnāga concisely formulates the *svasamvedanā*, the Buddhist theory of self-awareness, as part of his discussion of perception as a means of knowledge. According to his theory, self-awareness characterizes every act of consciousness: perception, thought, willing, feeling, judgments and so on and plays a central role in the very possibility of knowledge.[7]

Husserl's analysis of inner time-consciousness explains how it is possible to speak of pre-reflective self-awareness as a structural feature of experiences. He articulates the structure of inner time-consciousness from the manner in which temporal objects are constituted or become manifested to consciousness. In perceiving a temporal object such as a melody, the perception itself is not merely the awareness of the present phase of the object as an isolated note but rather it is also an awareness of the various phases of the object, those that have preceded the present moment and those that shall appear later. Awareness of the present phase is termed by Husserl "primal impression," awareness of the preceding phases is termed "retention," and awareness of the future phases is termed "protention." They are unthematic modes of awareness that do not constitute new objects (unlike recollection or expectation). They are contingent moments of the experience itself that make the constituting of its object possible (ITC 42-45). This threefold structure does not only explain the manner in which awareness of an object is possible, but also the manner in which experience is aware of itself in each of its phases. Retention is not only the preservation of the phase of the present object receding towards the past, but also the retention of this retention and those to come; as such, it is the basis for reflection. Reflection on the previous act of consciousness, such as perception, is possible since the different phases of perceiving the object are retained (CIT 122-123).[8]

By virtue of this threefold structure of primal impression-retention-protention an experience is aware of itself in each of its phases, and this is the structure of the pre-reflective self-awareness of experience. This awareness does not characterize a specific act or experience; it is rather a structural dimension of any acts and experiences. Despite the difference between experiences, be they perception, recollection, imagination, etc., all experiences are self-given pre-reflectively.[9]

Dinnāga arrives at his theory of self-awareness in his analysis of the structure of cognition. We can detect in all cognition, according to him, two aspects, the objectual aspect or appearance (*visayābhāsa*) and the self-appearance (*svābhāsa*) or the self-specifying.[10]

Thus, in the experience of seeing a blue stain, for instance, there is an act of perceiving and a perceived form of blue. But the perceiving of the perceived is always accompanied by self-awareness (*svasamvitti*), a third component in the event of cognition (PS 1.9). These three aspects are only nominally, not ontologically, separated. Thus, this self-awareness is not a further act that comes after perception. It is an intrinsic aspect of cognition itself, which forms together with the two others, *unity* (PS 1.10). Furthermore, if we understand self-awareness as a separate act, Dinnāga claims, the fallacy of infinite regress is unavoidable. Infinite regress would follow because in order to be aware of the additional act, a further act is required, which in turn should be brought to awareness and so on, ad infinitum. In fact, the theory of self-awareness helps to avoid the aforementioned fallacy: cognition is brought to awareness concurrently with its occurrence (PS 1.12). Self-awareness occurs simultaneously with the act of cognition. It is a feature of the experience itself and not an awareness of that experience as its *object*. In that sense, it is different from reflection, retrospection or introspection; all of which are separate acts of consciousness that direct their awareness towards a different act as their object. Thus, every experience is both aware of an object and self-aware in a non-objectifying way.[11]

What is the nature of this awareness? According to Dinnāga, it is a kind of perception (PS 1.6ab) and as such, according to his definition of perception, it is immediate and non-conceptual (*kalpanapod)ha*) (PS 1.3c, 1.6ab). Although awareness ordinarily implies attention, in this type of self-awareness there is no explicit attention to our acts. Thus, self-awareness, according to Dinnāga, is the awareness of consciousness to itself; it is immediate, non-conceptual, non-attentive, and non-objectifying. It takes place concurrently with cognition and thus accompanies each and every cognitive event.

III. The Status of Subjectivity in Theories of Reflexive Self-Awareness

The survey of the two theories shows that both philosophers agree that consciousness has a reflexive character. Both accounts of self-awareness result from a philosophical analysis of consciousness and intentional awareness. Both explain this self-awareness as a structural feature of consciousness. It is a part of the structure of experience and occurs with every cognition or directedness towards an object. The two positions explain reflexive self-awareness as intransitive self-awareness and are suggested as two versions of an account of first-order self-awareness, in contrast to higher-order accounts.

However, there are several points of disagreement between Husserl's and Dinnāga's theories, both thematic and methodological. Phenomenology, in contrast to Dinnāga's theory, is not an epistemology. Thus, the motivations and the purposes of these philosophical positions in formulating conceptions of self-awareness are different. Phenomenology, at least not explicitly, is not transformative philosophy, and its purpose is not to change the way we experience the world, only to describe the way it appears and the structures of consciousness that enable or constitute it (a notable exception is perhaps found in Merleau-Ponty). There are obviously other differences that stem from the different cultural contexts and time periods in which each philosopher worked. Thus, their conceptual frameworks and presuppositions are distinct. In the rest of the paper, I would like to focus on one central difference between the two accounts that concerns the status of subjectivity in relation to reflexive self-awareness.

According to the phenomenological account, as Dan Zahavi argues, although the primal self-awareness is understood as a passive and automatic awareness, which is not initiated by a *subject*, there is a sense in which subjectivity appears already at the level of pre-reflective self-awareness. Pre-reflective self-awareness is understood as the first-person mode of givenness of experiences: it is their experience in an immediate and non-inferential way as *my* experiences. The contents of consciousness change, there are different and distinct acts of consciousness, but there is one feature that remains constant. The constant and *invariant* feature of consciousness is that every experience is experienced as given from *a first-person perspective*. From this account it is possible to understand the subject or the self not as that which motivates or controls this type of self-awareness, but as the mode of givenness of each experience.[12]

According to this explanation, the self is not a separate entity that exists above or behind experiences; it is not their owner, but an experiential dimension of experiences. Subjectivity, then, is not separate from experience but a part of the very structure of experience. This is a minimal and basic sense of subjectivity that is distinguished from more developed and sophisticated forms of selfhood, such as the self that appears in reflection or in recollection, or a self that has biography, certain personal traits, and so on. In other words, the idea of a core self as experiential dimension does not exhaust the notion of self and it is complemented with other more developed notions of selfhood such as the narrative self. The point is that already at the level of pre-reflective self-awareness there is a basic sense of self, which is experiential and inseparable from experience, as Zahavi clarifies, "Self-awareness is there not only when I realize that *I* am perceiving a candle, but whenever I am acquainted with an experience in its first-personal mode of givenness, that is, whenever there is something it is like for me to have the experience. In other words, pre-reflective self-awareness and a minimal sense of self are integral parts of our experiential life."[13] Nevertheless, this account takes subjectivity as essential and necessary for an exhaustive description of consciousness.

In contrast to Husserl, Dinnāga formulates a theory of self-awareness *without a self*. However, with the minimal sense of subjectivity as a core experiential self that the phenomenological account suggests, it seems that the two positions draw near to each other and the question is whether the Buddhist could accept this minimal notion of experiential self or subjectivity to their account. In order to clarify the different conceptions regarding the status of subjectivity, I continue to examine the three interrelated characterizations of consciousness in the phenomenological account that form the core of the dispute: 1) the *perspectival* character of consciousness and in particular 2) the claim that experiences are given from *a first-person perspective*, and 3) the claim that this characteristic of first-person givenness is an *invariant* dimension of consciousness.

According to the first characterization of consciousness as perspectival, every experience embodies a certain perspective from which something, namely the intentional object, is experienced. This observation necessitates certain duality, namely, a distinction between the source of the perspective and the thing the perspective is about. Experience is about something which is distinct from itself. The idea that an object is always experienced from a certain perspective is (actually) expressed in Dinnāga's thesis about the dual structure of awareness of the grasping and the grasped aspects. Yet, this distinction is not ontological; it does not entail a subject and an object that exist separately from the experience but merely different aspects or structural features of experience. As we saw, the phenomenological description of pre-reflective self-awareness does not include the subject as a separate entity above and behind experience, and on this point there is an agreement between the two positions. The problem from a Buddhist point of view, however, is in the next issue, that the idea of the (constitutively) perspectival consciousness entails the first-person perspective and the notion of *mineness*, the claim that experiences experienced as one's own.

There is a dispute in contemporary Buddhist scholarship

whether the *svasamvedana* theory can coincide with the characteristic of first-person givenness of experiences or whether experiences are *anonymous*. Interpretations that claim that the Buddhist position accepts the characterization of first-person givenness explain that it is possible to reconcile it with the Buddhist doctrine of no-self since the first-person givenness of experience does not entail acceptance of a self as the subject of experiences or any substantial definition of an enduring self.[14] George Dreyfus contends explicitly that it is possible to speak in the Buddhist context about subjectivity without a self. Subjectivity captures the phenomenal nature of experience without a further requirement of a substantial self. Yet it is momentary and punctual and everything behind this minimal subjectivity would be an untenable construction. Dreyfus agrees that at each moment of experience there is a phenomenal sense and a synchronic unity of a single perspective. But the idea of diachronic unity, the enduring of the self across time requires an act-transcendent self that unifies the different experiences and this is untenable since it does not coincide with the experience of impermanence and interdependency. Diachronic unity, according to the account held by most Buddhist traditions, "is a fiction that conceptually stands for the complex causal connections that exist in reality. It is a convenient way to understand reality, what Buddhists call a conventional truth, not a causally effective part of the fabric of reality."[15]

Interpretations that take experiences to be anonymous, such as Chien-hsing Ho's, argue that the Buddhist position may accept the first-person perspective but only in a conventional way. That is, the first-person perspective itself is a construction that does not reflect the nature of consciousness. They agree that at the level of phenomenological description, a first-person perspective appears, but this is exactly what the Buddhists see as misleading since it leads to a more robust sense of self that they ask to avoid. For the Buddhist epistemologist, Ho writes, the phenomenological notion of self would "still be conventional or habitual. In its deep-lying nature consciousness is anonymous and pre-subjective, prior to the subject–object duality. And the core of consciousness belongs to self-awareness, not to the subjective and objectual aspects."[16] Moreover, rather than a primitive– the first person givenness is something that can be explained according to certain processes in consciousness that result in this feel of first-person manner of experiences, such as Vasubandhu's analysis.[17]

The third issue, the phenomenological claim that the first-person givenness of experience is an invariant dimension of experience should be finally rejected by the Buddhist view to my understanding, since it is an essentialist abstraction or conceptual fabrication (*vikalpa*) over reflexive self-awareness that is, according to the Buddhist account, non-conceptual. This approach suggests an understanding of experience without a self that rather than pathological is therapeutic since it concerns a genuine experience of reality that is constantly changing without any invariant element. To assume an invariant dimension of experience renders the Buddhist therapeutic project impossible. If there is no change, that is, no possibility to dispense with the sense of the self, even in its minimal manifestation, there is no way to be rid from the distorting construction that bring the sense of 'mine' or attachment and thus suffering. If the Buddhist goal is ending of suffering, then the sense of the self must be understood as a distortion of experiential reality and alternative way of experiencing must be possible, one that does not include the redundant but 'useful fiction' (to borrow Siderits's term for the Buddhist reductionist notion of the self)[18] of the first-person perspective.

Now, what challenge poses the Buddhist to the phenomenological account? To dismiss the Buddhist position since it does not share the same motivations and bring normative considerations to the description of consciousness such as the sense of first-person givenness as a distortion or construct, would be to miss its intriguing alternative about the very possibility of experience without a self, even a minimal sense of a self.[19] The very idea that 1) what seems to be experientially given can be explained and 2) that there are reports and evidence for experiences without the first person perspective (for-me-ness or mineness) – at least raise the question of whether this feature is invariant. Can phenomenology extend its investigation to include this kind of experiences? Can it accept that the first-person is not an invariant dimension of experience?

I end this section, before concluding, by sketching two difficulties in the insistence on the irreducibility of the first-person perspective. First, methodologically, the phenomenological reduction, on its various forms, takes as its point of departure the first-person perspective. Here lies also its significant contribution to the study of consciousness. Yet, how can phenomenological investigation begin from the first-person perspective and then arrive at the end to its irreducibility without begging the question? This, of course demarks the limit of the project exactly, to investigate what appears, i.e. the phenomena and the structures of experience, that is, conscious experience, while the Buddhists ask what produces this experience (or what enable it in a more Kantian formulation) and whether we can go beyond it to a more accurate, or even 'real', experience.

Second, is the idea of the first-person perspective as minimal or core self liable to a similar criticism as that of the Kantian notion of the unity of apperception? Zahavi claims that the experiential self can replace the Kantian notion of the unity of apperception, or the self as a pure identity-pole. He indicates that the former "just like the Kantian notion, is a very formal and minimalist notion, and it is obvious that far more complex forms of selves exist," yet, he sees it as pivotal and fundamental.[20] It is not clear, however, how different this formal dimension is from the Kantian one. It is supposed to demonstrate that the act-transcendent ego or the identity-pole is rooted in experiential reality contrary to the purely formal transcendental 'I-think.' Although the enduring self across time and different changing experiences, contrary to the self-givenness of a single experience, cannot be experienced directly since it is a result of synthesis, it is nevertheless grounded in experiential core, in the "pervasive dimension of first-personal experiencing."[21] But since the latter is a formal principle of individuation that requires a complementary more complex self,[22] it seems that the idea of an enduring self owes itself to a similar formal unity if not to 'some non-experiential enduring ego-substance.'[23] To put it differently, although the first-person givenness is presented as experiential dimension it is closer to the purely abstract formal identity-pole that is, as the Buddhists would claim, a result of inference or construction and is not available to experience proper. The sense of the self, then, is constructed over experience.

IV. Conclusion

Following the two approaches, we see that an account of reflexive self-awareness does not require subjectivity as a separate entity behind or above experience. There is no subject that controls or initiates this type of self-awareness. This self-awareness is also not awareness of the subject but awareness of the experiences themselves. However, according to the phenomenological approach there is still a sense of subjectivity in the account of self-awareness. It is found in the manner of experiencing the experiences; they are experienced as given from a first-person perspective. This phenomenological conclusion gives a weaker sense of subjectivity than the one the Buddhists seemingly rejects. This conclusion raises a challenge to the latter, since it claims that an account of self-awareness does require a sense of subjectivity, even if minimal. The Buddhist approach, to some extent, can accept the first-person givenness into its theory since it does not entail a substantial subjectivity. Nevertheless, this will be only a conventional sense of subjectivity that in the final account is not required and can be altered.

NOTES

1. I use 'subjectivity' and 'self' alternately at this point since this is exactly the subject in question. I examine what notion of subjectivity the theories below have when they reject or accept subjectivity into their account.
2. Several scholars have recently drawn attention to the similarity between the conception of self-awareness in the Buddhist school of epistemology and conceptions of self-awareness in the Western philosophical tradition, particularly phenomenology. Cf. Mark Siderits, Evan Thompson, and Dan Zahavi, eds., *Self, No Self?: Perspectives from Analytical, Phenomenological, and Indian Traditions*

(Oxford; New York: Oxford University Press, 2011); Dan Arnold, "Buddhist Idealism, Epistemic and Otherwise: Thoughts on the Alternating Perspectives of Dharmakirti," *Sophia* 47 (2008): 7-8; Georges Dreyfus, *Recognizing Reality: Dharmakirti's Philosophy and its Interpretations* (Albany: State University of New York Press, 1997), 401-402; Jonardon Ganeri "Self-Intimation, Memory and Personal Identity," *Journal of Indian Philosophy* 27 (1999): 469–483; Chien-hsing Ho, "Consciousness and Self-Awareness," *Asian Philosophy* 17, No. 3 (2007): 213-230; Dan Lusthaus, *Buddhist Phenomenology: A Philosophical Investigation of Yogacara Buddhism and the Ch'eng Wei-shih lun* (London: Routledge Curzon, 2002); Matthew MacKenzie, "The Illumination of Consciousness: Approaches to Self-Awareness in the Indian and Western Traditions," *Philosophy East and West* 57, No. 1 (2007): 40–62; J. N. Mohanty, *Explorations in Philosophy: Indian Philosophy*, ed. Bina Gupta (New Delhi: Oxford University Press, 2001), 164-170; Roy Perrett, "Intentionality and Self-Awareness," *Ratio* 16 (2003): 222-235; Stephen Priest, *The Subject in Question: Sartre's Critique of Husserl in The Transcendence of the Ego* (London ; New York: Routledge, 2000), 1-17. These studies, with some notable exceptions in the first volume, mainly present a comparison with Sartre's early phenomenology and not with Husserl's phenomenology based on similar accounts of consciousness without a self that are found in both Sartre and the Buddhist philosophy. This essay aims at a contribution to these studies by extending the exploration and examining the differences that can shed light on both accounts of self-awareness in Husserl's phenomenology and Dinnāga's Buddhist thought. In particular, this discussion aims at illuminating the Buddhist thesis of *anatman* and the subjective nature of experiences according to phenomenology by focusing on the debate on reflexive self-awareness.

3. The distinction between reflexive self-awareness and reflective self-awareness is parallel to the distinction between intransitive self-awareness and transitive self-awareness. *Intransitive self-awareness* is an elementary form of self-awareness in the sense that it does not require an additional act, such as reflection or introspection, but occurs concurrently with the awareness of an object. It does not involve judgment or belief and it is passive in the sense that it is spontaneous and involuntary. In contrast, *transitive self-awareness* is a result of deliberate reflection, introspection or inner-perception. In this kind of self-awareness,

there are two mental acts, for example, a perception of visual object and a reflection on that perception. My aim is not to discuss the strength and justification of such a theory vs. the higher-order thought alternatives but instead to look at the place of subjectivity in such a theory. See Uriah Kriegel, "Consciousness as Intransitive Self-Consciousness: Two Views and an Argument," *Canadian Journal of Philosophy* 33 (2003): 103–132; Evan Thompson and Dan Zahavi, "Philosophical Issues: Phenomenology," in *The Cambridge Handbook of Consciousness*, ed. Philip David Zelazo, Morris Moscovitch, and Evan Thompson (New York: Cambridge University Press, 2007), 76; Dan Zahavi, *Subjectivity and Selfhood: Investigating the First-Person Perspective* (Cambridge, Mass.: MIT Press, 2005), 17-32.

4. The simile of the lamp is used widely in Classical Indian and Buddhist philosophy but also, to a lesser extent, in phenomenology. Cf. Paul Williams, *The Reflexive Nature of Awareness: A Tibetan Madhyamaka Defence* (Richmond, Surrey: Curzon, 1998), xi-xii; Ho 2007, 223, Zahavi 2005, 61.
5. The dispute in terms of the framework that is set in the introduction to *Self, No Self?* is whether consciousness is fundamentally egological or non-egological. See Siderits, Thompson, and Zahavi 2011, 1-3. Specifically, I will look at the challenge that Dan Zahavi's phenomenological notion of a minimal self poses for the Buddhist view of consciousness as non-egological. See Zahavi 2005, 99-146; Zahavi, "The Experiential Self: Objections and Clarifications," in *Self, No Self?: Perspectives from Analytical, Phenomenological, and Indian Traditions*, ed. Mark Siderits, Evan Thompson, and Dan Zahavi (Oxford; New York: Oxford University Press, 2011), 56-78. The recent prolific discussion of the relation between reflexivity and self in the edited volume *Self, No Self?*, as well as previous work of the authors, inform my thought greatly. I want, then, to indicate where my focus is slightly different. First, my consideration is not ontological. My aim is not to argue for the existence or non-existence of the self but rather to investigate to what extent the premise of the self is required for an account of reflexivity. Turning to Husserl's phenomenology and Dinnāga's epistemology helps to avoid making ontological claims since both bracket them. It may well be reasonable that there are indeed ontological commitments behind their views but I attempt to dispense with them unless they come up from the dialogue itself. This is a possible consequence that relates to my second aim which pertains to the meta-philosophical implications

of such dialogue across philosophical traditions. There are indeed difficulties with such a project that stems from the different motivations and purposes of formulating the reflexive thesis in phenomenology and Buddhism. Yet, I hope that bringing these views together can help to shed light on their presuppositions and their boundaries and lead to examining their commitments and what they allow to take in or leave out.

6. See Edmund Husserl, *The Phenomenology of Internal Time-Consciousness*, ed. Martin Heidegger, trans. James S. Churchill (Bloomington: Indiana University Press, 1964), henceforth ITC; Edmund Husserl, *On the Phenomenology of the Consciousness of Internal Time (1893-1917)*, trans. John Barnett Brough (Dordrecht: Kluwer Academic Publishers, 1991), henceforth CIT, and Dan Zahavi's discussion of Husserl's conception of inner time-consciousness in *Self-Awareness and Alterity: A Phenomenological Investigation* (Evanston, Ill.: Northwestern University Press, 1999), 63-90. Also see Zahavi 2005, 49-72; Shaun Gallagher and Dan Zahavi, "Phenomenological Approaches to Self-Consciousness," *The Stanford Encyclopedia of Philosophy* (Winter 2010 Edition), ed. Edward N. Zalta, <http://plato.stanford.edu/archives/win2010/entries/self-consciousness-phenomenological/>.
7. See Dinnāga, *Dinnāga, On Perception*, trans. Masaaki Hattori (Cambridge, Mass.: Harvard University Press, 1968), henceforth PS. Dinnāga and Dharmakirti are traditionally identified with the Yogācāra school but they are also recognized under the title of the Yogācāra-Sautrāntika school due to the evident influence of the earlier Sautrāntika school. Buddhist epistemology, contrary to non-Buddhist schools, accepts only two means of knowledge, perception (*pratyaksa*) and inference (*anumāna*). The objects of perception are particulars (*svalaksana*) which are momentary, indeterminate, and non-conceptual. The objects of inference are universals and since they are conceptual fabrication (*vikalpa*) the knowledge of them is mediated and liable to distortion. Self-awareness is a type of perception (see below) and as such it is non-conceptual and immediate. Since every cognition, whether it is perceptual or conceptual, is also self-known, self-awareness is identified with the resulted cognition (*pramānaphala*) (PS 1.9a). For further discussion of the significance of self-awareness to knowledge and the *svasamvedana* theory, see Zhihua Yao, *The Buddhist Theory of Self-Cognition* (London: Routledge, 2005); Zhihua Yao, "Dinnāga and Four Types of Perception," *Journal of Indian Philosophy* 32 (2004): 57–79; Ho 2007; Williams 1998; Hattori 1968;

Richard P. Hayes, *Dinnāga on the Interpretation of Signs* (Dordrecht: Kluwer Academic Publishers, 1988), 140-142, Dreyfus 1997, 400-402; Georges Dreyfus and Evan Thompson, "Asian Perspectives: Indian Theories of Mind," in *The Cambridge Handbook of Consciousness*, ed. Philip David Zelazo, Morris Moscovitch, and Evan Thompson (Cambridge, New York: Cambridge University Press, 2007), 103-104; Dan Arnold, "Is Svasamvitti Transcendental? A Tentative Reconstruction Following Śāntaraks)ita," *Asian Philosophy* 15, No. 1 (2005): 77–111; "Self-Awareness (svasamÚvitti) and Related Doctrines of Buddhists Following Dignāga: Philosophical Characterizations of Some of the Main Issues," Special issue on Buddhist Theories of Self-awareness (svasamvedana): Reception and Critique, *Journal of Indian Philosophy* 38 (2010), 323–378.

8. Dan Zahavi, *Husserl's Phenomenology* (Stanford, Calif.: Stanford University Press, 2003), 89.
9. Zahavi 1999, 71; 2005, 65.
10. See Ho 2007: 216; Jonardon Ganeri, "Self-Representation and Mental Time Travel," paper presented in *International Conference on Problems of the Self: Debates in Consciousness Subjectivity and Otherness*, Center for Philosophy, School of Social Sciences, Jawaharlal Nehru University, January 24, 2013.
11. See PS 110-111. The notion of infinite regress is part of a more developed justification for the theory. The point in this context is that this is an account of a one-level awareness in a similar manner to the pre-reflective self-awareness. For a similar regress argument in Husserl see CIT; 123 Zahavi 2005, 59-61.
12. See Zahavi 1999, 138-156; 2005, 115-132; 2011.
13. Zahavi 2005, 146, 130.
14. Cf. Matthew MacKenzie, "Self-Awareness without a Self: Buddhism and the Reflexivity of Awareness," *Asian Philosophy* 18, No. 3 (2008): 245- 266; Joel W. Krueger, "The Who and the How of Experience," in *Self, No Self?: Perspectives from Analytical, Phenomenological, and Indian Traditions*, ed. Mark Siderits, Evan Thompson, and Dan Zahavi (Oxford; New York: Oxford University Press, 2011), 30-34.
15. Georges Dreyfus, "Self and Subjectivity: A Middle Way Approach," in *Self, No Self?: Perspectives from Analytical, Phenomenological, and Indian Traditions*, ed. Mark Siderits, Evan Thompson, and Dan Zahavi (Oxford; New York: Oxford University Press, 2011), 133. Also See Miri Albahari, *Analytical Buddhism: The Two-Tiered Illusion of Self* (Basingstoke; New York:

Palgrave Macmillan, 2006), 7, on the distinction between subjectivity and self. For Zahavi's reply to the notion of diachronic unity, see 2011, 71-76.

16. Ho 2007, 224. Also see John Dunne, "The Reflective Self: Egological versus Non-Egological Approaches to Consciousness," A Panel Discussion with Dan Zahavi, Evan Thompson, Georges Dreyfus and John Dunne, *The Columbia Society for Comparative Philosophy (CSCP)*, 2008, <http://www.cbs.columbia.edu/cscp/phenomenology>. A similar point is made by Jonardon Ganeri in relation to Vasubandhu: "A no-ownership theorist need not deny that a sense of ownership accompanies experience, a sense which is grounded in the subconscious activity of *manas*. One can deny that first-person present-tense ascriptions ascribe states of consciousness to subjects without falling into the incoherence, identified by P. Strawson, of denying that experience is necessarily experience as that of someone." "Buddhist No-Self: An Analysis and Critique," in *Hindu and Buddhist Ideas in Dialogue: Self and No-Self*, ed. Irina Kuznetsova, Jonardon Ganeri and Chakravarthi Ram-Prasad (Surrey: Ashgate, 2012), 73.
17. See Ganeri 2012, 70-73.
18. See Mark Siderits, "Buddhas as Zombies: A Buddhist Reduction of Subjectivity," in *Self, No Self?: Perspectives from Analytical, Phenomenological, and Indian Traditions*, ed. Mark Siderits, Evan Thompson, and Dan Zahavi (Oxford; New York: Oxford University Press, 2011), 310-312.
19. See Ganeri 2012, 74-75.
20. It is fundamental in the sense that "nothing that lacks this dimension deserves to be called a self." Zahavi 2005, 106.
21. Ibid., 132.
22. Such as the narrative self that enriches the minimal self with contents of autobiographical history, convictions, values, actions and decisions, all which make me the person I am. Zahavi indicates the connection between the experiential and the narrative self: "Owing to the first-personal givenness of experience, our experiential life is inherently individuated. It is, however, a purely formal kind of individuation. In contrast, a more concrete kind of individuality manifests itself in my personal history, in my moral and intellectual convictions and decisions. It is through such acts that I define myself; they have a character-shaping effect." Ibid., 129.
23. Zahavi 2011, 74.

REFERENCES

Albahari, Miri. *Analytical Buddhism: The Two-Tiered Illusion of Self.* Basingstoke; New York: Palgrave Macmillan, 2006.

Arnold, Dan. "Buddhist Idealism, Epistemic and Otherwise: Thoughts on the Alternating Perspectives of Dharmakirti." *Sophia* 47 (2008): 3-28.

——. "Is SvasamÚvitti Transcendental? A Tentative Reconstruction Following Śāntaraks)ita." *Asian Philosophy* 15, no. 1 (2005): 77–111.

——. "Self-Awareness (svasamvitti) and Related Doctrines of Buddhists Following Dignāga: Philosophical Characterizations of Some of the Main Issues." Special issue on Buddhist Theories of Self-Awareness (svasamvedana): Reception and Critique. *Journal of Indian Philosophy* 38 (2010): 323–378.

Dinnāga, *Dinnāga, On Perception, Being the Pratyakcapariccheda of Dignāga's Pramā Gasamuccaya from the Sanskrit Fragments and the Tibetan Versions*. Translated and annotated by Masaaki Hattori. Cambridge, Mass.: Harvard University Press, 1968. [PS].

Dreyfus, Georges. *Recognizing Reality: Dharmakirti's Philosophy and its Interpretations*. Albany: State University of New York Press, 1997.

——. "Self and Subjectivity: A Middle Way Approach." In *Self, No Self?: Perspectives from Analytical, Phenomenological, and Indian Traditions*, edited by Mark Siderits, Evan Thompson, and Dan Zahavi, 114-156. Oxford; New York: Oxford University Press, 2011.

Dreyfus, Georges and Evan Thompson. "Asian Perspectives: Indian Theories of Mind." In *The Cambridge Handbook of Consciousness*, edited by Philip David Zelazo, Morris Moscovitch, and Evan Thompson, 89-114. Cambridge, New York: Cambridge University Press, 2007.

Dunne, John. "The Reflective Self: Egological versus Non-Egological Approaches to Consciousness." A Panel Discussion with Dan Zahavi, Evan Thompson, Georges Dreyfus and John Dunne, *The Columbia Society for Comparative Philosophy (CSCP)*. 2008. <http://www.cbs.columbia.edu/cscp/phenomenology>.

Gallagher, Shaun and Dan Zahavi. "Phenomenological Approaches to Self-Consciousness." *The Stanford Encyclopedia of Philosophy* (Winter 2010 Edition), edited by Edward N. Zalta. 2010. <http://plato.stanford.edu/archives/win2010/entries/self-consciousness-phenomenological/>.

Ganeri, Jonardon. "Buddhist No-Self: An Analysis and Critique." In *Hindu and Buddhist Ideas in Dialogue: Self and No-Self*. Edited by Irina Kuznetsova, Jonardon Ganeri and Chakravarthi Ram-Prasad, 63-76. Surrey: Ashgate, 2012.

——. "Self-Intimation, Memory and Personal Identity." *Journal of Indian Philosophy* 27 (1999): 469–483.

Hayes, Richard P. *Dinnāga on the Interpretation of Signs*. Dordrecht: Kluwer Academic Publishers, 1988.

Ho, Chien-hsing. "Consciousness and Self-awareness." *Asian Philosophy* 17, No. 3 (2007): 213-230.

Husserl, Edmund. *On the Phenomenology of the Consciousness of Internal Time (1893-1917)*. Translated by John Barnett Brough. Dordrecht: Kluwer Academic Publishers, 1991. [CIT].

——. *The Phenomenology of Internal Time-Consciousness*. Edited by Martin Heidegger. Translated by James S. Churchill. Bloomington: Indiana University Press, 1964. [ITC].

Kriegel, Uriah. "Consciousness as Intransitive Self-Consciousness: Two Views and an Argument." *Canadian Journal of Philosophy* 33 (2003): 103–132.

Krueger, Joel W. "The Who and the How of Experience." In *Self, No Self?: Perspectives from Analytical, Phenomenological, and Indian Traditions*, edited by Mark Siderits, Evan Thompson, and Dan Zahavi, 27-55. Oxford; New York: Oxford University Press, 2011.

Lusthaus, Dan. *Buddhist Phenomenology: A Philosophical Investigation of Yogacara Buddhism and the Ch'eng Wei-shih lun*. London: Routledge Curzon, 2002.

MacKenzie, Matthew. "Luminosity, Subjectivity, and Temporality: An Examination of Buddhist and Advaita Views of Consciousness." In *Hindu and Buddhist Ideas in Dialogue: Self and No-Self*. Edited by Irina Kuznetsova, Jonardon Ganeri and Chakravarthi Ram-Prasad. Surrey: Ashgate, 2012.

——. "Self-Awareness without a Self: Buddhism and the Reflexivity of Awareness." *Asian Philosophy* 18, no. 3 (2008): 245- 266.

——. "The Illumination of Consciousness: Approaches to Self-Awareness in the Indian and Western Traditions." *Philosophy East and West* 57, No. 1 (2007): 40–62.

Mohanty, J.N. *Explorations in Philosophy: Indian Philosophy*. Edited by Bina Gupta. New Delhi: Oxford University Press, 2001.

Perrett, Roy. "Intentionality and Self-Awareness." *Ratio* 16 (2003): 222-235.

Priest, Stephen. *The Subject in Question: Sartre's Critique of Husserl in The Transcendence of the Ego*. London ; New York: Routledge, 2000.

Siderits, Mark. "Buddhas as Zombies: A Buddhist Reduction of Subjectivity." In *Self, No Self?: Perspectives from Analytical, Phenomenological, and Indian Traditions*, edited by Mark Siderits, Evan Thompson, and Dan Zahavi, 308-331. Oxford; New York:

Oxford University Press, 2011.

Siderits, Mark, Evan Thompson, and Dan Zahavi, eds. *Self, No Self?: Perspectives from Analytical, Phenomenological, and Indian Traditions*. Oxford; New York: Oxford University Press, 2011.

Thompson, Evan and Dan Zahavi, "Philosophical Issues: Phenomenology." In *The Cambridge Handbook of Consciousness*, edited by Philip David Zelazo, Morris Moscovitch, and Evan Thompson, 67-87. New York: Cambridge University Press, 2007.

Williams, Paul. *The Reflexive Nature of Awareness: A Tibetan Madhyamaka Defense*. Richmond, Surrey: Curzon, 1998.

Yao, Zhihua. "Dinnāga and Four Types of Perception." *Journal of Indian Philosophy* 32 (2004): 57–79.

——. *The Buddhist Theory of Self-Cognition*. London: Routledge, 2005.

Zahavi, Dan. *Husserl's Phenomenology*. Stanford, Calif.:Stanford University Press, 2003.

——. *Self-Awareness and Alterity: A Phenomenological Investigation*. Evanston, Ill.: Northwestern University Press, 1999.

——. *Subjectivity and Selfhood: Investigating the First-Person Perspective*. Cambridge, Mass.: MIT Press, 2005.

——. "The Experiential Self: Objections and Clarifications." In *Self, No Self?: Perspectives from Analytical, Phenomenological, and Indian Traditions*, edited by Mark Siderits, Evan Thompson, and Dan Zahavi, 56-78. Oxford; New York: Oxford University Press, 2011.

9

Reflexivity, Subjectivity, and the Enacted Self

Matthew MacKenzie

Introduction

I would like to take up three closely connected questions in the philosophy of mind. First, does consciousness necessarily involve subjectivity? Second, what is the connection, if any, between self-consciousness and subjectivity? And, third, does consciousness necessarily involve an ego or self? Of course, philosophers in both the Indian and the Western traditions have had much to say about these questions. In what follows, I will draw on both traditions to develop an account of the relation between consciousness, subjectivity, and the self. The account is inspired by the Yogācāra-Madhyamaka synthesis of Śāntarakshita (8th century CE), though I make no claims to follow him in every detail. In brief, I will argue, first, that phenomenal consciousness is reflexive or self-illuminating (*svaprakāśya*) in that conscious states present both their intentional object and themselves. Second, I will argue that consciousness necessarily involves subjectivity in that all phenomenal presentation is presentation-*to* a subject. Third, I will argue that neither the reflexivity nor the subjectivity of consciousness implies that there is any such *entity* as the self or ego over and above reflexive consciousness. Fourth, and finally, I will argue that what we normally think of as 'the self' is best understood as a complex, multi-layered *process* (*ahaAkāra*, 'I-making') that emerges within the embodied and embedded pre-egoic flow of subjective consciousness.

Ego and Consciousness

Let me begin with a familiar account of the debate between Buddhists and the Brahmanical schools over the nature and existence of the self: the Brahmanical schools accept the existence of the *ātman* (the substantial self), while the Buddhists reject the *ātman* while adopting a reductionist or irrealist account of persons. Thus while the Buddhists are similar to Hume, Locke, and Parfit, the *ātmavadins* are, though diverse, basically Cartesian in their approach to the self. Yet, as a number of scholars have pointed out, this view of the Indian debates on the nature of the self is far too simplistic. Indeed, as Chakravarthi Ram-Prasad argues, there are (at least) two distinct debates going on.[1] The first debate concerns the nature of the empirical person (*pudgala*) and the ego-sense (*ahaṃkāra*), whether the person (or ego) is constructed or ontologically fundamental, as well as questions of synchronic and diachronic personal identity. The second debate concerns the existence and nature of an 'impersonal subjectivity' which may constitute the (formal) ground of empirical personhood. In this debate questions such as the reflexivity, unity, and continuity of consciousness are emphasized.[2]

We can see the complexity quite clearly with regard to the first type of debate. On the one hand, some proponents of the self (*ātmavadins*) argue that personhood is a conceptually, linguistically, and socially constructed phenomenon and that the psychological ego-sense (*ahaṃkāra*) provides a false or distorted sense of self. On the other hand, self-sceptics (*anātmavadins*) such as the Buddhists argue that we do indeed have a relatively stable, persisting sense of self and that the notion of personhood is central to moral responsibility and the active pursuit of the spiritual life. With regard to the second type of debate, it is important to keep in mind that it was central to the *anātmavadins'* task to develop a philosophically and experientially adequate account of consciousness and the sense of self so as properly to diagnose and overcome what they took to be the deep-seated distortion and reification involved in *ātmad[cmi*, the 'view of the self'. Thus we can conceptually distinguish the genetic, constructive analyses of the phenomena offered by the self-sceptics from their deeper commitment to an anti-realism or error-theory about the sense of self.[3] Moreover, all parties agree that there is no simple answer to the question of the self's existence and that working out a viable position on the topic involves a number of interconnected questions in metaphysics, philosophical psychology, epistemology, and the contemplative exploration of experience.

Given these complexities, it may be useful to begin with a distinction drawn within the phenomenological tradition between egological and non-egological accounts of consciousness. As Dan Zahavi explains, on the egological view, "the self is some kind of unchanging soul substance that is distinct from, and ontologically independent of, the mental experiences and worldly objects it is the subject of. According to the second [non-egological] view, there is nothing to consciousness apart from a manifold of interrelated changing experiences."[4] Clearly, there are versions of *ātmavāda* and *anātmavāda* that correspond to the egological and non-egological views, respectively. However, my interest here is with views that occupy a position between these extremes. For instance, rejecting both views, Zahavi argues that the self is "immersed in conscious life; it is an integral part of its structure."[5] The self is not to be seen as some kind of *entity* either apart from or within conscious life, but is instead the very first-personal givenness of experience itself.

Zahavi further argues, in line with perhaps the entire phenomenological tradition, that consciousness is characterized by an immanent reflexivity or pre-reflective self-consciousness. Indeed, he thinks that reflexivity or self-givenness is the very mode of being of consciousness itself. And yet, the reflexivity or self-manifestation of experience has been given both egological and non-egological interpretations. On a non-egological view, reflexive awareness is simply the "acquaintance consciousness has with *itself* and *not* as an awareness of an experiencing *self*."[6] On a strong version of the non-egological view—a 'no-ownership' view—experiences are not *for* a subject at all. In contrast, "an *egological* theory," Zahavi explains, would claim that when I watch a movie by Bergman, I am not only intentionally directed at the *movie*, nor merely aware of the movie being *watched*, I am also aware that it is being watched by *me*, that is, that *I* am *watching* the *movie*.... Thus, an egological theory would typically claim that it is a conceptual and experiential truth that any episode of experiencing necessarily includes a subject of experience.[7]

As I understand him, Zahavi sees the usual distinction between egological and non-egological views as too crude and develops a more nuanced version of an egological theory of consciousness and the minimal self.

This view implies that conscious experiences have a dative of manifestation and are, in some appropriate sense, subjectively lived-through (*Erlebt*). This is the basic and irreducible subjectivity of consciousness. It also associates this with the basic *mineness* or *for-me-ness* of experience, the primitive sense of ownership or *ipseity* of experience. This sense of ownership is not explicit or thematic, but is rather a pre-reflective sense of ownership that is an invariant aspect of conscious experience.[8] Moreover, the reflexivity and *mineness* constitute the minimal, experiential self. Thus, while self-sceptics such as Thomas Metzinger or Vasubandhu may be right to deny the self either as a substantial, independent entity or as the basis of the unity of consciousness, they are wrong, on Zahavi's view, to hold that consciousness is fundamentally selfless. Self-sceptics reject a reified self, but to reject the minimal experiential self is to miss or misconstrue deep and perhaps necessary features of mental life.

In contrast to Zahavi's nuanced egological theory, I want to sketch and motivate a more nuanced non-egological account of consciousness drawn from Indian Buddhist philosophy of mind that may have wider scope than the egological alternative.

Luminosity and Cognizance

In classical Buddhist discussions, consciousness is defined as that which is *luminous* and *cognizant*. The metaphor of illumination is at the heart of Indian (and Tibetan) discussions of consciousness and subjectivity.[9] Just as light reveals those objects upon which it falls, consciousness has the unique capacity to make experientially present those objects to which it is directed. It is that by which there can be any phenomenal appearance. As the capacity for experiential manifestation, luminosity (*prakāśatā*) is linked to the phenomenality of consciousness. As Ram-Prasad puts it:

> Luminosity is the rendering of an event as subjective. It is that by which there is an occurrence, which it is something it is like to undergo. The subjective is the having of the experience (*anubhava*)....The [Indian] philosophers are agreed on all sides that consciousness is phenomenological; it is luminous. The debate is over the constitution of the phenomenality of consciousness. The debate is about what it is for there to be subjectivity.[10]

The luminosity of consciousness is also closely connected to its qualities of *clarity* (*prabhāsvara*) and *unobstructedness*. Consciousness is clear in that it has no colour, shape, size, weight, and so on; yet it is the condition of the possibility of experiencing these qualities. Indeed, when one searches for consciousness itself as an object or content, one is unable to find it.[11] The clarity of consciousness is also linked to its capacity to present accurately, when not clouded by cognitive and affective distortions. Consciousness is unobstructed in that, while not itself having a sound, colour, or shape, it has (it *is*) the capacity to present the whole open-ended range of experiences. That is, consciousness is unobstructed in that it can present indefinitely many experiences. The cognizance of consciousness is its capacity to grasp or apprehend its object. This aspect, then, is linked to the intentionality of consciousness. Conscious states not only present phenomena, but also are intentionally directed to objects (*vicaya*). Further, consciousness involves not just the capacity to reveal or phenomenally manifest, but also to identify, re-identify, and understand its objects.

The basic divide in Indian accounts of the luminosity of consciousness is between other-illumination (*paraprakāśa*) and self-illumination (*svaprakāśa*) theories. For advocates of other-illumination, the luminosity of consciousness consists in its capacity to present a distinct object. Thus, transitive, object-directed intentionality is the mark of consciousness. Conscious states, in order to be states the subject is conscious *of*, must be presented by a distinct, higher-order cognition. Hence, consciousness illuminates that which is other than itself, and conscious states themselves are apperceived by another state.[12] In contrast, for advocates of self-illumination theories, the luminosity of consciousness consists in its being reflexive or self-presenting. Consciousness presents itself in the process of presenting its object. Moreover, just as light does not need a second light in order to be revealed, so consciousness does not need a distinct state to present itself.

The Yogācāra-Madhyamaka philosopher Śāntarakcita (8th century CE) follows the Buddhist epistemologists in holding that consciousness is reflexive, but provides a distinct and (within Buddhism) innovative account of reflexivity.[13] In so doing, Śāntarakcita moves the Buddhist account of reflexive awareness closer to the accounts of pre-reflective self-awareness found in the phenomenological tradition. There are five features of Śāntarakcita's theory of reflexive awareness I will highlight here. First, reflexivity is identified with luminosity (*prakāśatā*) and asserted to be the very nature or defining characteristic (*svalakcana*) of consciousness. Indeed, he would agree with Sartre that this type of non-positional self-consciousness "... we ought to consider not as a new consciousness, but as *the only mode of being which is possible for a consciousness of something.*"[14] Second, it is, as Ram-Prasad puts it, 'the rendering of an event as subjective'—that is, all phenomenal presentation of an object is presentation *to* a subject, but that subject is just consciousness itself. Third, reflexive awareness is the condition of the possibility of object-directed intentionality, and indeed of any phenomenal appearance. Unless consciousness is self-manifesting, it cannot present a transcendent object. Fourth, reflexivity provides or is tightly bound up with the synchronic unity of consciousness. Fifth, reflexive awareness is compatible with the emptiness (*śūnyatā*) of consciousness—that is, its lack of inherent existence or ontological independence (*svabhāva*).

On this account, then, consciousness is luminous (self-presenting) and cognizant (intentional) and the luminosity of consciousness *just is* its basic subjectivity. All phenomenal appearances are appearances *to* a luminous consciousness and, these Buddhist philosophers insist, no object is ever given *apart from* the primary self-givenness of consciousness. There is no hetero-manifestation without auto-manifestation.

The Yogācāra thinkers further distinguish eight dimensions or aspects of consciousness and it is here that we find an interesting and sophisticated account of the sense of self. The first five dimensions are the basic forms of sensory awareness. The sixth dimension is called 'mental-consciousness' (*mano-vijñāna*), which allows for direct non-inferential access to one's mental states. It is also thought to serve a synthetic, apperceptive function with regard to the other types of sensory awareness. These six types or aspects of consciousness are accepted throughout Indian Buddhist philosophy of mind, but thinkers associated with Yogācāra posit two more types of awareness: afflictive mentation (*klicta-manas*) and base- or store-consciousness (*ālaya-vijñāna*). On this account, the *ālaya-vijñāna* forms the most basic stratum of the stream of consciousness against the background of which the six types of sensory awareness operate. Unlike the discontinuous flow of the six manifest types of awareness (*prav[tti-vijñāna*), the base-consciousness is taken to be a diachronically continuous flow. It is also the store or repository of the various habits, dispositions, and propensities that shape the experience of the individual. Finally, according to the Yogācārins, the base consciousness is central to the explanation of the synchronic unity of consciousness. In phenomenological terms the *ālaya* is a sedimented retentional continuum, an egoless streaming.[15]

The seventh consciousness, the *klicta-manas* is the basic sense of self, the felt sense of mental ownership that is built into our default mental architecture. Like the base-consciousness, it is taken to be pre-reflective, continuous, and stable. As an implicit sense of mental ownership it does not depend on the operation of mental attention associated with *mano-vijñāna* and it is more basic than the capacity for having explicit 'I-cognitions' (*ahampratyāya*). Its basis is the *ālaya-vijñāna* and it is argued that the *klicta-manas* involves a basic cognitive-affective illusion: it mistakes the egoless streaming of the base-consciousness for an enduring self-entity. This innate distortion in our mental architecture is thought to be the basis of various destructive emotions and other mental afflictions (*kleúas*)—hence the term 'afflictive mentation'.

I want to emphasize three key points from this too quick sketch. First, to take consciousness to be self-luminous (*svayam-prakāśa*) is to see that subjectivity and phenomenality are inseparable. Indeed luminosity in this sense is the very mode of being of consciousness. Second, conscious events are not isolated occurrences, but rather each is constitutively part of a stream of consciousness (*citta-santāna*), which is itself a retentional continuum. This primordial flow is the dynamic ground (*āśraya*) from which other conscious events arise. Third, the felt sense of mental ownership (*klicta-manas*), while pre-reflective and stable, is in fact an emergent construct within the stream of experience. It is a *product* of the passive syntheses within the base-consciousness, even while it provides the sense that there is a self that is the enduring owner and ground of the stream of experience. The sense of self, on this view, may *feel* fixed and fundamental, but it is in fact a malleable, emergent construct.

Self and Subjectivity

On the view just sketched, reflexivity is tied to perspectival ownership and this is thought to provide an account of minimal subjectivity. Experiences do not float free and are always *undergone* experientially. But, as I will argue, in itself what this gives us is more like experiential *hosting* than a sense of *mineness* or *ownership*.[16] Note that the issue here is not reflective, thematic, or robust narrative notions of ownership. The Buddhist thinkers I am drawing from here hold that there is, in the normal case, a pre-reflective, non-thematic sense of mental ownership (*klicta-manas*), what in current discussions is called a minimal self, built into the stream of consciousness. The ego-sense (*ahaṃkāra*) is not a product of reflection. It emerges from the egoless streaming of the retentional continuum (*ālaya-vijñāna*), but is itself a pre-reflective structure of consciousness and is the basis (*āśraya*) of the thematic or explicit 'I' and 'mine'. The question, then, is whether reflexivity can come apart from the sense of mineness.

There are two kinds of cases I would like to discuss here. First are cases where the subject reports being aware of experiences as belonging to nobody. These include both pathologies and certain types of meditative states. Second are cases where the sense of ownership is reconstituted or reframed and is no longer taken to be either central or fundamental to the nature of consciousness. In both types of cases, it seems to me reasonable to hold that the pre-reflective sense of ownership is distinct from sheer reflexivity and that it is neither invariant nor fundamental.

Zahn, et al., report the case of DP, a 23-year-old male who complains of having "double visions" which he finds distressing. It turns out that he does not in fact have double vision.[17] Rather DP reports that, "he was able to see everything normally, but that he did not immediately recognize that he was the one who perceives and that he needed a *second step* to become aware that he himself was the one who perceives the object." DP, it seems, is aware of visual objects, but is not immediately aware of himself as the subject of the visual experiences in which the objects were given. Only with an act of reflection does he come to have a sense of ownership of the experiences. Indeed, according to Zahn, it is precisely the absence of the usual pre-reflective sense of mental ownership that DP found so distressing.

If the basic description of this case is correct, it seems to be a counter-example to the idea that a pre-reflective sense of ownership or mineness is an invariant feature of consciousness. In DP's case the sense of mineness has dropped out of the visual modality and he must take a second step in order to feel the visual experiences as his own. In an important sense, DP's pre-reflective visual experiences are anonymous. On the other hand, this case is importantly unlike a case of blindsight. First, DP's visual experiences are phenomenally conscious; there is something it is like to undergo them. Second, it appears that DP is pre-reflectively aware of his visual experiences in that he does not need to reflect in order to be aware of their occurrence. The 'second step' is at the level of ownership, not awareness. Third, his visual experiences are available for report and memory just like his other types of perceptual experience. Therefore, the case of DP provides *prima facie* evidence that one can have experiences that are phenomenally conscious, of which one is pre-reflectively aware, but that lack the felt sense of for-me-ness or mineness typical of our conscious experiences.

So, are these visual experiences DP's or are they unowned? Some self-sceptics, including many Buddhist thinkers, hold a strong no-ownership view of conscious events, such that, in the final analysis experiences are simple occurrences, like states of the weather. However, one need not follow them in that more radical view in order to see the force of DP's case—lack of experiential ownership does not entail lack of ontological ownership.[18] The visual experiences can be said to belong to DP in that they are integral parts of his embodied stream of experience. They are lived-through only by DP and only DP is directly access-conscious of them. The experiences are structured by DP's bodily point of view—that is, the objects are perspectively given. Yet what this shows is that they are experientially *hosted* by DP, but they are not experientially *owned* by him. The experiences are lived-through by DP, but not lived-through *as his own*. An experience can be *for me* in the sense that it is lived through by me and not someone else and yet the experience may not be given, even pre-reflectively, *as mine.*

With these considerations in mind, we can now distinguish a range of positions. A strong no-ownership view will deny even minimal subjectivity to conscious events—conscious events *occur*, but are not in any meaningful sense lived-through by a subject. A non-egological subjectivity view will hold that experiences are lived through by the subject, but will deny that subjective experiences always involve even a pre-reflective sense of for-*me*-ness.[19] A weak (or sophisticated) egological view will hold that minimal subjectivity is both a necessary feature of experience and that it necessarily involves a sense of mineness or for-me-ness. A strong egological view holds that experience necessarily involves the experience of a more robust *self*, not simply the for-me-ness of first-personal givenness. Here the debate is between the second and third positions.

A more dramatic type of case is associated with a meditative state referred to in the current literature as a *pure consciousness event* (PCE). In general, PCEs, which are reported in a number of meditative traditions, are described as being conscious, but devoid of sensory and thought contents or objects. As Shear characterizes it, "when the mind has become completely settled (while nevertheless remaining alert) one steps outside all activity of perception, and, silent and fully awake inside, experiences pure, unmanifest, absolutely objectless, consciousness."[20] Moreover, in many cases (and according to many theoretical descriptions) the sense of self is significantly altered or is simply absent. In the latter case, consciousness is said to be free of all traces of the sense of self or ego—there is nothing but the sheer luminosity of consciousness itself. Of course, some self-sceptics take PCEs as evidence of the fundamental ontological selflessness of consciousness, while some *ātmavādins* argue that pure consciousness *just is* the true self. In any case, if the standard description of PCEs is right, we seem to have a state that is: 1) conscious, 2) subjectively lived-through, 3) memorable, 4) lacking positional intentionality, 5) lacking a sense of self, 6) lacking sense of the passage of time, and 7) lacking perspective (bodily or perceptual). Indeed, probably the central, though by no means uncontroversial, account of this type of state in Indian philosophy of mind is that it is an instance wherein the sheer self-luminosity of consciousness is no longer occluded by either objects or the ego. That is, in more phenomenological terms, the field of consciousness is no longer structured by transitive intentionality, the minimal self, bodily perspective, or temporal contents—what remains is simply the non-objectifying self-givenness of consciousness itself.

The second type of case arises out of the specifically Indo-Tibetan Buddhist contemplative practice of 'Open Presence' (*Rigpa Chog-zhag*), which, as John Dunne has argued, has its theoretical roots in the syncretic, broadly Yogācāra view I have sketched above.[21] The theoretical background of the view begins with the observation that intentional objects are only given in and through experience and, further, that objects are not given apart from the (non-objectified) givenness of the subject. Thus, subject and object are co-given in experience and are correlative and mutually specifying.[22] As Lutz, et al. write:

> *Chag-zog* practitioners are thus aiming to understand the nature of experience—that which is essential to any instance of experience, regardless of the accidental and changing features of the objects or subjectivities involved. To do so, they employ a set of techniques that are intended to make the practitioner aware of the invariable feature of all experiences. They speak of this invariable feature using various descriptions, including *Rigpa*, "Awareness," or, using the metaphor of light, *Selwa* (*gsal ba*), "Luminosity" or "Clarity." But whether called Awareness, Clarity, or some other synonym, the point is that the invariant element in experience is that which, from a phenomenal standpoint, makes it possible for the subject-object relation to be presented in experience.[23]

On this view, subject and object are co-given and correlative, but also variable across different experiences. Moreover, in so far as subject and object are variable contents of experience one may ask what makes it possible for these contents to be given. In this tradition, the answer is luminosity, the open space or phenomenal field that allows even the subject-object correlation to be presented.

The practice itself follows four stages. First, one must develop concentration or stable attention on an object of meditation. Second, one de-emphasizes the object-pole of experience and begins to attend to the subject-pole. That is, without shutting out the object one becomes mindful of the subjectivity of experience. One is then led to recognize that, while initially seeming quite independent of awareness, experiential objects are constituted in and through experience and are not given apart from subjectivity. One recognizes that 'appearances are not other than mind'. Third, one begins to de-emphasize subjectivity and in particular the sense of diachronic subjectivity, the sense of an 'I' that extends beyond the living present. This leads to a state in which, "The experience's content does not appear as an object over against a subject, and the experience also does not involve a sense of subjectivity that is articulated by conceptual or linguistic structures, even if those structures are only implicit."[24] Finally, in the fourth stage:

> [D]e-emphasis of both object and subject moves, at least theoretically, to a point where no elements of objectivity or subjectivity—whether in the form of conceptual structures, categories of time and space, or some other feature—remain in the experience. At this point, the invariant feature of cognition is said to be realized fully by the meditator, and this is the full-blown state of Open Presence... [The] stability [of this state] consists of one's ability to continue to experience phenomena without objectifying them and, ideally, without having a sense of an agentive or narrative subjectivity. The state thus seems to cultivate a type of *ipseity* or bare awareness.[25]

While this practice, in its advanced stage, may evoke a type of pure consciousness event, its overall character is quite different. The point is not to shut out experiential content, but rather progressively to undo the implicit and habitual reification of subject and object. Thus subject and object are no longer seen as fixed realities, but rather come to be experienced as dynamically co-emergent and correlative appearances within a pre-objective, pre-subjective field of experience. This field is then identified as luminosity, non-egological reflexive awareness. As the great *Chag-zog* master Karme Chagme puts it:

> When it [awareness] stares at itself, with this observation there is a vividness in which nothing is seen. This awareness is direct, naked, vivid, unestablished, empty, limpid luminosity, unique, non-dual clarity and emptiness. It is not permanent, but unestablished. It is not nihilistic but radiantly vivid. It is not one, but manifoldly aware and clear. It is not manifold but indivisibly of one taste. It is none other than this very self-awareness.[26]

Here again we *prima facie* evidence that the minimal self is not an invariant structure of experience, both in the sense that it can drop away and in the more subtle sense that one can potentially, through a kind gestalt shift, come to experience it as an emergent phenomenon within a larger horizon of awareness. Thus, the sophisticated non-egological model of consciousness, which can account for both our normal pre-reflective sense of self and its absence or modification in certain cases, may be have the advantage over egological models.

Now, do these cases *prove* that the minimal self, the pre-reflective sense of *for-me-ness*, is not an invariant feature of experience? We should be cautious here. Altered states, pathological or meditative, can be misdescribed and misunderstood. On the other hand, cases such as these remind us that even though a feature of our consciousness is invariant across a wide range of experience and, indeed, is so central to our usual way of experiencing that we can scarcely imagine its absence, it does not follow that it is a fundamental or necessary feature. This is one reason why I think careful phenomenological and neurophenomenological engagement with contemplative techniques and experiences can be quite fruitful.

The Enacted Self

It seems to me that a view must meet three conditions to count as a proper form of *anātmavāda* or self-scepticism. First, it must reject the existence of the self as a substance or enduring entity. Second, it must deny that the sense of self is a necessary and invariant feature of experience. That is, it must have, at bottom, a non-egological theory of consciousness.[27] Third, it must maintain that the sense of self, no matter how natural it seems, necessarily involves some kind of error, illusion, or distortion.

A strong motivation for self-scepticism both in India and the West is a broadly empiricist and reductionist objectivism. However, in the case of the Buddhist tradition, the motivation for self-scepticism goes deeper. On the Buddhist analysis, our innate tendencies towards affective and conative distortions such as craving and attachment drive a vicious cycle of frustration, suffering, and alienation (*saṃsāra*). The root cause of these distortions is the innate tendency to reify self (*ātmad[cmi*) and world (*satkāyad[cmi*). In the case of the Buddhist view I sketched previously, the pre-reflective sense of self is called the *klicta-manas*, 'afflicted mentation'. In itself it is ethically neutral, but it is the basis for the afflictions of greed, aversion, and so on. Moreover, as we have seen, it is argued that there is cognitive illusion built into the *klicta-manas* in that it mistakes the egoless streaming of the *ālaya-vijñāna* for an enduring self. In this respect, the Buddhists view the sense of self as comparable to visual illusions such as the "impossible fork" illusion. As a line drawing, of course, the fork is perfectly real, but what it depicts is impossible. Moreover, the illusion of the fork, like the illusion of the reified self, is cognitively impenetrable: merely changing one's beliefs does not dispel the illusion. Likewise, while the *klicta-manas* is a real psychological structure, its existence necessarily produces in us the cognitive illusion of a reified self. This is an important insight, even if one demurs from the idea that the sense of self is *necessarily* distorted or illusion-like. The idea that various tendencies to reification are built into our cognitive-affective-conative systems strikes me as very plausible. This brand of self-scepticism also has resources to contribute to a deeper and more integrated understanding of the kinds of experience, pathological and contemplative, that I discussed above.

My own view is more emergentist than illusionist about the minimal self. That is, I think the minimal self emerges from an embodied, reflexive, but pre-egoic stream of experience. Thus, I think the right way to approach the multi-layered phenomenon of self is enactive, processive, and emergentist. In this sense, the minimal self is neither a necessary and invariant feature of all experience nor simply an illusion.

NOTES

1. Ram-Prasad 2012.
2. MacKenzie 2011.
3. Ganeri 2012.
4. Zahavi 2011a: 59.
5. Zahavi 2005: 125.
6. Zahavi 2005: 100.
7. Zahavi 2005: 99.
8. Zahavi 2005: 125.
9. Ram-Prasad 2007: 53.
10. Ram-Prasad 2007: 54
11. This is one of the phenomenological uses of *śūnyatā*.
12. MacKenzie 2007.
13. Williams 1998.
14. Sartre 1956: liv.
15. Zahavi 2011b.

16. Lane 2012.
17. Zahn, et al., 2008.
18. The insolation of experiential from ontological issues cuts both ways. There might be a sense of self or experiential self, but no ontologically more robust self. Or, there might be an ontologically robust self even if it is not (always) manifest in experience.
19. They might, however, still accept the perspectival or indexical structure of experience.
20. Shear and Jevning 1999: 194-195.
21. Dunne (unpublished).
22. Lutz, et al., 2007: 513.
23. Lutz, et al., 2007: 513-14.
24. Lutz, et al., 2007: 517.
25. Lutz, et al., 2007: 517.
26. Quoted in Dreyfus 2011: 121–2.
27. Siderits (2011) has recently argued, in effect, that because consciousness is egological, an *anātmavādin* should be a fictionalist about consciousness itself. This view, however, has no Indian Buddhist proponents.

REFERENCES

Dreyfus, G. (2011), "Self and Subjectivity: A Middle Way Approach" in *Self, No Self?* (Oxford: Oxford University Press).

Dunne, J. "Towards an Understanding of Non-Dual Mindfulness," unpublished manuscript.

Robert K. C. Forman (1990), "Introduction: Mysticism, Constructivism, and Forgetting," in *The Problem of Pure Consciousness: Mysticism and Philosophy*, ed. Robert K.C. Forman (New York: Oxford University Press).

Ganeri, J. (2012), *The Self: Naturalism, Consciousness, and the First-Person Stance* (Oxford: Oxford University Press).

Lane, T. "Towards an Explanatory Framework for Mental Ownership," *Phenomenology and the Cognitive Sciences*, 11:251–286.

Antoine Lutz, John D. Dunne, and Richard J. Davidson (2007), "Meditation and the Neuroscience of Consciousness: An Introduction," in, P. David Zelazo, M. Moscovitch, and E. Thompson *The Cambridge Handbook of Consciousness* (New York: Cambridge University Press).

MacKenzie, M. (2007), "The Illumination of Consciousness: Approaches to Self-Awareness in the Indian and Western Traditions," *Philosophy East and West*, 57: 40–62.

——— (2012), 'Luminosity, Subjectivity, and Temporality: An

Examination of Buddhist and Advaita Views of Consciousness', in Kuznetsova, et al., *Hindu and Buddhist Ideas in Dialogue: Self and No-Self* (Surrey: Ashgate).

Ram-Prasad, C. (2007), *Indian Philosophy and the Consequences of Knowledge* (Aldershot: Ashgate).

——— (2012), 'Self and Memory: Personal Identity and Unified Consciousness in Comparative Perspective', in Kuznetsova, et al., *Hindu and Buddhist Ideas in Dialogue: Self and No-Self* (Surrey: Ashgate).

Sartre, Jean-Paul (1956), *Being and Nothingness,* trans. Hazel Barnes (New York, NY: Philosophical Library).

Shear, J. and R. Jevning (1999), 'Pure Consciousness: Scientific Exploration of Meditation Techniques,' *Journal of Consciousness Studies* 6: 189-209.

Siderits, M. (2011), "Buddhas as Zombies: A Buddhist Reduction of Subjectivity," in Siderits, et al., *Self, No Self?* (Oxford: Oxford University Press).

Williams, P. (1998), *The Reflexive Nature of Awareness: A Tibetan Madhyamaka Defence* (Delhi: Motilal Banarsidas).

Zahavi, D. (2005), *Subjectivity and Selfhood: Investigating the First-Person Perspective* (Cambridge, MA: MIT).

——— (2011a), 'The Experiential Self: Objections and Clarifications', in Siderits, et al., *Self, No Self?* (Oxford: Oxford University Press).

——— (2011b), 'Unity of Consciousness and the Problem of Self', in S. Gallagher *The Oxford Handbook of the Self* (Oxford: Oxford University Press).

Zahn, R., Talazko, J., et al. (2008), 'Loss of the Sense of Self-Ownership for Perceptions of Objects in a Case of Right Inferior Temporal, Parieto-Occipital and Precentral Hypometabolism', *Psychopathology* 41:397–402.

10

The Affected Subject and the Case of Individuating Pain

Siby K. George

> The subjectivity of a subject is vulnerability, exposure to affection, sensibility, a passivity... an exposure to expressing, and thus to saying, thus to giving... the caress in which pain arises, and then the contact... Of itself saying is the sense of patience and pain... If the subject did not run this risk, pain would lose its very painfulness. (Emmanuel Levinas, *Otherwise than Being, Or Beyond Essence*, 50)

Pain is enigmatic because it is experienced by the sufferer as inexpressible, bounded by the limits of selfhood, private and utterly individuating, but, at the same time, without understanding subjectivity as vulnerability and exposure to exteriority, the other, pain itself becomes inconceivable. Taking advantage of the phenomenology of the affected subject, constitutively open to its outside, vulnerable and exposed, this paper engages with the enigma of pain, arguing that the affectedness of subjectivity is the opening towards making sense of and meaningfully encountering the incommunicability and loneliness of intense pain.

The discussion below starts with a short exposition of the conception of affected subjectivity. I then very briefly go over the well-documented phenomenology of the inexpressibility and non-intentionality of intensely painful experiences. The third and central section dwells on the possibility within affected subjectivity to interrupt the privacy and solitariness of pain experience. The paper concludes with a discussion which treats this clue as significant for the sufferer and the carer in encountering the reality of pain.

1. Affected Subjectivity

A useful way of tracing the central tendency of modern Western thought is perhaps to point at the *subjectivist turn*. The construction of objectivity centered on subjectivity can be shown to be behind every modern pattern of thought, and achievement, varying from science, technology, development, social revolution, to modern ethics. In the 1938 essay, 'The Age of the World Picture', Heidegger characterized the interweaving processes of subjectivism and objectivism as 'decisive for the essence of modernity'. The processes of subjectivism and objectivism feed on each other in the sense that "the more completely and comprehensively the world, as conquered, stands at man's disposal, and the more objectively the object appears, all the more subjectively (i.e. peremptorily) does the *subiectum* rise up, and all the more inexorably, too, do observations and teachings about the world transform themselves into a doctrine of man, into an anthropology".[1] Hence, for Heidegger, the fundamental event of modernity is the conquest of the world, the object, as picture or representation by the human being or the subject, and modern humanism becomes a human-centrism in this sense.

In one of the most original approaches to a philosophical history of modernity (from the perspective of the human good purportedly occluded by the dominant view of modernity), *Sources of the Self* (1989) of Charles Taylor, inwardness or interiority, as against outwardness or exteriority, is spoken of as a source of the modern identity.[2] According to this strand of modern identity, he says, "[w]e are creatures with inner depths; with partly unexplored and dark interiors."[3] In the important and dominant strain of modernity, the human interior is the source of value, of knowledge and of being. That is, the interior castle of the human spirit is the ground of ontology, epistemology and ethics. Taylor traces this strand of modernity in its hermeneutical origin to Plato and Augustine but shows how it got consolidated as the mainstream vision in Descartes,

Locke and Kant. In another context, Taylor says that this view of the modern knowing agent is definitive for modernity: "speaking of the 'dominant' view I am thinking not only of the theories that have been preeminent in modem philosophy, but also of an outlook that has to some extent colonized the common sense of our civilization."[4] It means that the privileged knowing agent is disengaged from the world of cares and cultural horizon; she is a rational agent who picks up bits of information from her world, processes them in her mind —the interior castle—emerges with a representation of the world, and acts to meet her own instrumental calculus of ends and means in line with such a representation of the world. In Heidegger's later writings, the subjective turn, which gave rise to the modern understanding of the subject as disengaged and drawn inward, is itself shown as based on the technological or instrumental view of being as such.

A central argument in 20th century continental thought has been that this view of the subject is radically mistaken, or at least, that it is a partial view, and is conditioned on a more primordial understanding of the knowing agent "as engaged, as embedded in a culture, a form of life, a 'world' of involvements... as embodied."[5] Heidegger's *Being and Time* (1927) is the landmark text in formulating a comprehensive critique of the unaffected subject and its alternative. Abandoning the metaphysics of the disengaged 'subject', Heidegger called the agent, 'Dasein', to emphasize her situatedness within the world, context, language, culture. As being-in-the-world, Dasein's inwardness is impinged on by the outside, and her world, as the referential context of signification, is perceived and understood interpretively. Dasein takes issue with its own being, but this taking issue with 'mineness', or authentic existence, is itself produced by the process of negotiating the nebulous boundaries of the inside and the outside. The world affects mineness at least as much as the perception of the world is affected by selfhood. Since Heidegger thought of the world as a constitutive aspect of Dasein's manner of being, he characterized Dasein as a naturally lighted up rather closed off being. This existential lighting up of Dasein's world, constitutive of its manner of existence, is called disclosedness by Heidegger. It means that Dasein is itself the clearing, the field for phenomena to show up in one way or another. What is to be emphasized about disclosedness, for my purposes here, is this: its three constitutive existential conditions—state-of-mind, understanding and falling, all given form in discourse (language)—unveil the world in some manner as it affects Dasein. State-of-mind or attunement means Dasein's being in a mood in each case of its existence; it means *"a disclosive submission to the world, out of which we can encounter something that matters to us."*[6] We discover something as mattering to us because we are attuned towards the world in a particular manner, and so, first and foremost, no neutral, bare world is disclosed to us. Not even the purest theory has left all moods behind but has made itself possible within a tranquil mood. Heidegger notes that since Aristotle's *Rhetoric*, the ontological problematic of attunement has been philosophically discussed under the term affect/pathos/feeling. But they were never considered in their ontological significance and priority but, rather, were reduced to phenomena accompanying the rational animal. Understanding, on the other hand, means how our being-in-the-world is disclosed to us in its possibilities. All our cognition, meaningfulness and its absence as such, is possible because pre-cognitively our being-in-the-world is disclosed to us interpretively as a matter of Dasein's interest. Understanding is our engaged being towards the possibilities disclosed by our attuned being-in-the-world. If state-of-mind discloses our *factical* way of being, understanding discloses our *possible* way of being. By falling, the third ontological state of Dasein's disclosedness, is meant Dasein's everyday way of surrendering to its being-in-the-world, disclosed by state-of-mind and understanding, rather than seizing hold of its ownmost possibilities resolutely. After the analysis of disclosedness, Heidegger asks whether there is a single unitary phenomenon, an 'undestanding state-of-mind' wherein Dasein is disclosed to itself distinctively. If the disengaged vision of the human being often looks at calculative rationality as the defining feature of the human being, Heidegger wants to point at a more primordial ontological characteristic of Dasein, and his name for it is 'care'. The ontological term 'care' for Heidegger means, as Hubert Dreyfus puts it, *making being an issue*. It is because we, as engaged, involved, affected beings take issue with our being and the being of entities we encounter that a violinist can effortlessly produce melodies out of her instrument, a scientist can get engrossed in her lab, or even the musically inept onlooker could interestedly stare at the violin. Care means that 'beings get to me' in one way or the other.[7] "'Theory' and 'practice'", writes Heidegger, "are possibilities of Being for an entity whose Being must be defined as 'care'."[8] It is because the human being is the caring, affected animal that it can discover the world interestedly or disinterestedly.

Though Heidegger disputed the disengaged standpoint more than any philosopher before him, he is criticized for being not radical enough with regard to the perspective of the engaged agent, the affected subject in several respects. Rather than dwelling on the specific critiques of Heidegger, I shall very briefly here dwell on how the conception of the affected subject has progressed since Heidegger's ontology of the subject in the world.

Maurice Merleau-Ponty's contribution to the conception of the affected subject is remarkable in its articulation of the phenomenology of the embodied agent, the body subject of perception. Perception is not the decoding of signals received from exterior realities by the inner mind-machine; perception is the dynamic orientation of the animate body subject towards its world and the way the world affects the perceiving agent. What I need to emphasize here is the conception of perception as an interchange between the body and the world. "The sensible," writes Merleau-Ponty, "gives back to me what I lent to it, but this is only what I took from it in the first place."[9] Our perception of hardness and softness is recollected later not as sensory content but a kind of 'symbiosis', says Merleau-Ponty, "certain ways the outside has of invading us and certain ways we have of meeting this invasion."[10] Our embodiment contributes to our finite situatedness in terms of which we access the world and our own self; by the same token, certain other terms of accessing reality are not ours. Upon reflection on subjectivity we find it entangled in the body and the world because "my existence as subjectivity is merely one with my existence as a body and with the existence of the world, and because the subject that I am, when taken concretely, is inseparable from this body and this world."[11]

Emmanuel Levinas' contribution to our understanding of the affected subject is the notion of the embodied ethical subject. He begins with pointing out an inadequacy in Heidegger's thought: the phenomenon of the human other, being-with, is seen by Heidegger as a neutral ontological dimension of Dasein's being-in-the-world. For Levinas, on the other hand, the Other or the face, is an irreducible difference (from the same or ipseity) that puts into question the spontaneous existence of self or identity. It is the questioning face that makes possible the being of the moral self. Levinas calls the unwilled response that the other elicits from the self 'responsibility', and sees subjectivity as already substituted for the Other. By "substitution as the very subjectivity of a subject, interruption of the irreversible identity of the essence,"[12] Levinas means that the self is exposed to, claimed by and responsive towards human otherness. Before questions of choice and intelligibility (being) arise, the self is already constituted as social and ethical—that is, as responsible towards others. Before conscious phenomenological subjectivity arises, the subjectivity is already preontologically impinged on by the other, and hence subjectivity is 'other in the same'.[13] Since this formation of subjectivity is not traceable to a prior time period, Levinas says that subjectivity as substitution for the Other is before freedom and temporality. What Levinas means by the statement "[m]orality is not a branch of philosophy, but first philosophy"[14] is the phenomenological insight that if subjectivity itself is formed by something prior to ipseity and consciousness, namely ethics, all conscious endeavours of the subject are conditioned on that ethical rupture and questioning of ipseity. In a language reminiscent of the psychoanalytic tradition, Levinas writes: "I exist through the Other and for the Other, but without this being alienation: I am inspired. This inspiration is psyche."[15] In consideration of the conscious fact of ipseity, there is any possibility of ethical phenomena—pity, compassion, pardon, even little acts of consideration for others—only on account of substitution. For Levinas, substitution for the other of identity is the meaning of embodiment: "[a]n animate body or incarnate identity is the signifyingness of this non-indifference"[16] towards the other, the 'gravity of the body extirpated from its *conatus*'[17] (existence). Levinas is not prescribing a moral code but is showing the condition for the possibility of morality. However, his metaphysics of ethics points towards concrete practice, for the meaning of human corporeality and materiality is "for the other, despite oneself, starting with oneself, the pain of labour in the patience of ageing, in the duty to give to the other even the bread out of one's own mouth and the coat from one's shoulders."[18]

Further radicalization of the understanding of the affected subject is carried forward in several ways. Two most significant of these ways can be depicted by means of a dialogue with Levinas' characterization of the subject's pre-originary impingement. (Though similar radicalizations can be achieved with reference to Heidegger or Merleau-Ponty, that Levinas is the best known philosopher of the Other in recent times gains in importance in view of these two critiques from the standpoints of feminism and postcolonialism.) (i) Luce Irigaray observes that recognizing the Other as Other cannot be radical unless the feminine subject is recognized as other in relation to the masculine subject despite their species similarities. Without this, Irigaray contends, "the other is again reduced to a category of one and the same world, and to the possibility for a single subject to maintain, thanks to the category of 'alterity,' the permanence and development of that world."[19] The Other, the feminine other to begin with, has to be recognized as living in a world other than the self's. For Irigaray, sexual difference is equiprimordial with self-other difference; it means the difference in feminine and masculine ways of experiencing the world and relating to others both physically and psychically. She is interested in the way intellectual and cultural structures, which are already gendered, construct the sexed subject and affect subjectivity as such. Instead of arguing that feminine subjectivity is not the other of the masculine subject and should be his equal, Irigaray argues that Western intellectual culture has recognized only a single subjectivity. According to her, "[t]he question of the other has been poorly formulated in the Western tradition, for the other is always seen as the other of the same, the other of the subject itself, rather than an/other subject... irreducible to the masculine subject and sharing equivalent dignity."[20] (ii) A second differentiation that has come to light within subjectivity has its origins in race and postcolonial theory. Levinas is speaking primarily about subjectivity that is already substituted for the Other. Our responsiveness to others and responsibility for them is conditioned on a susceptibility to others that is unwilled and unchosen. This susceptibility is before consciousness and freedom, before memorable time and history, and so, it is the passive base for consciousness itself and ethics. Levinas speaks of responsibility as something that has "nothing to do with any acts one may really have committed. Prior to any act, I am concerned with the Other, and I can never be absolved from this responsibility."[21] But, it is often asked, if the other is she who is not the same, self or ipseity, then is not the other primarily that subjectivity farthest removed from the same—that is, radically other subjectivities? Levinas does not answer this question. Further, he has often privileged masculine, Western, Judeo-Christian subjectivities.[22] Given such valorization of Western subjectivity even in a philosophy of the Other, and in most other intellectual spaces, there is the concern with recovering the histories of peoples on the peripheries of the dominant history; that is, "[t]heir own particular forms of subjectivity, experience and agency, at present subjugated by these universalizing modes, are to be reconstituted and thus restored to history."[23]

Levinas, in the above two cases, is only a 'mark' because similar questioning is routinely performed today by theorists who revisit the texts of almost all the stalwarts of philosophy and theory. But, before proceeding to the next station in this argument I must add that the most radical perspective to enrich the project of imagining the affected subject centers on what non-human nature does to the human subject. This is perhaps the most revolutionary aspect of thinking about human subjectivity and moral life. If we are integral parts and products of nature as embodied, sentient beings, is not our subjectivity impinged on not only by other humans and the things that come in handy for our use (Heidegger's ready-to-hand) but the environing nature as such, the elemental natural world? Indeed, there is a flurry of scholarship aiming to recover the forgotten animality of the human. "The human mind," writes David Abram, "is not some otherworldly essence that comes to house itself inside our physiology. Rather, it is instilled and provoked by the sensorial field itself, induced by the tensions and participations between the human body and the animate earth."[24] There is the increasing tendency to return to a variety of naturalism even in theologically oriented phenomenology of human-nature relation. The imagination is to see "the being of humans as integrally linked to the being of nature, however conceived, treating humans as distinctive only as much as any distinct species is that, but as fundamentally *at home* in the cosmos, not 'contingently thrown' into it as into an alien context and 'ek-sisting' from it in an act of Promethean defiance."[25] According to the author of this quote, Sartrean existentialism typified the Western mindset of the time that saw the human being "as perplexed, perhaps defiant aliens in a strange, meaningless universe."[26]

To go over my attempt in this section, the affected subject is an already sensing subject, open to the world of both the gentle breeze and the scorching sun, of the warmth of companionship, the friendly gaze, the erotic touch, the maternal caress as well as to the pain of rejection and the look of disgust, to the assurance of recognition and acknowledgement as much as to the anguish of denial and rebuff. As embodied subjectivity I am "a sort of open circuit that completes itself only in things, in others, in the encompassing earth."[27] Subjectivity is knotted not only in intentional consciousness and being-towards-one's-self but in corporeality, sensibility, materiality, and as Levinas has argued, being towards the otherwise than being in the gesture of 'a denounement of being'.[28]

2. Pain and Interiority

If subjectivity, the intentional consciousness of mineness, of the temporal unfolding of my being within the intentional awareness of my world or horizon, is also a denouncement of being and openness to radical otherness, what is the constitution and meaning of one of the most individuating of experiences, the experience of pain? This is the question I intend to begin asking in this section: what does affected subjectivity mean to the constitution of pain experience?

Let me begin with the very starting point of the phenomenology of pain. It is a truism to say that if our subjectivity were not, in itself, exposed to otherness, we would neither have the world nor community, except as meaningless dream objects; if we were windowless monads or non-dual consciousness without an other, the possibility that the world and the others were internal differentiations within a narcissistic consciousness, actors in a delusionary drama, would have been real. Consciousness is intentional, that it takes objects indeed means that it is exposed to objects other than itself and always already *is* that exposure as such. Though there are exceptional non-intentional experiences (like Heidegger's anxiety about the nothing, Levinas's non-intentional exposure to the irreducible Other), pain is not an exceptional experience, except in that it is non-intentional. Such is the starting point of the phenomenology of pain. "[P]ain 'intends' nothing;" declares Elaine Scarry, "it is wholly passive; it is 'suffered' rather than willed or directed."[29] I love a beloved or a child; I hunger for food and thirst for drink; but I suffer pain. Physical pain does not point to anything outside of us. "Pain is not the injury itself, but the way we sense the injury," writes Abraham Oliver. "[P]ain cannot be an object of sensation, but is a quality or mode of sensation."[30]

A second departure in the phenomenology of pain is its inexpressibility and tendency to remain locked up within the intensely personal, private realm. Those in great physical pain and in intense trauma moan, groan, sob and grunt but cannot easily give words to the experience of pain. "English, which can express the thoughts of Hamlet and the tragedy of Lear," complains Virginia Woolf, "has no words for the shiver and the headache... let a sufferer try to express a pain in his head to a doctor and language at once runs dry."[31] In *The Human Condition,* Hannah Arendt speaks of great physical pain as 'intense to the point of blotting out all other experiences' but 'most private and least communicable of all'. According to her it is the only experience that cannot be dressed up for public consumption; pain deprives us of the sense of reality around us but is quickly forgotten as soon as it passes. It is the most amorphous form of intense subjectivity. "There seems to be no bridge from the most radical subjectivity, in which I am no longer 'recognizable', to the outer world of life."[32] In the account of David Biro, a doctor turned patient "pain shatters our sense of being as a being-in-the-world and isolates us from others...[33] The quintessential private experience, "pain severs our engagement with the world and thrusts us inward... In pain we are alone."[34] Pain experience is world-denying and solitary. Alphonse Daudet, the 19th century French novelist, who lived the last twelve years of his life in excruciating pain, writes: "Words only come when everything is over, when things have calmed down. They refer only to memory, and are either powerless or untruthful."[35] Pain is withdrawal to oneself; without adequate words the intelligibility of the world and others wanes.

Like David Biro, while undergoing an autologous stem cell transplant for multiple myeloma in near-complete isolation in a Mumbai hospital room, during a six-day bout of intense nausea and diarrhoea, insomnia and delirium, what I recollect as my answer to the recurrent question of doctors, nurses and dear ones, 'how do you feel now?' was simply a tired smile that yearned to ward off any further probing. No phone call to enquire how you are now as distinct from an earlier unfortunate moment was desired. This is different from the time after pain when I minutely described the ordeal and the details of my illness to friends and family. Intense nausea is weariness with being, when world, words and even self is depressing. One thirsts for forgetting with no avail, for the body-subject constantly reminds itself of what it wants to reject, and reject even being. Retentions and protentions, sounds and images that make life a pleasure with a desire to have more and more of it do not merely become disenchanting but absent, and thus, the sense of existence is no more available. Pain is not a withdrawing inward to recover a sense of self incommunicable to others; it is an experience of absurdity incommunicable even to self. In extreme physical pain or conditions like intense nausea there is only the throbbing, smarting, hurting, burning, stinging, tiring, sickening sensation; there is no way of making meaning out of that experience in a simultaneous moment. Arendt calls this inability to figure out the meaning of experience for oneself or for others' 'radical subjectivity' where ipseity is unrecognizable to the 'I'. To young Levinas, nauseous experience gives the inkling of the otherwise than being: "There is in nausea a refusal to remain there, an effort to get out... an impossibility of being what one is... [but] at the same time riveted to ourselves, enclosed in a tight circle that smothers."[36] This impossibility of being and yet clinging close to being, this radical subjectivity of not even recognizing the 'I', Levinas says, is the experience of pure being coterminous with the experience of being's 'internal antagonism' and the 'escape that foists itself on us'.

In the case of at least intense physical pain and nausea, are we then to conclude that affected subjectivity is sealed off to the outside, its meaning thwarted, its sense negated and denied? In a moment of agonizing pain, are we then alone and lost, making neither sense of the world, others nor even ourselves? Perhaps, then, Levinas is wrong that "the living human corporeality, as a possibility of pain, a sensibility which of itself is the susceptibi1ity to being hurt, a self uncovered, exposed and suffering in its skin... [t]he painfulness of pain... [is] the against oneself that is in the self."[37] To make sense of radical subjectivity in the most personal of painful experiences, the affectedness of subjectivity has no meaning; the outward push of subjectivity is absurd at least in the case of painful experiences wherein subjectivity rivets on itself.

3. The Interruption of Interiority

But, for sure, neither the intense pain experiences of, at least, the most perceptive sufferers nor humanities research on pain experience has left the most intense and harrowing of human experiences to a bleak site of inescapability and hopelessness. And the fact is even in the blankest of pain experiences, the flickering, even impossible, desire to 'cross over' from the torment of the body-subject to the remarkable human delighting in affected subjectivity is not totally absent. In fact, the provocation to get away from being and get into impersonal, anonymous existence of non-affected subjectivity in cases of intense pain arises from the 'impossibility of being what one is'. Doctors routinely advise patients in trauma and pain to *think* positively, but 'think' is what one does not do in pain; what one does in pain is exactly to be in pain, to be hurt, to be passively afflicted. Pain arrests, numbs, and takes possession of consciousness. In pain one 'suffers', and does not actively do anything. Impossibility of action and agency is pain in its most intense purity. Even desiring the end of being in acute, irredeemable pain is desiring to cross over from groundless, homeless, unbearable, unrecognizable existence to the anonymity of non-being in the event of the impossibility of being what one is.

In fact, humanities research often recognizes the non-intentional, utterly individuating and inexorably private, inexpressible texture of pain experience but goes on to build a project of encountering the absurdity of pain meaningfully. While there is no easy way out of intense and especially irredeemable pain, the emphasis is usually on the most human way of facing up to pain experience as such as an inevitable and integral part of being the affected body-subject, being-in-the-world, that the human being is. At the end of an erudite study of the indescribability of pain, Biro the doctor-patient, concludes that while language in the usual sense fails in the land of pain, we can still talk to others of our pain in metaphors and allegories, taking advantage of the most expressive use of language. Alluding to Wittgenstein's rejection of private language, Biro affirms that "[l]anguage can alleviate pain... As long as the conversation lasts, we are not alone."[38] What appears impossible, says Biro, is not impossible; metaphors come to our aid to speak of the unutterable. Only in communicating and struggling to tell the others of our intense experiences can we make sense of them in any meaningfully human manner. Oliver, who looks at pain as disturbed bodily perception from the phenomenological vantage point of Merleau-Ponty, concludes that various kinds of pain—hurt, affliction, agony—transform our perception of ourselves and the world. He argues that this change of perspective has liberating possibilities because we can gradually begin to see pain itself from a different but radically personal perspective. Pain experiences are not identical; they vary according to personal and cultural perspectives. "If the nature of pain is such that it can be changed by our perceptual perspectives," argues Oliver, "our purpose might be to explore in pain perspectives of change... [that will] not only help to bear the pain better, or to escape its impact, but also to paradoxically find sense in senseless suffering."[39] However, talk about the 'management' and finding meaning in pain comes too easy and empty if the intrinsic uselessness of innocent suffering, the inappropriateness of theodicy is not recognized. "[T]he least one can say about suffering," remarks Levinas, "is that, in its own phenomenality, intrinsically, it is useless: 'for nothing'."[40] After going over the cases of painful illnesses, the pain of mental deficiencies, irremediable sufferings and the Holocaust, 'for nothing' is Levinas's answer to the question 'why suffering'. For him, the only meaningful suffering is "suffering for the useless suffering of the other, the just suffering in me for the unjustifiable suffering of the other."[41]

Even still, as I have shown above, Levinas recognizes the phenomenological texture of pain in the materiality, corporeality, vulnerability, 'exposure to affection' and the outward(or other)-directedness of subjectivity in general. He speaks of 'caress in which pain arises' to say that if it were not for the inherent passivity to the touch of the outside or the other, both human and natural, pain would not have been. Paradoxically, then, pain reaffirms the texture of subjectivity to the point of its non-recognition, revulsion and, thus, renders itself useless and unjustifiable. While inflicting the impossibility of being oneself, intense pain points towards the shadows upon which subjectivity is woven. On the other hand, subjectivity as openness to the other, the outside as such, already includes within itself the rupture of pain, the internal differentiation and antagonism within subjectivity, of passively suffering the impinging of the other on the self, the body-subject. What is useless is innocent intolerable suffering that destroys word, world and self. Scarry has incisively explored the hand of pain in unmaking and making the being-in-the-world of subjectivity.

If intense pain closes the self to the outside, then it reconstitutes the self as a windowless monad. But Levinas exclaims '[h]ow the adversity of pain is ambiguous!' The torment of pain is ambiguous because as the being that is able to feel sensations, a being with the skin and open to otherness, a being with porous boundaries and passive receptivity, pain is integral to being human, being the body subject, the worldly entity persecuted and menaced in its identity by the other. But as an identity, an ipseity, recovering itself in spontaneity, enjoyment and sensibility, being human is disrupted and held to ransom in pain, and with intensity, pain announces the uselessness of being oneself. But the uselessness of suffering is not only because of the impossibility of being oneself, the spontaneous ipseity. The ambiguous integration of pain into the innermost recesses of our existence, into our corporeal, menaced, porous ontological architecture, burdened with piercing sensible awareness and expressive recollection, attests the affectedness of subjectivity, at least as much as pleasure and delight is made possible by the open, other-directedness of our identity, the porosity of skin. If this is so, pain is useless and 'for nothing' not only because it renders being oneself impossible; pain indubitably attests the for-the-other architecture of identity. "The for-the-other (or sense)," writes Levinas in a revealing passage, "turns into by-the-other, into suffering by a thorn burning the flesh, but *for nothing*. It is only in this way that the *for-the-other*, the passivity more passive still than any passivity, the emphasis of sense, is kept from being *for-oneself*."[42] The being of pain is ambiguous because without it subjectivity is for-oneself and that alone. While intense pain reverts to radical subjectivity and aloneness unrecognizable even to oneself, the 'for nothing' of suffering pain, the texture of subjectivity as for-the-other, susceptibility to being affected, is always already attested by the experience of intense pain and deep suffering. Undoubtedly, sensibility is savouring and enjoying, nourishing and quenching, sustaining and being, filling and satisfying, pleasure and delight, gratification and completion, spontaneity and being oneself; but this being oneself of sensibility is interrupted and ruptured by the impact of alterity. Pain disrupts the complacency and abandon of being oneself. Being affected means being wounded and outraged as much as being filled and satisfied. Because this interruptive texture of our subjectivity is unwanted, unwilled, unchosen, Levinas speaks of it as coming from before freedom, an immemorial past, before and otherwise than being.

Heidegger speaks of pain as opening up the most intimate gathering of the meaning of being, existing, and its internal differentiation and inherent antagonism.[43] Pain is integrated into our existence as affected subjectivities. To create and have the world means pain as well. "[E]verything that is alive...," observes Heidegger, "is imbued with pain... Everything that is alive, is painful... By virtue of this power it is fit to join in that harmony of mutual bearing by which all living things belong together. In keeping with this relation of fitness, everything that lives is fit, that is to say, good. But the good is good painfully."[44] Pain interrupts the predilection of human subjectivity and unites it with life and nature as such. Since being human also means being open to the inclemencies of the weather, the hardness of the earth and the eventuality of being jabbed as well as caressed on the skin, without pain the texture of our ambiguous subjectivity is incomplete.

Pain, hardly expressible, barely intelligible, forces a retreat to radical subjectivity in the most extreme manner of unravelling the possibility of neither being oneself nor being for the other. Because being oneself or inwardness is thus disrupted, pain is 'for nothing' and useless, not for self, and because pain radically reveals the affectedness of subjectivity, the for-the-other, in this most troubling and private of experiences, paradoxically, our subjectivity is touched and awakened from the outside.

4. Conclusions: Encountering Pain

I have been arguing that inherent to our subjectivity is an outward turn, and the deeply intense experience of pain, rather than denying this texture of subjectivity, attests it, albeit ambiguously and obscurely. Intense pain is, therefore, not a negation of affected subjectivity but its most extreme attestation. Our moods and sensations of pleasure and pain are, in Heidegger's idiom, ontical markers of the ontological state of our being affected by the world, by alterity. The difference in Heidegger and Levinas is on the way human otherness impinges on the self. For Heidegger there is no element of surprise, irreducibility and asymmetry in the encounter with otherness. Being-in-the-world, the inside-outside fusion that subjectivity is, negotiates human otherness in its own terms, within its space or world, in as much as this same space negotiates mineness. For Levinas, while the navigation within the familiar ontological space of being-in-the-world is true for our meeting with phenomena in general, the face, or the human other, is an exception. It surprises subjectivity, torments its ontological space of spontaneity and demands a response by the height and strength of its affecting or impinging on the self. Except for this difference, they both agree that if the subject were not to be affected, pain would not have been. Pain is forgetting the 'outside' of my subjectivity that affects me, and nakedly facing the 'inside' of my subjectivity in its utmost intolerability. The full passive weight of my subjectivity is never as burdensome as in the state of intense pain.

The conclusion that intense pain is the absolute negation of otherness and affectedness is too early. We have noted that at the back of the eagerness to turn away from otherness and even to escape and evade being in intense pain and nausea lie the burdensome intolerability and, thus, impossibility of being oneself. And yet, pain as such is grounded on affected subjectivity. When the body-subject closes the eyes of her being and turns within in intense pain, this turning away from alterity is possible only because existence as such, affected and impinged on, open and porous, is insufferable. The turning within does not open the door to a deeper recess, but to the impossibility of being oneself. Pain opens the door to unrecognizable oneself. I know I am the experiencer but the excruciating experience closes out the nudge of otherness knocking at my selfhood and takes me towards my insufferable being. Paradoxically, the door within my selfhood through which pain as well as otherness is accessible to me, namely sensibility and sense or meaning, the affectedness of my subjectivity, is closed to otherness in intense pain on account of the insufferability of being in pain, which is itself conditioned on sensibility.

But the desire for otherness, the Levinasian metaphysical desire for the 'alien outside-of-oneself',[45] is the lingering other side of even the most intense and individualizing pain.

Though Daudet's claim that memories of intense pain are 'either powerless or untruthful' is right, what I recollect, hopefully without the original force rather than with no tinge of truth, about my recent experience of pain was the reluctance to speak and the desire to be left alone. But it was not really a desire to be *left alone* but left untroubled, left without having to respond; in short, without having to do anything. But the surrender of agency, is it equal to shutting off all presence, presence of the other person? No. Presence, at least presence, was desired; if not wilfully desired and demanded, the faint, indistinct awareness of the presence of the other lingered at the back of painful consciousness. Desire for otherness is possibly the only content, even if faint and indistinct, other than the pain-sensation itself, that a consciousness in intense pain could possibly have. The perceptive apparatus of the body-subject in pain is still affected by otherness. In intense pain, the embodied subject is gripped and held by the sensation of menacing pain penetrating that subjectivity in its entirety. With increasing intensity of pain, nothing and no one else seems to matter except oneself and one's pain; one's world seems to shatter in pain. But the terror of my aloneness in the isolation ward of the hospital seems to belie this recoiling upon the self as something definitive. While concerned prodding and inquiring after did lead to restiveness and annoyance, the terror of aloneness was an attestation of the desire for the other. The arresting sensation of pain is not, thus, the non-sensing of otherness. The grip of pain wards off only the more overt gestures of Levinasian responsiveness demanded of every self-other encounter, and neither otherness nor responsiveness as such is warded off by the subject of intense pain. In fact, in my experience of severe prolonged nausea and diarrhoea, when powerful cancer drugs began to work in my body, the empty isolation of the hospital ward required to fight chances of infection, intensified the depressing tendency to surrender, not specifically to the end of existence or nothingness, but simply to the grip of pain and, if at all, to a lack of agency, leading to nightmarish delirium and anguish that only reinforced the painfulness of pain. Even then, the presence of the other, at least of strange faces, was appealed to.

The unsharability of pain and the loneliness of this unsharability are burdensome and depressive to the body-subject of pain because of the very affectedness of subjectivity. If otherness were not to matter to the subject, the individualizing loneliness of pain would have been sufferable. The insufferability of the loneliness of pain buttresses affected subjectivity, and does not negate it.

From the point of view of this conclusion, our approach to pain, both of the sufferer and of the carer, should be informed by the affirmation of the affectedness of subjectivity. Suffering, whether of the self or of the other, is aggravated or alleviated, in proportion to the affirmation of otherness and the affectedness of subjectivity. Empathetic and careful attention to the other's suffering alleviates that suffering is perhaps a truism, but what is to be emphasized is Scarry's observation that there are difficulties with carers and acquaintances of sufferers in recognizing and appropriately responding to the other's suffering. This is complicated by the utter muteness of pain when it comes to showing itself to the other, its proverbial inexpressibility. The vacuous aloneness in intense pain is not the occasion to withhold attention to the person in pain because her reciprocal responsive gesture is absent or inadequate. The sufferer's pre-cognitive awareness of the attentive, empathetic presence of the other, the sense that her world has not completely collapsed, contributes to the alleviation of pain even in the most hopeless cases of individuating, world-denying pain. Long, chronic pain of another could numb the responsiveness of the carer, but pain brings ever new surprises to the self; further, with its inadequate exhibition pain could easily be trivialized, misunderstood, ignored by onlookers and carers. "It is attention to the suffering of the other," says Levinas, "that... can be affirmed as the very nexus of human subjectivity..."[46] Hence, from mere helpless but empathetic presence to all humane gestures and artifacts that Levinas intends to institute for relieving suffering is to be affirmed. There is justification probably for one's suffering; but for the suffering of the other, there is no justification; it is useless suffering.

The other part of the thesis linking affectivity and inexpressible pain is the hope to find expression for one's own pain, in small ways and big. From grunts and wails, metaphors and allegories, to painting and every form of self-expression, the victim of pain is invited to find positive attestation in affected subjectivity for the articulation and expression of one's pain to the other. As affected and affecting subjects, as sharers of the affective life, as beings unable to complete themselves except in the shared life, the possibility of finding expression to the most world-shattering experience of pain is never absent.

As long as the journey of the subject is on—of the affected, afflicted, impinged on, caressed subject—there is a reason for comfort. Because our subjectivity is constituted affectedly, when our expressive powers fail us, when the 'inside' is dark and vacuous, the reason for comfort could still lie 'outside' the subject. This reason for comfort is not only the human other, the face; it is also the things we make, the most creative products of our self-expression, the fruits of our labour, the works of the most fertile human/ humane imagination. I would reduce the core thesis of Elaine Scarry's *Body in Pain* to this affirmation. The rending, rifting, tearing asunder, differentiating, separating movement of pain in life as such, in the Heideggerian idiom,[47] also gathers and joins. Creative self-expression directed towards the human culture of the artifices and technologies may be said to be this gathering and joining, painstaking in itself. While excruciating pain shatters and unmakes one's world, and silences her expressive powers, Scarry shows, pain is integral to all our efforts at making and creating, which in turn are self-extensions or self-expressions. Hence, Scarry concludes that "[d]irected against the isolating aversiveness of pain, mental and material culture assumes the sharability of sentience."[48] For Scarry, our artifices—images, metaphors, gods, technologies, art, social and political structures—are conditioned on the double movement of the pain necessary to bring them forth and the pain they necessarily alleviate. If it is not for the encountering of pain, our artifices have no meaning. For this reason, even if all technologies become superfluous and creative culture is detechnicized, medical technologies and techniques would be justifiable. Alluding to Heidegger's influential critique of technology, Levinas observes that "medicine as technique, and consequently the technology as a whole that it presupposes... does not drive solely from the so-called 'will to power'."[49] In Scarry's account human imagination divests the objects of the world of their inanimateness and animates them literally by putting them in pain by conceiving them as aware of human pain and designing them accordingly as artifacts. If a chair were not imagined as aware of the pain of managing and adjusting the human body weight, it would not have been made in such a manner as to hold the body and eliminate the pain of managing body weight in the uncomfortably bent position. Imagination, expression, metaphor, artifice, technologies —they are all mobilized for encountering the problem of pain, at once basic, complicated and inexpressible. "[I]t is the benign, almost certainly heroic, and in any case absolute intention of all human making to distribute the facts of sentience outward onto the created realm of artifice, and it is only by doing so that men, and women are themselves relieved of the privacy and problems of that sentience."[50] It is not only people that affect us and relieve our pain but also things we make and create.

Intense pain occurs to the affected, sentient subject as an alterity-denying experience that reverts back to the self, unrecognizable even to itself. But attentive, caring human presence and painstaking creation of artifacts in the most humane self-expressive tradition encounters the pain of the other in responsibility. Hence, pain is encountered by affirming the affectedness of subjectivity, understanding our affective life as the condition for the possibility of pain and pleasure, acknowledging the baffling non-intentionality, inexpressibility and the reversal of the very affectedness of our subjectivity in experiences of intense pain, and by surmounting these contradictions by reaffirming our affective constitution that makes possible imaginative expression of painful experiences by the sufferer, empathetic attention to the other's pain by carers and by the mindful creation of artifacts, which themselves are imagined as conversations with the other in pain.

NOTES AND REFERENCES

1. Martin Heidegger, The Age of the World Picture (1938), trans. Julian Young and Kenneth Haynes. In Martin Heidegger, *Off the Beaten Track*, eds. Julian Young and Kenneth Haynes, 57-85. Cambridge: Cambridge University Press, 2002, 70.
2. But, for Charles Taylor, the subjective turn is not the only constitutive layer of the modern identity or sense of the self. He narrates three constitutive layers of the modern identity: "first, modern inwardness, the sense of ourselves as beings with inner depths, and the connected notion that we are 'selves'; second, the affirmation of ordinary life which develops from the early modern period; third, the expressivist notion of nature as an inner moral source" (Charles Taylor, *Sources of the Self: The Making of the Modern Identity*. Cambridge, MA: Harvard University Press, 1989, x.).
3. Charles Taylor, *Sources of the Self*, 111.
4. Charles Taylor, 'Engaged Agency and Background in Heidegger'. In *The Cambridge Companion to Heidegger*, ed. Charles B. Guignon, 317-336. Cambridge: Cambridge University Press, 1993, 319.
5. Charles Taylor, 'Engaged Agency and Background in Heidegger', 318.
6. Martin Heidegger, *Being and Time*, trans. John Macquarrie and Edward Robinson. New York: HarperCollins, 1962, 177.
7. Hubert L. Dreyfus, *Being-in-the-World: A Commentary on Heidegger's Being and Time, Division I*. Cambridge, MA: MIT Press, 1995, 238.
8. Martin Heidegger, *Being and Time*, 238.
9. Maurice Merleau-Ponty, *Phenomenology of Perception*, trans. Colin Smith. New York: Routledge Classics, 2002, 249.
10. Maurice Merleau-Ponty, *Phenomenology of Perception*, 370.
11. Maurice Merleau-Ponty, *Phenomenology of Perception*, 475.

12. Emmanuel Levinas, *Otherwise Than Being, or Beyond Essence*, trans. Alphonso Lingis. Pittsburgh, PA: Duquesne University Press, 1998, 13.
13. Emmanuel Levinas, *Otherwise Than Being*, 25.
14. Emmanuel Levinas, *Totality and Infinity: An Essay on Exteriority*, trans. Alphonso Lingis. The Hague, The Netherlands: Martinus Nijhoff Publishers, 1969, 304.
15. Emmanuel Levinas, *Otherwise Than Being*, 114.
16. Emmanuel Levinas, *Otherwise Than Being*, 71.
17. Emmanuel Levinas, *Otherwise Than Being*, 72.
18. Emmanuel Levinas, *Otherwise Than Being*, 55.
19. Luce Irigaray, What Other Are We Talking About?, trans. Esther Marion. *Yale French Studies*, No. 104: Encounters with Levinas, 67-81, 2004, 68.
20. Luce Irigaray, The Question of the Other, trans. Noah Guynn. *Yale French Studies*, No. 87: Another Look, Another Woman: Retranslations of French Feminism, 7-19, 1995, 8.
21. Emmanuel Levinas, Ethics and Politics, trans. Jonathan Romney. In Emmanuel Levinas, *The Levinas Reader*, ed. Sean Hand, 289-297. Malden, MA: Blackwell Publishing, 2007, 290.
22. The most balanced treatment of this subject, I think, may be found in: Robert Bernasconi, Who is My Neighbour? Who is the Other?: Questioning 'The Generosity of Western Thought'. In Claire Katz and Lara Troute, eds., *Emmanuel Levinas: Critical Assessments of Leading Philosophers, Vol. IV: Beyond Levinas*. New York: Routledge, 2005, 5-30. See also: Judith Butler, *Giving an Account of Oneself*, Capter 3. New York: Fordham University Press, 2005; and, Andrew McGettigan, The Philosopher's Fear of Alterity: Levinas, Europe and Humanities 'Without Sacred History'. *Radical Philosophy*, 140, 2006, 15-25.
23. Rosalind O'Hanlon, Recovering the Subject: Subaltern Studies and Histories of Resistance in colonial South Asia. *Modern Asian Studies*, 22: 1, 189-224, 1988, 190.
24. David Abram, *The Spell of the Sensuous: Perception and Language in a More-than-human World*. New York: Vintage, 1997, 262.
25. Erazim Kohík, *The Embers and the Stars: A Philosophical Inquiry into the Moral Sense of Nature*. Chicago, IL: The University of Chicago Press, 1984, 8.
26. Erazim Kohak, *The Embers and the* Stars, 5.
27. David Abram, *The Spell of the Sensuous*, 62.
28. Emmanuel Levinas, *Otherwise Than Being*, 77.
29. Elaine Scarry, *The Body in Pain: The Making and Unmaking of the*

World. Oxford: Oxford University Press, 1985, 164.

30. Abraham Oliver, *Being in Pain*. Frankfurt, Germany: Peter Lang, 2007, 70.
31. Virginia Woolf, *On Being Ill*. Ashfield, MA: Paris Press, 2002, 6-7.
32. Hannah Arendt, *The Human Condition*, Second Edition. Chicago, IL: University of Chicago Press, 1998, 51.
33. David Biro, *The Language of Pain: Finding Words, Compassion, and Relief*. New York: W.W. Norton & Company, 2010, 41.
34. David Biro, *The Language of Pain*, 47.
35. Alphonse Daudet, *In the Land of Pain*, trans. Julian Barnes. New York: Alfred A. Knopf, 2002, 15.
36. Emmanuel Levinas, *On Escape (De l'évasion)*, trans. Bettina Bergo. Stanford, CA: Stanford University Press, 2003, 66.
37. Emmanuel Levinas, *Otherwise Than Being*, 51.
38. David Biro, *The Language of Pain*, 219.
39. Abraham Oliver, *Being in Pain*, 169.
40. Emmanuel Levinas, Useless Suffering, trans. Michael B. Smith and Barbara Harshav. Emmanuel Levinas, *Entre Nous: Thinking-of-the-Other*, 91-101. New York: Columbia University Press, 1998, 93.
41. Emmanuel Levinas, Useless Suffering, 94.
42. Emmanuel Levinas, *Otherwise Than Being*, 50.
43. Martin Heidegger, On the Question of Being (1955), trans. William McNeill. In Martin Heidegger, *Pathmarks*, ed. William McNeill, 291-322. Cambridge: Cambridge University Press, 1998, 306.
44. Martin Heidegger, The Way to Language (1959), trans. Peter D. Hertz. In Martin Heidegger, *On the Way to Language*, 111-136. New York: HarperOne, 1982, 181.
45. Emmanuel Levinas, *Totality and Infinity*, 33.
46. Emmanuel Levinas, Useless Suffering, 94.
47. Martin Heidegger, Language (1950), trans. Albert Hofstadter. In Martin Heidegger, *Poetry, Language, Thought*, 185-208. New York: HarperCollins Perennial Classics, 2001, 201-2.
48. Elaine Scarry, *The Body in Pain*, 326.
49. Emmanuel Levinas, Useless Suffering, 94.
50. Elaine Scarry, *The Body in Pain*, 288.

11

Facing the Other: Merleau-Ponty and the Ethical

T.V. Madhu

Where is the other in this body that I see? She is (like the meaning of the sentence) immanent in this body (one cannot detach her/him from it and to pose her/him apart) and yet, more than the sum of the signs or the significations conveyed by them. She is that of which they are always the partial and non-exhaustive image — and also nonetheless is attested wholly in each of them. Always in process of an unfinished incarnation—beyond the objective body as the sense of the painting is beyond the canvas.

From Merleau-Ponty's Working Notes, September 1959

I

The strength of Merleau-Ponty's mode of thinking the other is that it is radical enough to break off from what is called the horizontality of the phenomenological approach. It escapes the conventional paradigm where the existence of the other has been looked at analogically or by any other means that treat the other in terms of how they appear to the subject rather than in their genuine alterity. Usually the question of the other is posed as an epistemic question, as how it is that we come to 'know' the interiority of the other. Husserl also is not free from this convention even though he gives a different dimension to the question of the other which is significant in many respects. He attempts to address the question by employing the concept of 'analogical apperception'. By the concept of 'apperception' Husserl points to the manner in which our perceptions go beyond what we perceive, to incorporate the invisible dimensions. Our perception always contains an excess or surplus, that when I perceive something it contains more than what I actually see. For example, when I perceive a house what is authentically perceived is one of the sides, usually the front-side, of the house. The rear-side is hidden from my present perception, but is implied in it. I see what I see but by adding in some unseen dimensions or aspects. This process is *apperception*, where I habitually couple past experiences with present experiences. In the strict sense, the things which I perceive, each moment when I open my eyes, are strange to me. However, I do not usually feel this strangeness because I habitually couple them with the experiences from my past, and thereby the world becomes familiar to me.

What follows from the above account is that the concept of apperception clarifies how we see the concealed aspects of the perceptible things. Husserl believes this concept could explain how we are able to experience the interiority of the other person as well. But the difficulty here is that the apperception involved in the latter case is clearly different from the apperception in the context of our sense experience of physical things. In the case of sense-perception of a physical thing there is a possibility of verification that, from a different perspective, the 'rear-side' becomes the 'front-side'. In the case of the apperception of the other person, this possibility is excluded *a priori*.

The other person enters into the field of my visibility as a body. This body is being apprehended as lived body by transferring my sense of embodiment to the other and this takes place at a pre-cognitive level. This is what Husserl calls the 'apperceptive transfer'[1]. Let us try to unpack this slightly complex argument. My lived body is the only body that is and can be authentically experienced as a lived body. So the body of the other person which is apprehended as a lived body must have this sense only in a roundabout manner. This sense is something that is being transferred from my lived body, that is, by means of an 'apperceptive transfer'. The behaviours of the other person appear similar to mine, and only by this similarity that I connect the other body with my body. The crux of the argument is that taking an external material thing to be another center of subjectivity is founded upon a perceived similarity that motivates a 'transfer of sense' from my body to the external thing, whereby the latter is apperceived as a lived body. It is true that Husserl views this not as an analogical *inference,* since it takes place at a pre-reflective level. He explains this basing on the notion of habitual coupling, that one 'pairs' the bodily behaviours of the other person with his own and habitually attributes interiority to them on the basis of his own.

Husserl's explanation seems to be convincing at this level. However, the very posing of the question of the other, that is, conceptualizing the other within the parameters of phenomenology, remains problematic. One of the difficulties is the horizontality of the phenomenological approach itself that it begins with the subject and looks at the other on the same level. It necessarily results in treating the other as equal to, not *different from,* the subject. In other words, it results in denying that the other is *different*. Husserl's account, as we have seen, begins with the perspective of the subject who apparently meets others, as a visual datum.[2] Obviously, there are two presuppositions here: one knows oneself, from within, and, one has a sense of self, prior to his/her sense of otherness. These presuppositions imply the conventional paradigm, which is very much Cartesian in spirit, where consciousness is given to itself directly; a thesis that contradicts the spirit of Husserl's own thesis of the intentionality of consciousness where there is nothing pre-given in consciousness. Merleau-Ponty's project is to resolve this tension which, as we shall argue, marks a moment of interruption, where phenomenology interrupts its own horizontality and also its subject-centrism.

II

In his early writings, Merleau-Ponty proposes the concept of body-subject, a theory of body as the locus of intentionality which is in direct contrast to the Cartesian paradigm where there is no fundamental distinction between lived body and object-body possible. In Merleau-Ponty's early formulation, lived body is *sub-ject*, that which is thrown under (*Subjectum*) as the condition of experience, rather than the object (*ob-ject*) experienced. 'I am my body, at least wholly to the extent that I possess experience, and yet at the same time my body is as it were a 'natural' subject, a provisional sketch of my total being.'[3]

Merleau-Ponty is well aware that the expression 'body-subject' could be misleading that the 'sub' of the 'subject' might refer to an 'inside'. One of the main concerns of Merleau-Ponty's later writings especially of his incomplete work, *The Visible and the Invisible*, is to clarify the meaning of the subjectivity of the subject. Our relation to the visible world, according to him, is irreducible to consciousness-object distinction. Primarily, we *inhabit* the visible world. We belong to the visible, and the visibility is not the result of a cognitive act on the part of the subject. There is no experience of object, as *objectum*, at this level. It implies that there is no subject as well. I am not a subject, a thinking substance, detached from the material substance. The world is not composed of dead matter, but is 'fleshy'. I am inescapably *in the world*, and of the *flesh of the world*. Subject is made of the flesh of the world. This is what Merleau-Ponty actually means by the expression 'incarnate subject' or carnal subjectivity. One of the implications of this view is that the conventional notion of intersubjectivity indicating the *interspace* between the two subjects is inadequate to think the self-other relation.

Interpreting the last phase of Merleau-Ponty's work was quite puzzling for the scholars until when his notes for his lecture at College de France began to appear. Italian philosopher Mauro Carborn,[4] by drawing heavily from the materials published on Merleau-Ponty's last writings, provides an excellent account of the ontological implications of the above mentioned concept of flesh. The central theme of Merleau-Ponty's last lectures, according to him, is concerned with a wide generalization of his earlier concept of the incarnated subject. The carnal subjectivity is to be understood as a domain where the duality between passivity and activity is blurred. It actually refers to *the passivity of our activity*, by which what exists shows itself *through* a subject which is part of it, for it is carnally bound to Being. Merleau-Ponty's key-word, the chiasm, is to be understood as indicating the complexity of the mutual relationship between carnal subjectivity and Being. There are two implications here. 1) To accept the notion of the subject's circular bond with the flesh of the world then means to upset the image of a subject in full possession of itself. 2) It is also to follow the affections of the subject up to the point of its being dispossessed by the carnal world.

The second point is more explicit in Merleau-Ponty's statement "I 'am of the world' and I am not it".[5] Obviously, to say 'I am of the flesh' is different from saying 'I am the flesh'. This difference is crucial for Merleau-Ponty. It can be argued that we have here 'an instance of vertical being, of a "surpassing which does not leave its field of origin". Each layer of being is 'of' proceeding layers while, simultaneously, being irreducible to it'[6]. By arguing that I am of the flesh and that I am not the flesh, Merleau-Ponty thus moves to a radically different ontological framework where the so-called horizontality of phenomenology is deeply problematized. His much discussed perspective that self and the other like 'two hands touch each other' and his concept of inter-subjective relation where both self and the other are 'like organs of one, single intercorporeality'[7] are to be understood in the backdrop of the ontological implications of the notion of flesh. We shall come back to this point in the concluding session where an attempt will be made to defend Merleau-Ponty against the Levinasian line of criticism.

III

Levinas's concept of ethical subject is different from Merleau-Ponty's notion of body-subject or flesh in a significant sense. His attempt is to radically reject, not merely to reformulate, the horizontal or the interactionist model of conceptualizing the inter-subjective. The *ethicality* of the subject, for him, is to be understood in terms of transcendence, the implications of which are clearly brought out in some of his interviews and speeches published under the title *Alterity and Transcendence*.

Transcendence means a kind of surpassing; but the notion obtains a special significance in Levinas' account of intersubjectivity. Etymologically transcendence points to a movement of crossing over (*trans)*, but also of ascent (*scando*). Levinas relies on this etymological sense to capture the meaning of upward movement, or of a gesture that moves beyond itself. Levinas' philosophy, as pointed out by Pierry Hayat in the preface to *Alterity and Transcendence*, is constructed on a non-constructed intuition: that of the upsurge of transcendence as a '*question* to the Other and about the other.'[8]

What is it to think transcendence in terms of the Other? In a sense, Levinas' entire philosophical endeavour is to explain this point. True transcendence, for him, is not born of the interiority of a being, but of *exteriority*. In facing the other, I am always already *out of myself*. It is in finding me inescapably facing other's face, the meaning of which is beyond my grasp, that I am born *as subject*. Hence, subjectivity is challenged from the very start; transcendence can be felt only as subjectivity in constant challenge. The face of the other is the locus of transcendence that it calls *me* into question and this questioning is constitutive of what I am. It is precisely in 'taking the other as one's point of departure' that transcendence can emerge. It is in this exteriority or alterity that averts the *I* from enduring within itself, human subjectivity as *responsible for the other* is formed.

The transcendence that Levinas talks about is 'ethical' transcendence; it is not the movement of intentional consciousness. One of his major concerns, especially in *Otherwise than Being*, is to problematize the primacy accorded to the intentional consciousness in conventional phenomenology. Phenomenology, by thinking consciousness *as* intentionality, depends on the primacy of the epistemic relation where the subject maintains an objectifying relation to the world at the fundamental level. What Levinas attempts is to radically interrupt the spirit of phenomenological thinking by moving from the primacy of the *epistemic* to what he calls *the ethical*. Ethical subject is the embodied being of flesh and blood; intentional consciousness is not primary since it is always already embodied, habituated by our conditions of living. We live primarily by eating, drinking, working, sleeping and so on and these are not intentional acts in the strict sense. Transcendence is to be seen not at the level of intentional consciousness but at the level of embodiment. As Levinas puts it, only this embodied being, who enjoys eating, drinking and so on 'can be for the other', capable of being called into question by the other. Ethics is nothing but *this calling into question of my embodied self by the other*. Ethical subject is not *subjectum,* referring to that which is thrown under, but is always already a *subjected* body and the form that this subjected embodiment assumes is that of unconditional vulnerability. To be precise, it is through subjection that the ethical subject is formed *as subject*.

On the basis of this notion of subjection and the vulnerability of the subject Levinas puts forward two points which put pressure on the interactionist model, and more specifically, on Merleau-Ponty's concept of intertwining: One, ethical relation is not a question of need; two, it is not chiasmic. At the fundamental level, my relation to the other is not based on the fact that I need the other in order to become what I am. It is not the case that 'I need the other' where my primary concern is myself. In the ethical relation, 'thinking the other person is a part of the irreducible concern for the other.'[9] I am inescapably open towards the other and the movement here cannot be reduced to a need that returns to self. In the inetractionist model, everyone needs the other to achieve his/her psychophysical integrity and thus is always already entangled in the system of interactions. Merleau-Ponty's account of intertwining does not escape this horizontality and thus remains 'ontological' where alterity is reducible to 'the same'. Secondly, ethical intersubjectivity is not of the nature of intertwining; the relation is a relation of irreducible difference that it cannot be reduced to a symmetrical system of equality and mutuality. In other words, the ethical relation is not horizontal, the relation between the self and the other is not similar to two hands touching—ethics is not similar to a handshake.[10]

IV

Does Merleau-Ponty really advocate an 'imperialism of the same' that ignores difference? To answer this question, we need to understand what it actually means for Merleau-Ponty *to face the other*. The event of me meeting the other is to be understood primarily as *my gaze meeting another gaze*, where the other is conceived of neither as incomprehensible nor as reducible to me. I find myself facing the other means, as James Haltey puts it, "the gaze of the other reveals an alterity that is already articulated in my own visibility"[11]. That is, in facing the other, the alterity is being re-enacted in a sort of incarnate reflection. It is not that I consciously reconstruct the other, rather, the reflection here is a tacit acknowledgement of the other as an *other* and it does not involve a rational or cognitive judgment on a self-conscious level. The other is not a mirror for me to see myself, providing an occasion to work out my rational ego. It is not the case that the other is there, simply in front of me, as a discernable person. The other is originally encountered without having a personal address, as anonymously.

What does Merleau-Ponty mean by 'anonymity'? As he made it clear in *Phenomenology of Perception*, every perception takes place in a non-personal, and hence natural horizon and is presented to us anonymously. "Non-personal" perceptual existence underlies and intertwines with my life *as a person*. I am thrown into a mortal situation where I find myself '*already* born' and 'still living'. Just as birth and death are non-personal horizons, so is there a non-personal body, systems of anonymous functions, blind adherences to beings that I am not the cause of and for which I am not responsible. I am always already *worldly*, "conatural" with the world through no effort on my part. The other also, like me, is a field of anonymous forces structured by the fact of being embodied. Most importantly, it is this concept of the anonymity that leads Merleau-Ponty to form a common ontology, say, ontology of flesh, concerning self, other, and thing. The commonality is due to the fact that the world belongs to flesh, a prepersonal, anonymous subject, or *element* that is common to all bodies[12].

Through the fact of having a visual field, I am already 'fleshy'. To be fleshy is to be in touch with the other, *visible for the other*. 'To feel one's body is also to feel its aspect for the other'. This is what Merleau-Ponty means when he says self and the other are always already intertwined together (or reversible). Let us try to unpack this slightly mysterious claim.

According to Merleau-Ponty

> The self and the non-self are like the obverse and the reverse, and since our own experience is this turning around that installs us far indeed from ourselves, in the other, in the things. Like the natural man, we situate ourselves in ourselves, in ourselves *and* in the other, at the point where, by a sort of *chiasm*, we become the others and we become the world.[13]

It is clear from this passage that Merleau-Ponty proposes what can be called a chiasmic ontology which endorses an infringement between self and other. However, the proposal is not to admit a fusion, or a merging together of self and the other. Rather, his point is that of an ambiguous intertwining between self and other. This is also clear in Merleau-Ponty's celebrated account of the relation between touching and being touched. When I touch something, I am also being touched. It is not simply a matter of oscillation between these respective polarities, between subjective and objective poles. There is also an overlapping and infringement, such that 'the experience of being touched is always betrothed to the experience of touching, and vice versa'.[14] When one hand touches the other, there is never a situation where touching is radically conflicting to being touched. Rather, there is always an ambiguity, and Merleau-Ponty hence argues that 'to speak of touching as if it could be dissociated from being touched is to represent the phenomenon falsely'.[15]

Looking at another person always also involves the tacit recognition that we too can be looked at. However, rather than simply swinging between these two modes of being—looker and looked upon, each experience is betrothed to the other in such a way that we are never simply a disembodied looker. Rather, the alterity of the other's look is always already involved in us. Two significant consequences of Merleau-Ponty's position are as follows: 1) The other cannot be conceived 'as freedom that transcends my freedom'; the other can be concieved only with reference to the subjectivity with which it is always chiasmically intertwined. 2) The relation between self and the other can be conceived only as *intertwining* that involves these categories overlapping and intertwining with one another, but without ever being reduced to each other.

If alterity is something that can only be appreciated in being encountered, it amounts to saying that there can be no absolute alterity. Absolute alterity is inconceivable in the strict sense, and what needs to be considered, according to Merleau-Ponty, is the paradoxical relation where self and the other are intertwined, and yet also, at the same time, divergent. If this relation is of such a nature, then what is it to be responsible towards the other? Obviously, responsibility, within Merleau-Ponty's account, cannot be of the nature of acknowledging the incomprehensibility of the other. It is precisely about immersion in an intimate relation where self and other chiasmatically encroach upon and transform or alter one another. The other alters what I think of myself making me realize that I am the other for the other. Alterity, thus, implies the sense of 'alteration'.[16]

Facing the other implies the possibility of influencing and changing the other. But, however, it does not necessarily amount to a denial of their alterity because we are open to the possibility of being influenced and altered by the difference that they bring to bear upon our interaction with them. This is the ethics that his ontology of the flesh tacitly presupposes, and it is a position that is importantly different from that of Levinas. As against Levinas's line of criticism it can be argued that this concept of reversibility escapes the paradigm of *horizontal intersubjectivity* and provides a different platform to think 'the ethical' suggesting an important conception of responsibility, that is, what is to be responsible towards the other. There is a conception of ethical intersubjectivity available in Merleau-Ponty where respecting the alterity of the other should involve the imperative to alter what I think of myself into 'the other of the other'. To recognize myself as the other of the other could be a precondition for the most non-violent attitude possible towards the other.

It is true that Merleau-Ponty's concept of reversibility does not leave any space for the other as 'absolute', as 'absolving' in the Levinasian sense. The other is embodied like me and this embodiment does not mean the other is entirely in the world as an item among other items in the world. Rather, the other is an alter-ego for whom *there is a world.* And it is this recognition of the other as *having a world* that could make my attitude non-violent, realizing myself to be the other for the other. As Derrida pointed out in *Violence and Metaphysics,* if the other were not recognized as ego, 'an origin of the world', its entire alterity would collapse.[17] The other is other precisely because it is an alter ego. Its irreducibility is due to the fact that 'it has the form of an ego'. For Merleau-Ponty, embodiment is the necessary precondition for *having a world.* The ego and alter ego must be commonly embodied; without presupposing the commonality in terms of embodiment, flesh as *general thing* or an *element* of Being, no relation between the two can be conceived at all. Finally, this flesh makes possible the reversibility between self and the other, i.e. the possibility of being the other of the other.

NOTES AND REFERENCES

1. Husserl, Edmund. *Cartesian Meditations: An Introduction to Phenomenology.* Trans. Dorion Cairns. The Hague: Martinus Nijhoff, 1977, p. 111.
2. See Crossley, N. *Key Concepts in Critical Social Theory,* p. 173.
3. Merleau-Ponty, M. *Phenomenology of Perception.* Trans. By Colin Smith, Delhi: Motilal Banarasidas Publishers,1996, p. 198.
4. Carborn, Mouro. *The Thinking of the Sensible.* Evanston, IL: Northwestern University Press, 2004.
5. Merleau-Ponty, M. *The Visible and the Invisible.* Evanston: Northwestern University Press, 1968, p. 127.
6. Adamo, Christopher. 'Merleau-Ponty: Reversibility, Phenomenality and Alterity', *Philosophy Today,* Vol.46:5, p. 56.
7. Merleau-Ponty, M. *The Visible and the Invisible.* Evanston: Northwestern University Press, 1968, p. 168.
8. Hayat, Pierre. 'Philosophy Between Totality and Transcendence', Preface to Levinas's *Alterity and Transcendence,* p. xii.
9. Ibid., p. 98.

10. On Levinas' critique of Merleau-Ponty, see, Simon Critchley's essay, 'Post-Deconstructive Subjectivity?' in *Ethics-Politics-Subjectivity: Essays on Derrida, Levinas and Contemporary French Thought*. London: Verso, 1999, pp. 50-65.
11. Haltey, James. "Recursive Incarnation and Chiasmic Flesh", in *Chiasmus*, Albany: SUNY Press, 2000, p. 237.
12. Merleau-Ponty says: 'The flesh is not matter, is not mind, is not substance. To designate it, we should need the old term "element" in the sense it was used to speak of water, air, earth and fire, that is, in the sense of a *general thing*, midway between the spatio-temporal individual and idea, a sort of incarnate principle that brings a style of being wherever there is a fragment of being. The flesh is in this sense an "element" of Being'. *Visible and the Invisible*, p. 139.
13. Merleau-Ponty. *Visible and the Invisible*, p. 160.
14. Merleau-Ponty. *Visible and the Invisible*, 123.
15. Ibid., 93.
16. Jack Reynolds, in his essay 'Possible and Impossible, Self and Other, and Reversibility of Merleau-Ponty and Derrida', argues Merleau-Ponty's philosophy affirms the transformation of self and other, a mutual devouring, and alterity is best construed as that which literally alters. See *Philosophy Today*, Volume 48:1, Spring 2004, p. 46.
17. Derrida says: "If the other were not recognized as a transcendental alter ego, it would be entirely in the world and not, as ego, the origin of the world. To refuse to see in it an ego in this sense is, within the ethical order, the very gesture of all violence. If the other was not recognized as ego, its entire alterity would collapse". See *Violence and Metaphysics*, p. 125.

12

Subjectivity and History

David Carr

My mentor and friend J.N. Mohanty once told me that there was no philosophy of history in classical Indian thought. This is remarkable, since he believes that practically every aspect of Western metaphysics and epistemology is anticipated in classical Indian writings, and he has argued this vigorously in many of his works. But according to him the thinkers of this tradition had little interest in history as a problem or as a concept that needed philosophical attention. History is not everywhere in the Western tradition, but it is fair to say that it has always had an important place in Western thought, and since the 19th century it has occupied a central place.

The Hebrew Bible is often mentioned as a source, because Judaism introduced the very concept of historical time into a world dominated by cyclical and ahistorical views of time. Indian, Persian and Greek traditions are portrayed as being characterized by notions of timeless patterns and eternal recurrence, in which individual events, both natural and human, get whatever significance they have from reflecting, imitating or instantiating these timeless forms. (See Eliade, 1956) Neither individual events nor sequences of events seem to be "going anywhere." Their essence, what gives them their being, we might say, lies outside of time altogether. Even political arrangements—constitutions like aristocracy, democracy, monarchy, etc. —are portrayed, in the classical texts of Plato and Aristotle, for example, as following cyclical patterns of rise, fall, and repetition.

By contrast, for the ancient Jews events both political and religious get their significance not from a "vertical," imitative or cathectic relation to eternal patterns, but from a "horizontal" relation backward and forward to other events in real time: backwards to creation, Adam's fall, the covenant establishing God's people; its captivity, exile, return, rulers and heroes; forward to the salvation of God's people with the coming of the Messiah. Time is the story of a people's progress from creation through perils, dangers and risks to final salvation. Christianity takes up this historical conception of time and intensifies it, first by affirming the coming of the Messiah as a central, real historical event, in the *middle* of history, as it were, pointing ahead to a final salvation in the second coming; and second, by extending the promise of salvation to all mankind through a progressive spread and universal triumph of Christianity. Creation, the fall, incarnation, and last judgment are unique, unrepeatable occurrences, and individual events and deeds in which both human and divine, are arrayed along a line of time that extends from beginning to end. Given this conception, events are coming from somewhere and are going somewhere in time—from past to future. They get their meaning from their place in this linear time. Their being is a function of their past and future.

There is no doubt that this historical (as opposed to ahistorical) view of time and human events has characterized much of Western thinking, even though it was always in competition with the equally important, and essentially ahistorical view of the Greeks. No one denies time and change; the question is whether they are important, whether they constitute the being or essence of things and events. The historical view thinks that they do; and it is this view that largely triumphed in 19th century Western philosophy.

This triumph was manifested in the great speculative and substantive philosophies of history, notably those of Hegel and Marx. But the same period saw the emergence of history as an academic research discipline with scientific methods, supposedly capable of attaining some measure of objectivity. Both developments, though opposed to each other, shared the deep conviction that everything human is essentially historical. The key to human nature is now to be found neither in religion nor in reason, but in history.

Philosophically, with the collapse of the metaphysical systems, the interest shifted to epistemology and the problem of how the past can be known. This has led in most recent times to theories of representation, especially narrative representation. While I have been interested in theories of historical narrative, as a phenomenologist I am more interested in the experience that lies behind it. What is the presentation behind the representation? What is the experience of history, how does it enter our lives, how do we encounter it directly? In other words, what is the connection between subjectivity and history?

At first glance, this connection might seem to involve a simple four-step progression. Subjectivity is essentially temporal; subjectivity is essentially intersubjective; history is intersubjective temporality; thus subjectivity is essentially historical. But each of these steps, especially the third, needs elaboration, and this is what I propose in the following.

First, temporality: The temporal flow of consciousness is essential to the concept of subjectivity, and phenomenology, beginning with Husserl, has developed an account of consciousness that is unified while spanning past, present and future. This concern with the unity of consciousness over time is not new, of course, and existed in classical Indian thought, both Buddhist and non-Buddhist. Mohanty has made connections in this regard between phenomenology and Indian thought, and recent discussions by such authors as Miri Albahari, Evan Thompson, Wolfgang Fasching, and Chakravarthi Ram-Prasad, have explored these connections in great detail.

As many of these authors acknowledge, Husserl's great accomplishment is his introduction of the notion of retention and the sharp distinction he makes between it and memory in the usual sense, which he calls "recollection" or sometimes "reproduction." What Husserl is trying to describe here is the experience of both the presentness of the present and the *continuity* of the present. Retention is definitely a consciousness of something past: the previous note is gone forever. Yet I am conscious of it *together with* the present and it makes the present possible.

The use by Husserl of small-scale, compact examples like hearing a melody is valuable because it permits us to focus on the main features that are new in Husserl's account, namely retention and the temporal *Gestalt.* But Husserl chose it partly because it allows him to abstract, for purposes of analysis, from elements that belong to the larger sphere of our experience. Our experience is not in our heads but relates us to a world. Consciousness, as Husserl famously recognized, is not wrapped up in itself, but is always *of something.* As Sartre would later insist, interpreting Husserl, consciousness is entirely outside of itself, *in the world.* The account so far is abstract because it has left out what these phenomenologists call *intentionality.*

The concept of subjectivity which emerges from this discussion is one that has been enriched by recognizing and describing its temporality and its intentionality. Consciousness flows, and has its retentional-protentional structure. It is of the here-and-now, the present, but only because the present stands out from a kind of temporal field that encompasses past and future. And it is *of* the here-and-now in the sense that it relates intentionally to objects that are other than and outside itself.

The introduction of intentionality into the discussion of experience means that we cannot properly speak of experience without discussing *what* is intended, *as* it is intended. It is not just that we want to consider those "objects that are other than and outside" the intention; we *must* consider them if we want to understand experience. Husserl spoke of "temporal objects" (*Zeitobjekte*) as a special class of objects—things that take time or unfold in time, and must do so in order to be what they are, and to be experienced *as* what they are. The melody is one example, but so is the dancer's twirl, the tree's sway in the breeze, a conversation. But we have a perfectly good word to describe such "objects:" they are *events.* Things that do not take time, or just persist through time, like my pen, can be distinguished from events. Of course, my experience, even of my pen, is itself an event; that is, it unfolds in time, even if my pen just sits there. So, when we talk of experiencing an event, like hearing a melody, we must distinguish between the event of hearing and the event that is heard, the melody itself.

As we further develop our treatment of subjectivity in relation to history, the concept of event assumes major importance, and needs to be further broken down and elaborated with some subtlety. For the moment it is sufficient to say that the experience, of the here and now, is intentionally related to things and events as its "objects," in the broadest sense. But as *intentional* objects, things and events have *meaning* and this leads us to the concept of *world.*

This is one of those terms that have developed a special sense in the context of phenomenology, largely thanks to the works of Husserl and Heidegger. "World" can mean just the totality of what is, the universe, all the things that exist, and so on. The phenomenological understanding of world retains the sense of totality, but includes the idea of things and events *as intended*, that is, as having meaning—for consciousness, for someone, for human existence—meanings they have in relation to one another and in relation to the totality itself. Things and events added together may make up a universe, but things and events that have meaning for someone make up a world, at least in the phenomenological sense. This does not mean that these things and events, or their meanings, or the world itself, are "merely subjective." Indeed one of the meanings they have is, as we have seen, that they are other than or outside consciousness. In virtue of intentionality, experience relates itself to what is beyond itself. In this sense, the subject is in the world, and the world, as a complex of meaningful things and events, is as essential to it as intentionality itself.

The phenomenological account of time and subjectivity is initially tied to the first-person singular point of view. And yet this focus seems highly inappropriate for talking about history. History, it is fair to say, is not itself focused on individuals, but concerns the social world. If we are to find a connection between subjectivity and history, then consciousness is in some sense going to have to concern more than just the individual. This is where intersubjectivity comes in. We are going to have to talk about the experience of the social world, and, at the limit, about experience itself as something that occurs *socially*.

A significant part of *what* we experience, among the things and events that make up our world, are 1) other people and groups of other people; 2) events involving other people; 3) the actions, sufferings, and experiences of other people; 4) human artifacts and other productions, not only physical but also institutional, procedural and developmental. The concept of subjectivity in modern philosophy came into prominence in response to epistemological concerns, and these were conceived in relation to the newly developing sciences of nature. The only *objects* of experience that were considered important, accordingly, were physical and natural objects. This focus on *things* meant that our encounter with other people was conceived in terms of our perception of their bodies as physical objects and led to the notorious problem of "other minds."

This supposed problem, certainly insoluble as it is formulated, has long been recognized as bogus. We experience persons as persons, their bodies as human bodies, not as physical objects. Thus our world is primarily, indeed overwhelmingly, a human and social world. So far we have distinguished between the experience of the social world and that of the natural world. But it must be noted that human events occur against the backdrop of the natural world. Thus nature plays an important —though secondary—role here as the location and theatre of human events. In this sense nature belongs to the human world. But this sense of nature is somewhat different from that of directly experienced nature, since it gets its meaning from the actions and experiences of individuals and social groups. A landscape can be directly experienced, but it can also be understood as the specific environment of some community and the source of its nourishment and building materials. Its geographical features influence the development of settlements and towns. Here the landscape is given indirectly to our experience, namely by way of the interests and activities of this particular group.

Once this human world moves to the center of our concern, and becomes more fully elaborated, we can return to the *temporality* of experience in relation to the social world and to social existence. We can now shift our attention from the simple act of hearing a melody to the music itself as a product belonging to the inventory of our cultural environment. We and our contemporaries live in a world that includes, besides music, also literature and art, pop-culture, the financial system, businesses, trends, movements, etc. But the material inventory of our cultural world is much nearer to us and more pervasive. Most of us live in a world of houses and buildings, of streets, traffic and means of transportation. Houses and streets (except when they are being torn down and built up) are more or less immobile objects, but they provide the surroundings for the movements and actions of those who live in and use them. As artifacts, they also refer implicitly to the activity of their builders. The human world is thus a world not just of things but of events and processes, of actions and developments, which we experience as continuities thanks to the retentional-protentional structure. Like the natural world the human world is temporal, and we experience it as temporal continuity, but the temporality of the human world is different from that of the natural world.

Houses and streets, cities and their configurations, have a past which is given with them as horizon and background when we experience them in the present. Indeed, we can say the same thing of other people. This horizon of pastness is given in retention, and thanks to retention we have something like an experience of the past—but only as background for the present. Further, we can say that many of these objects, and many of these people, are older than we are—i.e. older than I, the particular subject of any given experience. In these cases the horizon of pastness reaches back nto the time before our birth. Thus the depth and breadth of this past, receding into the indefinite, as horizon and background for the present, is always given in every experience of the human world. In this sense what is experienced is not limited to the lifetime of the experiencing subject.

Merging the phenomenological account of temporality with that of the social world we can say that the direct experience of persons, groups and other social entities, such as artifacts, buildings, streets, etc. bears its past along with it in the manner of retentional consciousness. To have an experience in this first sense is to be in the presence of an object that stands out from its temporal background. To experience an action or event is likewise to see it emerge from its antecedents. In each of these cases the retained past is part of what gives meaning to the present and makes it what it is. Each object and event, in other words, comes to us with its past attached. Without this past it would not only be meaningless, it could not even be an item in our experience. If it is true that our experience is in the present and connects us with the present, it is equally true that it gives an unmediated connection with the past.

This past extends indefinitely into the temporal "distance" and has its contours and features, some more distinct than others. The retained past has patterns that accumulate and bear upon the present. One way of stating this is that what is given in immediate and direct experience can make sense or have meaning for us in virtue of falling into a pattern or structure. It is recognized as an exemplar or instance of a type provided by our past experience. As Hume pointed out, we build up expectations. Yet because consciousness is also open to the future, those expectations can be rudely disappointed, or happily surprised, by the new and the unexpected.

To correctly describe and fully understand this relation to others, we need to introduce an indispensable new term, namely that of the group to which I and the others belong. It is precisely as fellow members of a group that others are encountered in this way, and so we need to explore what "group" means in this context, to understand how it exists, how far it extends, etc. What we have in mind here is not merely an objective collection of individuals, united by some common characteristic like size, shape, hair colour or complexion. The relevant sense of group for our purposes is united from the inside, not from the outside. The word most often used to convey this sense of group is *community, Gemeinschaft.* These terms derive from the common or the shared, but this must be understood in a special way.

If the community makes possible a certain kind of encounter

with others, how do I encounter the community itself? It too is not primarily an object standing over or against me as something to be perceived or known, as if I were an anthropologist or sociologist. I relate to it rather in terms of membership, adherence or belonging. The sign of this relation is my use of the "we" to characterize the subject of certain experiences and actions. The possibility that the community can emerge as a "we"-subject affords a way of understanding not only the nature of the community but also the peculiar character of being with others that makes it up.

One thing to be noted is how such a community relates to the possibility of phenomenological understanding. Phenomenology is often characterized by the first-person character of its descriptions. By shifting our attention from the "I" to the "we," it is not necessary to leave the first-person point of view behind; we merely take up the plural rather than the singular first person. [This shift from the I to the We reveals an interesting connection between 20th century phenomenology and Hegel's phenomenology, a connection that has always been murky and not understood. In the *Phaenomenologie des Geistes* the author introduces the key notion of his work, that of Geist, by calling it "an I that is We, a We that is I," in other words, a plural subject. It is Geist that forms the true subject of the dialectical forms that Hegel describes in his phenomenology, and which later figures as the central concept in his philosophy of history.]

Describing this plural subject phenomenologically involves reflecting on those occasions and experiences in which I identify myself with a group or community by enlisting, so to speak, in the "we." It happens when the experience or action in which I am engaged is attributed not just to me but to "us," when I take myself to be a participant in a collective action or experience. But the action or experience must be enduring or ongoing, and with it the existence of the collective subject, the "we." To say that we build a house is not equivalent to saying that I build a house, you build a house, she builds a house, etc. The common project is articulated into subtasks distributed among the participants such that the agent cannot be any of the members singly but only the group as such.

To say that I enlist in or participate in such collective endeavours or experiences is to say that I identify myself with the group in question, and this sense of "identifying oneself" deserves our attention. The identity of the subject is not a given but constitutes itself over time as a sort of project, and I identify myself in relation to others. This is often taken to mean that I gain my identity in opposition to others, but it is also true that one asserts one's identity by joining with others. This brings us into the territory of "identity" as it is used in such phrases as "identity crisis" and "identity politics." As an individual I identify myself with certain groups and thus construe my identity in terms of my belonging. Among these are family, profession, religion, nationality, culture, etc.

Thus individuals identify themselves with groups that range from small and intimate to larger and more encompassing. But it must not be thought that these groups nest easily inside each other like a series of concentric circles. Groups criss-cross one another, and I identify myself sometimes more with one than another, depending on circumstances. Furthermore, participation in one may not always be compatible with participation in another. Family may conflict with profession, class with country, religion with civic duty, etc., to name only a few of the classic conflicts. These conflicts can be personal and psychological, "identity crises" in which the individual is torn between conflicting commitments and allegiances; and through the individuals involved the conflicts can be social as well, pitting groups against each other in collective action and enmity.

Much more could be said about various aspects and implications of the We-relation, but I want to turn now to its relevance to our topic. We have been looking for a connection between subjectivity and history that could be described as the experience of historical existence. I want to contend that it is in the experience of membership in communities that time is genuinely historical for us. As a member of a community, I become part of a We-subject with an experience of time that extends back before my birth and can continue even after my death. Since the We is experienced as genuinely subjective, it has the same sort of temporality as the I-subject. That is, it is not just an entity persisting in time, or a series of nows, but it occupies a prospective-retrospective temporal field encompassing past and future. Just as we attribute agency and experience to the we-subject, so we can speak of its expectations and its memories. History is sometimes spoken of as "society's memory," the manner in which a community retains its past such that the past plays an enduring role in the life of the present. To put it another way: just as the present is for the I-subject the vantage point which gives access to a temporal field encompassing past and future; likewise, for the we-subject, the present similarly functions as a vantage-point. But the field which is opened up in this case is much broader. It is to this field that I gain access in virtue of my membership and participation in a community.

But there is more to it than this. Engaged in a community by using the term "we," I enjoy a special relationship with my fellow members, as we have seen. But these fellow members are temporally differentiated in significant ways. Alfred Schütz spoke of the difference between contemporaries, predecessors and successors, but this distinction is much too simple. My contemporaries are further differentiated into elder and younger, distinctions which are more than just chronological. In both family, ethnic and professional contexts, elders are traditionally considered more knowledgeable and more experienced, and act as parents, guides and mentors to the younger. In any case, these intergenerational relations show that being a member of a community means belonging to a temporally continuous entity whose temporality exceeds that of my own subjectivity. With regard to the past, its reach gradually expands in a kind of relay-form from elders to ancestors and predecessors who came "before my time," that is, before my experience and before my birth.

One thing to be emphasized about our account of subjectivity and history is that it remains anchored, like the concept of experience itself, firmly in the present, the here-and-now. But one great advantage of the phenomenological approach to temporality, on which we have drawn extensively, is that it shows there can be no experience of the present, and no presence as experienced, without its horizon or background of past and future. The "here-and-now" is possible only as emerging from the past and anticipating the future. This is true of the flow of our experience itself, and it is true of the meaningful events, objects, persons and other entities that occur around us and make up our world.

There has been much emphasis on continuity in what I have said so far: the continuity of time-consciousness, which brings past and future into our purview; the continuities of intersubjectivity, especially in the solidarity of membership in the community. But I think the relation between subjectivity and history is marked as much, if not more, by discontinuity, and I want to conclude by mentioning four sorts of discontinuity peculiar to historical experience.

1) First, the establishment of the we-subject is not possible without otherness. The community demarcates itself from other communities, just as the individual subject must distinguish itself from others. The intersubjective character of the individual is also affected: I relate to my fellows as members of the same community, with whom I say "we." And I relate to others not just as other individuals but as members of an opposing group: "them" versus "us."

2) The intergenerational continuity of predecessors and successors is also marked, perhaps necessarily, by discontinuity as well: Just as important as the benign relationships of filiation and tradition is the agonistic, indeed, Oedipal struggle, in which the young rebel against the domination of the old, break away and establish their independence. So often, of course, this classic youthful rebellion, instead of securing the emancipation of the individual from the group, only reveals the individual's deeper, inextricable dependence and adherence.

3) The "historical" is often experienced more by the discontinuity than the continuity of events. Think of the fall of the Berlin Wall in 1989, and the attacks on New York and Washington in 2001. Both were shocking and unexpected, taking everyone by surprise. They were immediately recognized as marking historical turning points, playing out, thanks to

television, before our very eyes.

4) This suggests a fourth discontinuity, this time in temporality itself. Claude Lévi-Strauss wrote that history, like any other science, uses a code to gain access to its objects, and that history's code is that of dates and chronology. But dates, he said, are not arrayed along a single axis but belong to different levels or strata. 1610, 1648, 1715 belong to one sequence, that of the French monarchy; the first and second millennia belong to another; ancient, medieval and modern make up a third, and so on. The point, which has been made by others as well, is that human temporality occurs on different planes, perhaps starting with the bodily cycles of sleep, waking and digestion. Superimposed on this is the personal history of the individual life-story. Events are experienced within these frameworks, and get their meaning from them. The idea of different levels or strata of temporality introduces a significant new feature to our whole account of temporality and historical time. It suggests that the experience of these large-scale historical events, in which we participate as members of the community of spectators, catapults us onto a different plane of temporality, that of historical time.

What we have been trying to describe here is what the German philosophers called the *Geschichtlichkeit*, or historicity, of human existence. Dilthey wrote that "we are historical beings first, before we are observers [*Betrachter*] of history, and only because we are the former do we become the latter...The historical world is always there, and the individual not only observes it from the outside but is intertwined with it [*in sie verwebt*]." Dilthey, Husserl, Heidegger and others who used this term thought of historicity as something like an essential human trait, something bound to subjectivity itself. But now I return to my remark at the beginning, and to a question I have never been able to answer: Is historicity essentially human, or is it essentially Western? Could it be a feature, not of subjectivity as such, but of a religious tradition based on historical time and a European 19th century obsessed with history? Is it just a sign of Western provincialism, or is it more than that?

13

Science and the Promise of Objective Knowledge: Husserl's Intersubjective Renewal

Nishad Patnaik

In the *Crisis*, Husserl claims that at the very juncture of their greatest theoretical and practical success, the positive sciences (including the 'humanistic sciences') have ceased to function as a source of meaning for us. For, "Merely fact minded sciences make merely fact minded people".[1] The "positivistic restriction of the idea of science" and the type of objectivity that comes to dominate our conception of 'nature', and of ourselves, excludes in principle, what is closest and most vital to us—questions "[...] concerning the meaning or meaninglessness of the whole of this human existence".[2] These questions have their original impetus or 'primal establishment' (Urstiftung), in the ancient ideal of a rationally constituted humanity in self-reflective freedom, i.e. in "nothing less than the philosophical form of existence".[3]

This ideal in turn, finds its animating sense in our capacity for autonomy—our irreducibility to the natural realm, through which we are nevertheless conditioned and in which we are situated. To *have* a world, with its discernible patterns of becoming, its consistencies and the practical and cognitive interests it holds for us, is to be in a 'subjectively' mediated, meaningful relation with 'nature'. Yet, despite the rediscovery and 're-establishment' (Nachstiftung), beginning with the renaissance, of this ancient ideal, its very pursuit, in the quest for founding a rational humanity—one that would reflectively clarify its own mediated relation to nature, results in its inevitable distortion and reification. In modernity, with the positivistic reduction of the idea of universality, and the sceptical and nihilistic tendencies to which it inevitably gives rise, the process of the 'inner dissolution' of this ideal reaches a certain critical mass, a tipping point, or precisely, a 'crisis'.[4]

Yet, transcendental–genetic inquiry, which as a response to this crisis of modernity, is to reanimate and reshape this ideal, and therefore reconstitute the sense of objectivity ('nature') as such, in intuitive self-evidence (*Endstiftung*),[5] cannot imply a return to the 'immediacy' of the 'world of lived experience' ('life–world' or '*Lebenswelt*') and its passively pre-given (doxic) modalities of 'sense'. As Husserl noted in *Experience and Judgment*, the world in which we live and cognize, "[...] is already pre-given to us as [...] the precipitate of logical operations".[6] For modern consciousness, the 'world' *is* the '*objective*' world of natural science—with its logico-mathematical modes of determination, in which an objective 'in-itself' is posited insofar as it admits measurement and quantification. This means that in principle, there is no 'immediacy' of the life-world to return to, if 'immediacy' is understood as a fundamental, a-historical mode of experience (such as 'sensuous perception' in the ordinary, naive sense) over against the modern natural sciences. Rather, the natural sciences are an intrinsic part of the life-world, and constitutively determine, at least for modern consciousness, its basic mode of encounter with the world (and itself)—the sense of 'objectivity' that the world has for such a (scientifically determined) subjectivity.

Further, this argument can clearly be generalized, since the modern natural sciences are only the latest in the series of historical modes of understanding/encountering the world. Consequently there is no possibility of undoing this historical mediation and returning to the 'immediacy' of lived experience prior to the advent of the natural sciences; rather, the life-world is historically mediated through and through—it is *constitutively* historical. It is this *historicity* of the Lebenswelt—its essentially temporal and intersubjective becoming that rules out, in principle, the possibility of a return to 'immediacy'.

It is within the context of this problematic (which indicates a generalized 'hermeneutical circle') that I will trace the possibility of a certain *mediated* re-appropriation and renewal of the 'originally' *constituted* sense of 'objectivity' prior to its positivistic reduction, to Husserl's account of the intersubjective, embodied co-constitution of spatiality as the "being-there-for-everyone" (das *Für-jedermann-da*),[7] intrinsic to my perceptual experience. The paper will therefore, also deal with some of the problems attendant upon this apparent shift in the trajectory of Husserl's thinking from phenomenological analysis understood primarily as 'transcendental egology', to a transcendental genetic, historicist and intersubjective account, discernible in the writings on spatiality.

In order to catch a glimpse of transcendental constituting (inter) subjectivity, genetic analysis qua reflective-intuitive re-constitution must occur in two stages. First, it must trace the sedimented, idealized world of natural science, with its mathematized conception of nature, to its emergence in the life-world, *understood in its historicity*. However, since the life- world is also a spatio-temporally constituted horizonal structure, within which all experiencing unfolds, it calls for a second stage of retrogression (Rückgang), which moves from its constituted spatio-temporal horizon to constituting transcendental subjectivity.[8]

Thus, from the transcendental-genetic perspective, once the world of natural science is bracketed, it becomes possible to see that before any movement of judgmental articulation, and before any objectification/modalization into conjecture, possibility, etc., the perceptual world and its objects are there for us in *simple certainty*, corresponding to a "simple believing consciousness" (*schlichten Glaubensbewußtsein)*.[9] Yet, this pre-thematic, pre-predicative *'thereness'* of the object is nothing 'immediate' in any positivistic sense, but a certain noematic structure of intentionality, where while "[...] the object of cognition is already present [...]", it is present "[...] as a *dynamis* which is to turn into an entelecheia."[10] The object affects us—attracts our interest, and motivates us towards its fulfilling entelecheia, only because it stands out within its surrounding world, which is passively co-intended, even when it is not thematically grasped. All praxis, whether practical, axiological or cognitive, arises from this passively pre-given perceptual domain, with its simple belief character and horizon of familiarity. Every experiencing has its infinite *internal* and *its* infinitely open *external* horizon, with its typical fore-knowledge (Vorwissen)—its possibilities of experience which are more or less indeterminate, and yet not completely empty, since the indeterminacy is limited by the one spatio-temporal horizon of possible experience.[11] This 'indeterminate *a priori*' of possible experience, or anticipatory fore-knowledge of the life-world, is the unity of an open-ended spatio-temporal horizon.[12]

Husserl underscores this pre-given, pre-reflective and 'indeterminate *a priori*' character of the spatio-temporal horizon, as the presupposed starting point of cognitive (judgmental) and at a higher level of abstraction, logical-rational articulation in *Experience and Judgment*. It is however, the theme of inquiry in Husserl's writings on spatiality and temporality, which span his entire philosophical career.

An analysis of the "[...] self-constitution—the self-manifestation [...] of experiential objectivity at the lowest level of experience,"[13] thus, of the reflective-constitutive emergence of spatiality (and temporality), along with that of Husserl's reflections on embodied consciousness and intersubjective co-constitution shows, I argue, how the inextricable interconnection between these three themes (space-time, embodiment, intersubjective co-constitution), reopens Kant's problematic of 'noumenal' transcendence in Husserl's phenomenology. By explicating the possibility of the constitution/emergence of 'objectivity' as such, as it structurally conditions, and is conditioned by, the problematics of the body and intersubjectivity, I outline the manner in which the non-phenomenal, non-representational 'beyond' may *function* (and qua posited, must be understood in a 'functional' sense), as the basis for the articulation of the phenomenal world of objective sense.

1. Husserl's Analyses Concerning the Origin of the Sense of Spatiality and Temporality as Interconnected, yet Distinct Realms

Let us consider Husserl's reflections on spatiality, understood as the open-ended unity of the perceptual- intentional field. The sense of the transcendence of objects in space with respect to appearances immanent to the stream of consciousness is captured in the notion of *perspective*. The latter refers to both my situatedness within a spatial horizon and the opening up of the horizon as such. The spatial field opened up is thus always *oriented* around a perceptual center; yet, as the very opening up, the perspectival center itself cannot be encountered within the spatial/perceptual field. The perspectival opening implies an *absolute "here"* in relation to which everything is oriented as "there", as "near" or "far", in motion or at rest, in a harmonious unfolding of *possible* perspectives.

Essential to the opening up of a spatial horizon is the situated, embodied character of my perceptions, and the *possibility* of my own bodily kinesthesis—the possibility of occupying different positions or perspectives, such that the "there" becomes a new "here". *Oriented space* is a system of actuality and potentiality, constantly open to re-orientation and reorganization with the unfolding of perspectives according to the transformation of a "there" into a "here" and vice versa.

Yet does this sense of the "I can" that is constitutive of perceptual objects given in space, and of spatiality itself, not render talk of an "absolute here" meaningless? Does it not entail that every "here" (and "now") is a spatio-temporally relative determination, and presupposes the uniform, objective space (and time) of Newtonian mechanics, within which every position may be encountered, and all motion and rest determined? The very sense of "perspective" seems to have these consequences built into it. The *awareness* of my visual field as perspectivally determined creates the requisite distance between the "subjective" and the "objective", "appearance" and "reality", etc. constitutive of our sense of spatiality.

Husserl points to these implications in his *Foundational Investigations*. The modern, Copernican conception of the world rests on the relativization of the immediately given realm of spatiality as perspectival, where not only our own animate organism, but the earth itself, loses its status as the original *'basis-body' (Boden-Körper).* The moment the earth is thematized/objectified *as* 'basis-body', its implicit sense as basis-body is necessarily nullified. The earth becomes one amongst other planetary bodies.[14] The objectification of the earth as 'basis–body', hence the emergence of objective space (and time), involves an objectification of motion and rest.[15] They are also understood in a relative sense—determined in relation to some *basis-body* picked out from the plurality of possible basis-bodies. The objectification of the basis-body, and the conception of 'nature' as an 'infinite totality' is inseparable from the formation of the modern 'natural sciences'.[16]

However, the origin of the Copernican world view may be traced to the implicit sense of spatial transcendence inherent in everyday experience within the life-world. "Already a certain relativity of rest and motion is fashioned here [...]"[17], for, my own bodily position forms the basis-body in relation to which motion and rest are apprehended. Yet, since my body can also be in motion, relative to the unthematized earth as basis-body, it is necessarily a *relative basis-body*. This relativity becomes explicit when we are aware of ourselves as moving, as in a railway car, but it is the landscape that appears to rush past. Where such awareness is missing, we are, for an instant, taken in by the appearance. For instance, sitting in a railway car which was stationary, the train on the track next to us appears to move, but it is we who have started moving. Under normal circumstances this discontinuity between 'appearance' and our awareness is an implicit feature of our experience—to which we adjust, without giving it a second thought.

Yet, whereas all such relative distinctions of motion and rest have their basis in the 'non-relative' earth–body, how do things stand when the latter itself becomes thematized in relativistic fashion? For Husserl, this does not constitute the nullification of the unrepresentable absolute positionality of the perspectival opening of the spatial horizon, within which the earth comes to be represented as a 'moved body' amongst others. For, the unrepresentable opening is again unthematically presupposed as the condition for the very conceivability of the earth qua spatial body.[18]

This suggests that although the earth is the original basis-body upon which our sense of spatiality as an oriented system of possible resting places, with its inherent sense of relativity and transcendence, is constituted, the earth is not to be understood literally as a *body* in the material sense, nor as a horizon in some specifically limited sense, but as a *stand in* for the spatial horizon itself. The impossibility of transcending the *earth*–horizon, is the impossibility of transcending the spatial horizon—of bringing *my* (non-spatial) embodied absolute "here", which constitutes the opening up of phenomenal, oriented space, to unmediated spatial representation.[19] Yet, the earth can always be conceived as a planetary body—a possibility inherent in the oriented space constituted within the earth-horizon such that the earth loses its pre-thematic, horizonal status qua basis-body.

To emphasize this, Husserl uses a series of locutions that at first glance, appear quite paradoxical.

> I have no motion away; I stand still or go. [...] My animate organism has extension but no change and non-change of place in the sense of the way whereby an outer body is presented as in motion receding or approaching, or not in motion, as near, far away. But the *basis* on which my animate organism goes or does not go is also not experienced as a body, as *wholly* to be moving away or not moving away.[20]

But how can the animate body be in motion or rest within the spatial realm, while, as the perspectival opening of spatiality as such, maintaining an unmoved reserve?[21] The question is connected to the problem, at the logical/epistemological level, of how the transcendental ego (or noumenal "I" in the Kantian sense) can be given to itself, i.e. represent its own modes of synthesis as (empirical or *a priori*) 'object'. The difference here is that we are dealing with the pre-objective, pre-thematic emergence of objectivity as such, namely, the horizon of spatiality (and temporality). At this level, it is not intentional consciousness, with its accomplished conceptual objectivities and cognitive interest in 'fulfilment', nor even its perceptual/ synthetic objectivities in space-time and motivated perceptual fulfilment that predominates, but a mode of 'reflection' belonging to the animate body.

In *Ideas II* Husserl illustrates this with the example of one hand touching the other.[22] When I touch my left hand with my right, I experience certain sensuous perceptions in my right hand, which I immediately objectify as attributes belonging to the left hand. Yet, in touching the left hand, the latter in turn, comes to be awakened, not as sensed but as sensing; in turn touching the right hand.[23]

This constant interchange between the touching and the touched, due to the *localization* of sensations, indicates a pre-thematic, corporeal awareness of unity in simultaneity. The animate body is a multiplicity of sensible *loci* of orientation, and while a certain orientational disposition predominates, determining the direction of "touching" and the "touched", it can do so only against the background awareness of other localizations of sensation. While there is an inescapable temporal priority of one perspectival kinaesthetic orientation over another, the sense of this internal perspectival self-differentiation within the animate body is such that there can be no "ontological" priority, since the predominant kinaesthetic orientation contains the others in an implicit manner.

This implicit sense of the *simultaneity* of a plurality of potential perspectives, inherent in the animate body, is the pre-cursor to the awareness of spatial objects and of spatiality. The awareness of *simultaneity* at the corporeal level brings into play a uniquely spatial differentiation—not the past and future of temporal distance, but the "near" and "far", "here" and "there" of spatial distance. This 'distance of the simultaneous' lies in the inability, within the internally differentiated unity of the animate body, of occupying two perspectivally oriented positions at once. The hand that touches cannot, without losing its oriented character as *touching*, thematize the touch sensations generated in it by the hand that is being touched, and similarly, the latter cannot thematize, without losing its sense as *touched*, the sensations that arise in it from being touched.[24]

Yet, one must not be too quick to extract from the internal orientational differentiation within the pre-phenomenal unity of the animate body and its implicit sense of simultaneity, a developed sense of the spatial horizon. The difference between the unity of the animate organism and of the oriented spatial field is that the latter is given independently of sensation, whereas bodily unity is essentially sensible.[25] The perspectivally oriented space that emerges even with the "subject" solipsistically considered, involves a mode of idealization unavailable at the corporeal level. The ideal unity of the oriented spatial horizon, with its kinaesthetic *possibilities*, has its basis in a passive *synthesis*, which is necessarily temporal. Ideality is temporally generated—it has a temporal form. I will come back to this point.

This is not to suggest that the unified spatial field is reducible to the temporal, even if it is constituted in a temporally extended synthesis. Spatial synthesis involves passive association of all that is given/posited in simultaneity. Unlike temporal synthesis where, with the advent of each new "now", what is intentionally retained of the previous "now" continually sinks into an increasingly undifferentiated past, until it is completely assimilated into the indeterminate unity of the temporal horizon[26], *associative synthesis* maintains the differentiation of each "now". Being confined to the present, association shows the "besides one another in simultaneity" (Außeinander–im–Zuglich) of the spatial horizon.[27] At the level of pre-phenomenal, bodily synthesis, the *'primal present'* with its differential affectivity, contains an implicit plurality of *Urimpressionen*, and thus a multiplicity of implicit kinaesthetic orientations. This originary "stratification of the present" is what lets prominences, contrasts, similarities, etc. emerge as affective differentiations, and thus motivations that may be taken up in a 'turning towards', within the domain of passivity. However, if this constitutes the unity of the *hic et nunc* of originary spatial differentiation, such differentiation must be merely posited. The *affective* differentiation of the primal present is always already past—transformed into a retentional modification, and on its way to assimilation in the undifferentiated horizon of the remote past.

Husserl underscores this *phenomenal* inseparability of time and space on the one hand, and its functional dependence on pre-phenomenal space–time (*hic et nunc*) on the other, in terms of the interrelation between immanent and 'phantom time'. "The style of the perspectives, including spatial and then qualitative perspectives, is already constituted in spatio-temporality, which is the form of realities [...]; we have here already a difference between 'immanent time', the 'time of perspectival progressions' and the 'phantom time' of the perspectivally appearing unities."[28] He continues: "But what about phantoms? Is it not the case that phantom perceptual fields and temporal fields are not separate and only combined by immanent time; and that immanent time and phantom time are still undivided even though the phantom as a possibly constituted unity of appearances and time itself are already separated?"[29] This irreducible interrelation between immanent and phantom time is key to understanding the emergence of the spatial horizon as a unified, *a priori* system of kinaesthetic possibilities.

All 'alterations', along with my corresponding bodily kinaesthetic possibilities, are constituted in a continuous *immanent* temporal flow of perspectives. The flow involves *passive synthesis*, as a continuity of retentional and protentional intentions, in their reciprocal interrelation. Two points must be emphasized here. First, this continuity depends on the retentional modification of each new "now", and therefore, both presupposes and constitutes the passage of time, hence, temporal difference/discontinuity. Temporal continuity is founded on the discontinuity of *place*—the unrepeatable position of each instant; such that, "Even a God cannot alter the temporal positions of events in the past".[30]

Second, the retentional-protentional continuity of the flow in passive synthesis does not yet amount to an *explicit* awareness of the past and the future, i.e. the *unity of duration* or 'phantom time'. The explicit sense of the passage of time requires the active power of recollection. Recollection is constitutive of 'phantom' time, the phenomenal time of *re-presentation* and all perceptual unities/phantoms, including the unity of the acts of consciousness itself, given in time.[31]

Recollection, and the determinate/representational unity of the 'object' and the 'subject', is made possible only on the basis of the 'double intentionality of retention'.[32] Consciousness retains both what it experiences originally in a 'transverse' intentionality (*Querintentionalität*), for instance, a particular tone, and *itself* as having experienced the tone, in a 'longitudinal intentionality' (Längsintentionalität). Without such pre-reflective self-awareness or continuous retentional self-differentiation in the temporal flow of consciousness, there would be no synthesis of the flow, hence no synthetic unity of representation of the flow either in the 'object' or the 'subject'. The flowing series of perspectival adumbrations (Abschattungen) would not be adumbrations pertaining to the *same* object, but unconnected points of experience. Correlatively, the temporal flow of consciousness would be unconnected and not retained as *my* experiences. Thus, any attempt to account for the unity of consciousness that does not presuppose an implicit self-consciousness, leads to an infinite regress.[33]

The *representation* of the unity of the 'object' or the 'subject', in and through the temporal flow of consciousness involves an idealization based on active recollection—the *reproduction* of the past in the present, and the *recognition* of the reproduced *qua reproduced*. In such explicit recollection in the present, of the past as *my* past, the unity of 'phantom' time, hence of all 'objects' and 'subjects' as determinate durations, is constituted.

Husserl implies that this idealization that remains implicit in the perceptual unfolding internal to the horizon of the unitary perceptual object becomes explicit when the external (spatial) horizon is in question. The external horizon, as the totality of the spatial domain, is presupposed in the experience of any spatial object. The object is never experienced in isolation, and with each perspectival alteration the whole oriented perceptual field that forms the background against which the object stands out, is also altered to some degree, while remaining the "same".[34] However, if there is break in my continuously unfolding series of perspectival experiences, the perspectivally oriented field around me may be altered to an extent where certain "perceptual phantoms" drop out of the field, while others come into view. Yet despite this, a certain continuity persists between the earlier and later fields;[35] moreover, an ideal unity emerges between the no longer perceived 'phantoms' in the earlier field and those given in the present field. It is always possible to "return at will" (*zurückzukehren*) to the earlier, lost phantoms.[36] This ability to "return at will" is, in the first instance, a mode of recollection, through which the new object within the present perceptual field is identified as of the 'same' *type*, as the earlier object. This continuity of perceptual transitions constitutes the "unity of the total experience of a phantom world" (*Einheit der Gesamterfahrung einer "Phantomwelt")*;[37] of all *co-existent* phantoms, whether actually perceived or not.

Yet, since 'recollection' belongs to the temporal horizon, it is not clear how it leads to the emergence of the spatial horizon, as the ideally articulated domain of *co-existence*.[38] However, the possibility of *actually* returning to objects, places, etc. experienced in the past, which constitutes the essence of spatiality qua co-existence, leaves the question of what constitutes their 'sameness',[39] unanswered. Moreover, this 'sameness' cannot be the strict identity of the mathematical-logical sciences. If I return to places I had known in my childhood, I find that much has changed—and yet I experience the surroundings as more or less the same, as altered but still the same. How is this loose sense of 'sameness' to be understood? The 'same' in this case pertains not only to temporal continuity but to spatial continuity—the sense of persistence, despite the lapse of time and alterations 'in' time, of places as co-existent in the world, and of the persistence of the spatial world as such.

Further, the actual return to a place experienced earlier does not amount to a reversal of the flow of time itself; the *present* experience of the 'same' object/place still comes later in the unified temporal series that constitutes my life–history, in relation to its experience earlier.[40] Yet despite this we recognize objects, places, persons, etc., as the *same*, not through some abstract ideality (arising from the temporal aspect of idealization) but as 'concretely individual types'.[41] As opposed to the ideality specific to temporal objects, which is constituted only with the loss of the perceptual present and its retentional and recollective intentional modification, the perceptual 'immediacy' of the concrete type has the sense of spatial co-existence built into it.

To account for this irreducible sense of spatiality, irreducible, that is, to the temporal synthesis through which it is necessarily constituted, requires an essential consideration which, while implicit, has gone unmentioned—that of transcendental intersubjectivity and its foundational, constitutive function.[42]

2. The Problem of the Other qua Co-constituting Transcendental Consciousness: Its Implications for Husserlian Phenomenology as a Whole

In the fifth Cartesian Meditation, Husserl introduces the theme of intersubjectivity by taking up a "grave objection"—one that arises as a consequence of the transcendental reduction. The latter transforms all 'real' or ideal transcendence into its meaning for the experiencing ego, and thus, into the problematic of the constitution of meaning within the sphere of egoic life. Yet, the claim that the question of the objectivity of the world is best approached through the "[...] constitutional problematic and a theory moving within the transcendentally reduced ego [...]"[43] immediately leads to the problem of solipsism. Phenomenology, insofar as it makes claims concerning the status of objective being as a whole, is threatened by its own methodological procedure.

How can the other, as another constituting transcendental ego, be constituted within my intentional life, while still retaining its sense as other? [44] If the purpose of the reduction is to illuminate the transcendental sources of meaning/sense, clearly such a method cannot tolerate the loss of a dimension of the meaning it tries to illuminate. Yet, is there not a loss in the sense of the other qua other, the moment one attempts to explicate it in terms of a constitutional analysis of transcendental consciousness?

To appreciate the paradox that the being-sense of the other

qua subject poses for any constitutive explication within the sphere of 'ownness', we may contrast it with the 'otherness' of objects in the perceptual world. Objects according to their very sense as spatio-temporal objects transcend my immanent conscious life, while being given and constituted within it. However, such intentional transcendence is 'transcendence' in the weak sense, since it involves the mere deferral of experiential givenness.

To be sure, the being–sense of a perceptual object, its very transcendence, lies in the *necessarily* perspectival unfolding in which it is given to consciousness, such that it can never be given "all at once". If it were, it would lose its sense as an object, and the perceptual world itself would lose its *depth* dimension. Yet, despite the impossibility in principle, of the object being experienced *all at once* and the potentially infinite number of possible perspectives that remain over, these perspectives can always be actualized. This impossibility of being given from all sides is the inverse complement of the possibility of the ever further exploration of the object and the perceptual world in general, in potentially inexhaustible perspectival unfoldings and modes of givenness. This constitutes the predominant sense of the unified spatio-temporal horizon. The latter, it seems, is nothing but the potentiality for ideal articulation/ representation.

The same cannot be said of the otherness of a subject. Even in ordinary, pre-analytical perception, the other is never experienced with the sense "for me", but as another constituting subjectivity, with its own life-history, thoughts, etc. The other ego signifies an independent opening on to the world. It occupies a particular perspective, within my 'here and now', through which it experiences the *same* spatio-temporal world that I experience, although with different experiential content owing to its perspective from "over there"; moreover, it experiences me too, as another ego within this world.[45] The alter ego is not 'present' merely as a 'correlate' of my egoic, constitutive consciousness, but as *co-existing* alongside it. Intersubjective coexistence harbours a certain reserve, an absolute *inwardness* that escapes the actual and possible grasp of my consciousness.

However, even as Husserl appears to draw a strict line of demarcation between the intentional constitution of the spatio-temporal world and the experience of the alter ego, he also undermines it. It turns out that the co-existence of the other is intimately connected with the sense of objective space/nature. For, we noted, intentional synthesis considered merely temporally, cannot account for the sense of 'objective' space, as the realm of 'simultaneity' and intersubjectively accesible co-existence. Since 'objective' space is intentionally constituted, and its meaning qua coexistence is built into such intentionality, the conception of intentional consciousness must be revised, to accommodate this sense of absolute alterity. This is the strategy that Husserl adopts in the fifth Meditation.

3. The Relation Between Spatiality and Intersubjectivity

The problem therefore, is how one should understand the relation between spatiality and intersubjectivity. Must the constitution of objective space be traced back to intersubjective constitution as foundational?[46] Husserl seems to imply this: "The existence–sense [Seinssinn] of the world and of nature in particular, as Objective Nature, includes after all, [...] thereness-for-everyone. This is always co-intended whenever we speak of Objective actuality".[47]

However, the relation between objective space and intersubjectivity, and with it, the possibility of intentional constitution, as both immanent to my conscious life, and simultaneously indicating the independent, co-constitutive activity of a multiplicity of egos, is further complicated, if one keeps in mind that the intentionally constituted 'other', is not *necessarily* an existent other encountered in the world.[48] Rather, within the transcendentally reduced sphere, it is a question of *possible* others, and the "thereness for others" that is *co-intended* in any objective experience, is also the possibility of my occupying the "there" as my new "here" and of imaginatively grasping what the object would look like from "there", i.e. from the perspective that a possible other may occupy *now*.[49]

This suggests that the alterity of the other escapes my actual and possible conscious grasp in the same way that the alterity/ co-existence of *place* escapes it. It is true that I can always change my perspective—move from "here" to "there", in the case of spatial perception, in a way that I can never replicate in the experience of the other. I can never literally *have* their thoughts or experiences. Yet, just like the alterity of the other, it is the differentiation of place—the specific 'here and now' and 'there and now' that escapes my synthetic-constitutive activity. Further, my own 'here and now', as the embodied perspectival opening onto the world, remains outside the ambit of possible presence to my (self) consciousness.

Moreover, just as the specificity of *place* is differentiated only insofar as it is apprehended, hence transformed into the oriented 'there', of a possible perspectival experience, similarly, the breach within my experiential field that the *other* represents, must also be somehow experienced by me. Otherwise the alterity of the other would have no meaning for me, since it would be either wholly other, or wholly immanent to my consciousness.

These considerations suffice to indicate the difficulties inherent in any attempt to unambiguously differentiate between the transcendence of nature and of the alter ego. Yet they also hint at the basic coordinates within which Husserl's strategy for addressing the paradox that the experience of the other presents, is going to be charted. If, as Husserl wants to argue, intentional constitution should not be misunderstood as a form of solipsism, where the latter implies the impossibility of any reciprocal relation to the other, then, conversely, the reciprocal relation to the other should not be mistaken for the complete dissolution of ipseity.[50]

The irreducibility of the '*sphere of ownness*' (Eigenheits-sphäre) in relation to the problematic of intersubjectivity (and the 'objective' world) means that Husserl's strategy remains that of intentional analysis of *my* singular egoic life. Yet, the systematic explication of the intentionality in which the other is constituted proceeds via a "*peculiar kind of epoche*"[51] that initially leads, paradoxically, to an "[...] exacerbation of the solipsistic illusion".[52] Husserl proposes that "[...] we disregard all constitutional effects of intentionality relating immediately or mediately to other subjectivity and delimit first of all the total nexus of that actual and potential intentionality in which the ego constitutes within himself a peculiar owness".[53] The argument proceeds via a *reductio ad absurdum* and requires a *novel* epoche—that operates within the perspective of the transcendental epoche while going a step further.

In the transcendental attitude the naive certainty in the existence of the world and the other, is bracketed and treated as phenomena, in order to uncover the intentional processes in which their *sense* is constituted. However, transcendental reduction does not bracket the objectivity of the reduced, phenomenal world; rather intentional analysis shows the irreducible interdependence between the ideal objectivity of the intended sense and intending/constituting subjectivity. "But in the case of our abstraction," Husserl writes, "[...] the sense 'objective', which belongs to everything worldly as constituted intersubjectively [...], *vanishes completely*".[54]

The reduction to ownness, although reminiscent of the Cartesian method of doubt, is motivated not by the desire to secure a foundational principle in the ipseity of the ego, but by the need to explicate the always already constituted *sense of objectivity* as such. Moreover, the sphere of ownness thus revealed is not the pure, disembodied "I", but my *animate organism* and the *corporeal* reflexivity through which "I" am given to myself as a psychophysical unity, situated in, and affected by, the world.[55] This embodied character of thought and reflexivity is crucial to the intentional explication of the alter ego.

It is through the transcendental reduction that I become aware of myself as transcendental constituting ego. However, it is when the transcendental reduction is pushed to its limits in the attempt to isolate a "pure" inwardness that it reveals the impossibility *in principle*, of any immediate encounter with such 'inwardness'. The relation between the transcendental ego and the empirical ego, along with the entire objective-phenomenal world, involves a *"mundanizing self-apperception"* (verweltlichende Selbstapperzeption). "By virtue of this mundanization everything included in this ownness belonging to me transcendentally [...] enters, as something *psychic* into 'my psyche'."[56] As correlate of consciousness, the objective–intentional world is a mode of self-objectification.

On the one hand, the reduction to ownness preserves all the distinctions inherent in *objective* experience through their transformation into phenomena—by allowing us to see them as objective correlates of intentional consciousness, or as self-objectifications of transcendental consciousness. On the other, this very transformation in the modality of experience, points to a deeper differentiation or alterity—one that cannot be represented within the phenomenal realm, as constitutive of the sphere of ownness, hence of objective experience. This *non-phenomenal* ("noumenal") differentiation articulates not only the distinction between 'ownness' and the alter ego, but also the perceptual spatio-temporal world. Thus, the initially sharp contrast implied between spatio-temporal modes of experience, as reflective-constitutive self–experience (in the transcendental attitude), and the experience of the other, must be viewed as provisional—a strategic ploy that frames the *paradox* of the givenness of the other in the context of the problematic of transcendental solipsism.

Husserl suggests this in drawing a parallel between self-apperception and the perception of the external world. The perception of an empirical object unfolds in an "articulated synthetic course" of perspectival intuitions, and the object is never given "all at once". Moreover, the intentional explication of the object in its perceptual unfolding, through which it acquires determinate content is "[...] only generally and horizonally anticipated beforehand [...]".[57] Similarly, in transcendental self-reflection, the ego is discovered "perceptually", through a process of internal explication, whereby the transcendental ego gradually acquires determinate figuration(s), through a mundanization of self-apperception. Further, just as with external perceptual idealities, in self-apperception, "I become aware that, although not grasped before this perception, I was 'already given', already there for myself as an object of original intuition (as 'perceived' in the broader sense)".[58] This *indeterminate* self-awareness is the "[...] open infinite horizon of still undiscovered *internal features of my own*".[59]

The transcendental ego is therefore, a mode of self-awareness qua horizon of possible determination. It is never encountered immediately as a perceptual *object*, but only mediately, in and through its determinate *re-presentations/* figurations, constituted in mundanizing self-apperception. This self-differentiation and mediation, inherent in, and constitutive of, what is *'ownmost'*—my awareness of myself as an identical "I", lies in the (spatio) temporal structure of (self) experience.

> [...] when explicating the horizon of being that is included in my own essence, [...] what I run into is my immanent temporality, and with it, my existence in the form of an open infiniteness, that of a stream of subjective processes, and in the form of all those 'ownnesses', of mine that are somehow included in the stream, one of which is my own explicating. Since it goes on in the living present, self-explication can find, strictly perceptively, only what is going on in the living present. In the most original manner conceivable it uncovers my own past by means of recollections. [...] Thus alone can my stream of subjective processes, the stream in which I live as an identical ego become accessible to me [...] in respect of its actualities and then in respect of the potentialities that manifestly are likewise moments of my own essence.[60]

Two points are worth mentioning here. First, the point of differentiation within ownness, namely, the 'here and now' of the living present, still requires a perceptual element, even if, within the immanent temporal stream the 'living present' is always already past, and merely posited as a differential limit. However, from this differentiating limit, common to external perceptual experience and self-apperception, it does not follow that 'external' perception is reducible to 'internal' perception; rather, both, qua phenomenally mediated, are dependent on the (*"noumenally"*) posited particularity of the 'here and now' for their modes of articulation. Second, the self-apperception founded on this differentiation is constitutive of the "I". Since the identical ego pole is nothing but a mode of continuous self-awareness, it is a continuous process of self-constitution through self-temporalization. The sense of the "I" (whether indeterminate or determinately figured) is continuously constituted in the passive and active syntheses of the just past (through retention) and the distant past (through recollection).

It is thus impossible to isolate a pure 'inside', wholly cut off from any 'outside', and solipsism is ruled out in principle. The very attempt to isolate, through the reduction to ownness, a pure "I", in the immediacy of inner self-experience, brings to light the process of self-objectification and mediation through which I am given to myself. It points to the irreducible 'otherness' at the heart of 'ownness' that is constitutive of my sense of continuous existence and identity over time.

If this continuous self-differentiation constitutive of the 'I' indicates a possible mode in which the otherness of the other may be maintained in and through the manner in which it is given as an intentional constituent of my consciousness, then this still does not tell us *how* the alter ego comes to be so constituted. For, the very possibility of my becoming "[...] aware of someone else, presupposes that *not all my modes of consciousness are modes of my self-consciousness*".[61]

Yet, the insight gained from the analysis of 'ownness' and its self-*transcendence* does not come to nought in the face of the persistence of the problem of otherness. Now Husserl can claim that although the other is encountered within my visual field only as mediated through its body "*over there*", and as such is only a "determining part of myself: an immanent transcendency,"[62] it gets its sense as *animate organism* indirectly, through an *apperceptive analogical transfer* based on my own intrinsic otherness with respect to myself—my situated animate organism (*over here*).

However, if the divide between 'ownness' and 'otherness' is absolute, how is any analogizing apperceptive transfer possible?[63] Explicating this possibility, Husserl first rules out the interpretation of appresentation as inference. Despite the fact that it *indicates*, through what is perceptually present, what is not (and can never be) present, appresentation is not inference, since it is not a "thinking act." Rather, it is a mode of mediation in which the "[...] *primally institutive original is always livingly present*, and the primal instituting itself is therefore always going on in a livingly effective manner [...]".[64] The peculiarity of such analogical apprehension is that although the other is never immediately present to my consciousness, it is somehow apperceived as "livingly present"—as the originally institutive co-presence *'paired'* with my 'Ur-Ich'. This *sense* of co-presence is also a continuous *primal instituting* (Urstiftung) on my part, and essential to the continuous constitution of my own ipseity.

To understand such analogical appresentation and its relation to spatiality, the concept of 'pairing' requires explication. "Originary pairing" (*ursprünglicher Paarung*) is a mode of passive synthesis that is associative, rather than 'identifying'.[65] 'Identification' is primarily a temporal synthesis (although dependent on a 'noumenal' "here"), based on passive retention, and active recollection/recognition; whereas the synthesis of association, as a "continuous primal institution in living actuality"[66], is primarily spatial (although dependent on the noumenal "now"). In associative pairing, two or more data are not only *intuitionally* given, but *simultaneously* intended.[67]

In the analogical appresentation of the other this leads to a "living mutual awakening" (*ein lebendiges, wechselseitiges Sich-wecken*) and a "mutual transfer of sense" (*Sinnesübertragung*).[68] This transfer involves an 'intentional *over reaching*', whereby the other appears with the being-sense—"animate organism *similar* to mine".[69] Intrinsic to this sense of 'similarity', is the possibility of my experiencing my own being 'other' than myself—the capacity to conceive that although I am *now* here, I could have been over there. Yet why is this relation of appresentation, based on associative pairing, not merely a mode of intentional appresentation? "What makes this organism another's, rather than a second organism of my own?"[70]

I am suggesting that Husserl's response invokes the "noumenal" dimension of spatiality—space as a system of co-existent *places* each of which, according to its sense as co-existent, could be my absolute "here". Yet, the simultaneity of my absolute, non-representational *"here"* in relation to any co-present *"there"*, means that I cannot be there *at the same time* as I am *here*.[71] However, since this oriented "there" can be 'freely changed' through my movement, I can always envisage what I would perceive (or what someone else is *now* perceiving), if I were "over there". The absolute difference of place becomes appropriated as *my own* kinaesthetic possibility, leading to the emergence of *ideal* space as a system of kinaesthetic possibilities. This spatial *associative pairing* of the "here" and the "there" both maintains the absolute separation between places, while setting up an appresentation of the "there", in the mode "if I were there", is intimately connected with experience of the otherness of the other.[72]

The manner in which the other retains its own absolute "here", while being given within *my* oriented spatial domain as "there", sheds light on the irreducible and dynamic interrelation between the "noumenal" and the phenomenal. Within the phenomenal domain, insofar as the *absolute* difference of the "here" of the other is transformed (though not without remainder) into the *relative* difference of the (oriented) "there" *for me*, appresentation becomes a mode of *continuous verification*. What is presented "originally", namely, the body of the other, continually points beyond itself to what is not present and can never be made present—its status as an animate organism, with its own primordial sphere, corresponding to its absolute "here". The alterity of the other is given to me as a harmoniously unfolding "horizon of appresentations," with its systematic "non-intuitive anticipations" and possible verifications. The general "style" of these appresentations provides the basis for higher order apperceptive transfers, through which relations of empathy, anger, love, etc.—the analogical association of specific psychic contents, becomes possible.[73] The other, in its embodied, animate character, continually confirms its otherness within my phenomenal experience.[74]

This mediate givenness of the other in the *expressive* character of its body should not be mistaken for a kind of behaviourism. Behaviourism operates within the "inner" and "outer" divide, and privileges the former, since it implicitly takes the realm of "inner" (self) evidence as the criterion for cognition, and thus gives an account of the other only in "outer", behaviouristic terms. However, for Husserl, the expressivity of the body would have no significance for me without my own 'capacity for *self*-alienation'[75]—my capacity to reflectively apperceive my own mediated, appresentational mode of givenness to myself. The process of self-temporalization is at the heart of this non-self-coincidence constitutive of my ipseity, and underlies the analogy between my self-transcendence and the transcendence of the other.

If this process of self-constitution is considered purely in its temporal form, it provides insufficient grounds, not only for the analogical transfer through which the alterity of the other is continuously appresented and established, but also for the constitution of my own 'primordial sphere'. In the former case, as long as the possibility of such appresentation is not clarified in terms of its "noumenal" *spatial* condition—the absolute "here" (or "there"), the chasm between 'ownness' and alterity remains unbridgeable. For, the non-originary presentations within 'ownness'—memorial presentifications, still belong to the "one identical I myself"; to the continuity of my conscious life. They are recognized as *my* past—as what was once originally present to my consciousness. This is why Husserl underscores the "need of a supplement"[76] the inextricable and irreducible condition of (noumenal) "place" which attaches itself to temporal differentiation. Just as it is impossible to conceive the absolute "here" without the "now", it is impossible to conceive the "now" without the "here".

Conclusion

If the 'positivistic restriction of the idea of science' represents the reification of human rationality, and with it, represents 'nature' and human beings as (self) alienated, then Husserl's uncovering of the processive genesis of 'objectivity', in and through the embodied, intersubjective co-constitution of the spatio-temporal horizon, amounts to the recovery of a non-reified, non-alienated source of the sense of objectivity, in the (transcendentally reduced) life-world. This 'source' is nothing but the undecidable movement of reason between the phenomenal and the "noumenal". Such a thematization signifies the recovery of a positive, as opposed to "positivistic" conception of freedom—one which could sustain the irreducible interrelation between autonomy and heteronomy, such that contingency is not understood as the dissolution of meaning but as its very 'condition of possibility'. It thus marks the renewal (*Endstiftung*), in an essentially transformed sense, of the guiding spirit of enlightenment rationality, where reason becomes explicitly aware of its own task as infinite, and takes this awareness as its "apodictic starting point".[77]

NOTES

1. Husserl, 1970. p. 6; *Krisis*, pp. 5-6.
2. Ibid., *Krisis*, p. 6.
3. Ibid. p.8; Krisis p. 8.
4. Cf. Ibid. pp. 7-14; Krisis p. 12ff.
5. On the interrelation between Urstiftung, Nachstiftung and Endstiftung, see *Crisis*, pp. 70-73. Cf. J. Dodd, 2004, pp. 61-72.
6. Husserl, 1973, p. 42, *Erfahrung*, p. 39.
7. Cf. Husserl, 1999, p. 92, *Cartesianische Meditationen*, p. 124.
8. Cf. Ibid. Zahavi indicates this by underscoring the distinction between the 'epoche' and the 'transcendental reduction'. The former is the 'condition of possibility' of the latter (cf. Hua 6/154) insofar as it functions negatively in suspending our naive natural attitude. This prepares the way for the reduction which thematizes the transcendental– constitutive correlation between subjectivity and the world. (cf. Zahavi, 2002, p. 46)
9. Cf. Husserl, 1973, p. 29, *Erfahrung*, p. 23.
10. Ibid., *Erfahrung*, p. 24.
11. Cf. Ibid., p. 32; *Erfahrung*, p. 27.
12. Cf. Ibid., p. 34; *Erfahrung*, p. 29.
13. Cf. Ibid., p. 7, *Ding und Raum*, p. 8.
14. Cf. Husserl, 1981, pp. 222-23, *Grundlegende*, 308-09.
15. Cf. Ibid., p. 223, *Grundlegende*, pp. 310-11.
16. Cf. Ibid., p. 229, *Grundlegende*, p. 321.
17. Ibid., p. 224, *Grundlegende*, p. 311.
18. Cf. Ibid., p. 224-25, *Grundlegende*, p. 312.
19. Cf. Ibid., p. 230, *Grundlegende*, p. 323.
20. Ibid., p. 226, *Grundlegende*, p. 315.
21. Zahavi raises the same problem (Cf. Zahavi, 2002, p. 101). However, despite acknowledging that the body constitutes the "zero point", the "indexical here" of my perceptual experience, he explicates this structural relation between the body qua

transcendental-subjective condition of spatial experience and its objective givenness in space, *primarily* in terms of the distinction between the "unthematic, pre-reflective lived bodily awareness" and "the subsequent thematic experience of the body as an object". Thus, Zahavi does not touch upon the problem of 'noumenal' difference. The latter is hinted at, for example, in Elisabeth Ströker's work, where the "incipient aporia" or "paradoxical structure" of the corporeal constitution of space, which also constitutes itself as a body in space, confronts us as an "[...] ultimate relationship beyond which thought cannot progress". (Cf. Ströker, 1987, pp. 147-48) This relation, I am claiming, points to a differentiation inherent in embodied 'place'. This 'noumenal difference', as the position or opening of the body on to the world, that escapes even my pre-reflective synthesis, and not merely the (secondary/subsequent) objectification of the body in space (cf. Zahavi, 2002, p. 102), is thematized in the problem of intersubjective co-constitution. Zahavi here again primarily emphasizes the relation between intersubjectivity and constituted, i.e. objectified (relativized) space and the body (as an object in space). (cf. Ibid.)

22. For a discussion of the theme of the body, see James Dodd, 1997. For a general discussion of the constitutive interrelation between corporeality and spatiality *see* Elisabeth Ströker, 1987, part one ("Lived Space", pp. 13-172).
23. Cf. Husserl, (Book II) 1998, p. 152.
24. Cf. Dodd, 1997, p. 52.
25. Cf. Ströker, 1987, p. 148.
26. For an analysis, in the context of the Bernau manuscripts, of both the fading (Abklang) or decay of the immediately retained past as well as the coming to fullness of protention, that together constitute the sense of temporal distance, along with its genetic-horizonal implications, *see* Nicholas De Warren (2009, p. 182ff), on 'near and far retention' and near and far protention.
27. Cf. Ibid.
28. Husserl, 1981, p. 240, *Die Welt*, p. 326.
29. Ibid., *Die Welt*, p. 327.
30. The passage reads:

    What is it that makes intelligible the marvellous distinction between 'now' and the 'just past', as well as the eternal drama of the now perpetually generating itself anew and the now perpetually sinking back anew into the past? In turn every past, just like every now is seized by an eternal movement: it constantly sinks back further, and the past becomes a further past, etc. If time thus appears as an eternal stream which precipitates everything temporal into the abyss of the past, yet on the other hand time has validity as an eternal and fixed form, since every being maintains its position in time. Even a god cannot alter the temporal positions of events in the past. (cf. Husserl, 1997, pp. 54-55, *Ding und Raum* p. 64)

Thus, it is the unrepeatability of the instant, its absolute differentiation that paradoxically, is the reason for its progressive lack of differentiation at the level of phenomenal time, as it is retentionally modified and sinks into the obscurity of the more and more distant past.

31. Cf. Husserl, 1981, p. 241, *Die Welt,* pp. 327-328.
32. Cf. Husserl, 1964, pp. 55-57; *Zeitbewusstseins,* p. 80ff, *See also*, De Warren, 2009, pp. 203-206.
33. On the problem of infinite regress inherent in traditional (non-transcendental) theories of reflection, *see* Zahavi, 1999, pp. 14-37. *See also* Nicholas De Warren, 2009, p. 202 ff.
34. Cf. Husserl, 1997, pp. 177-185; *Ding und Raum,* pp. 209-212, cf. Husserl 1981, p. 241, *Die Welt,* p. 327.
35. Cf. Ibid., 179-182; *Ding und Raum,* pp. 212-216, Cf. Ibid., *Die Welt,* p. 327.
36. Cf. Husserl, 1981, p. 241, *Die Welt,* p. 327.
37. Ibid., *Die Welt,* p. 327.
38. This is precisely the reservation that Husserl voices: "And yet we have given no justification for what makes phantoms into real objects, into objects that persist in objectively real alteration and non-alteration, and as such are persistent in themselves" (Ibid., p. 242, cf. pp. 242-43, *Die Welt,* p. 330). There are thus two problems that, while interconnected, must still be distinguished. The first is that of the constitution of objective –phenomenal time in and through the flow of immanent 'subjective' time. Put differently, since "the perception of [objective/ideal] duration itself presupposes duration of perception" (cf. p. 24, *Zeitbewusstseins,* p. 22), and since objective time is phenomenally given only in a temporal object (objects which are not only unities in time but include temporal extension in themselves), the problem is that of explaining the constitution of the ideal unity of specifically temporal objects (thus of objective/'phantom time as such) in the subjective temporal extension of consciousness. The second problem concerns the possibility of constituting the ideal identity of specifically spatial objects—the 'types' that may co-exist within

the spatial field.

39. Husserl, 1981, p. 243, *Die Welt*, p. 331.
40. Cf. Husserl, 1999, pp. 126-127, Cartesianische Meditationen, p. 155.
41. Cf. Husserl, 1981, p. 244.
42. While Husserl had been occupied with the problem of intersubjectivity from as early as 1905, he confronted the question of the link between intersubjectivity and spatiality in the years 1921-28, and the analysis appeared in 1929 in the fifth of the *Cartesian Meditations*. The extended analysis appeared in, *Zur Phenomenologie der Intersubjektivitet* (Vol. II). For a brief outline of the development of Husserl's thought on the problem of intersubjectivity, see Bernet, Kern and Marbach (1993, pp. 154-55).
43. Husserl, 1999 p. 89, *Cartesianische Meditationen*, p. 121.
44. Cf. Ibid., *Cartesianische Meditationen*, p. 121).
45. Cf. Ibid., p. 91, *Cartesianische Meditationen*, p. 123.
46. Zahavi emphasizes this reading. (cf. Zahavi, 2002 p. 115 ff)
47. Husserl, 1999, p. 92, *Cartesianische Meditationen*, p. 124, Cf. *Phänomenologische Psychologie*, p. 344, Cf. *Intersubjectivität II*, p. 289, p. 390, Cf. *Krisis* 469.
48. Cf. Ibid., pp. 92-93, *Cartesianische Meditationen*, p. 124.
49. Cf. Ibid., pp. 116-120, *Cartesianische Meditationen*, p. 146-147.
50. Cf. Dodd, 1997, p. 15; Zahavi, 2002, p. 114.
51. Cf. Husserl, 1999, p. 93, *Cartesianische Meditationen*, p. 124.
52. Cf. Dodd, 1997, p. 17.
53. Husserl, 1999, p. 93, *Cartesianische Meditationen*, pp. 124-125.
54. Ibid., p. 96, *Cartesianische Meditationen*, pp. 127-128.
55. Cf. Ibid. p. 97, *Cartesianische Meditationen*, p. 128.
56. Ibid., p. 100, *Cartesianische Meditationen*, p. 130.
57. Ibid., p. 101, *Cartesianische Meditationen*, p. 132.
58. Ibid., *Cartesianische Meditationen*, p. 132.
59. Ibid., *Cartesianische Meditationen*, p. 132.
60. Ibid., p. 102, *Cartesianische Meditationen*, pp. 132-133.
61. Ibid., p. 105, *Cartesianische Meditationen*, p. 135.
62. Ibid., p. 110, *Cartesianische Meditationen*, p. 140.
63. Cf. Ibid, *Cartesianische Meditationen*, p. 141.
64. Ibid., p. 112, *Cartesianische Meditationen*, pp. 141-142.
65. Cf. Ibid., *Cartesianische Meditationen*, p. 142.
66. Ibid., *Cartesianische Meditationen*, p. 142.
67. Cf. Ibid., p. 113, *Cartesianische Meditationen*, p. 142.
68. Cf. Ibid.
69. Cf. Ibid.

70. Ibid.
71. Cf. Ibid., p. 119, *Cartesianische Meditationen*, p. 148.
72. Ibid., p. 117, *Cartesianische Meditationen*, p. 146; Cf. Bernet, Kern, and Marbach, 1993, pp. 163-64.
73. Cf. Ibid., p. 120, *Cartesianische Meditationen*, p. 149.
74. Cf. Ibid., p. 114, *Cartesianische Meditationen*, p. 144.
75. Cf. Dodd, 1997, p. 29.
76. Cf. Husserl, 1999, p. 116, *Cartesianische Meditationen*, p. 145.
77. Cf. Husserl, 1970, p. 72, cf. *Krisis*, p. 147.

REFERENCES

Husserl, Edmund. 1954. *Die Krisis der Europäischen Wissenschaften und Tranzendentale Phänomenologie: Eine Einleitung in die phänomenologische Philosophie*. Ed. Walter Biemel. Husserliana, Vol. 6. The Hague: Martinus Nijhoff.

———, 1970. The *Crisis of the European Sciences and Transcendental Phenomenology*, Trans. David Carr, Evanston: Northwestern University Press.

Husserl, Edmund. 1938. *Erfahrung und Urteil: Untersuchungen zur Genealogie der Logik*. Ed. L. Landgrebe. Prague: Academia –Verlag; (Hamburg: Classen, 1954).

———, 1973. *Experience and Judgment: Investigations in a Genealogy of Logic*. Trans. James S. Churchill and Karl Ameriks, Ed. Ludwig Landgrebe, Evanston: Northwestern University Press.

Husserl, Edmund. 1960. *Cartesianische Meditationen und Pariser Vorträge*. Ed. Stephen Strasser. Husserliana, Vol. 1. The Hague: Martinus Nijhoff.

———, 1999. *Cartesian Meditations: An Introduction to Phenomenology*, Trans. Dorion Cairns, Dordrecht/Boston/London: Kluwer Academic Publishers.

Husserl, Edmund. 1966. *Zur Phänomenologie des inneren Zeitbewusstseins (1893-1917)*. Ed. Rudolf Boehm. Husserliana, Vol. 10. The Hague: Martinus Nijhoff.

———, 1964. *The Phenomenology of Internal Time Consciousness*, Trans. James S. Churchill, Ed. Martin Heidegger, Bloomington: Indiana University Press.

Husserl, Edmund. 1940. Grundlegende Untersuchungen zum phänomenologischen Ursprung der Räumlichkeit der Natur, in: *Philosophical Essays in Memory of Edmund Husserl*, ed. M. Farber, Cambridge: Harvard University Press.

———, 1981. Foundational Investigations of the Phenomenological Origin of the Spatiality of Nature, in: *Husserl, Shorter Works*, Ed.

Peter Mccormick and Frederick A. Elliston, Indiana: University of Notre Dame Press.

Husserl, Edmund. 1946. Die Welt der lebendigen Gegenwart und die Konstitution der ausserleiblichen Umwelt. Ed: Alfred Schutz, *Philosophy and Phenomenological Research*, Vol. 6, No. 3.

———, 1981. The World of the Living Present and the Constitution of the Surrounding World External to the Organism in: *Shorter Works*, Ed. Peter Mccormick and Frederick A. Elliston, Indiana: University of Notre Dame Press.

Husserl, Edmund. 1907. *Ding und Raum Vorlesungen 1907*. Ed. Ulrich Claesges. Husserliana, Vol. 16. The Hague: Martinus Nijhoff.

———, 1997. *Thing and Space Lectures of 1907*. Trans. and Ed. Richard Rojcewicz, Dordrecht/Boston/London: Kluwer Academic Publishers.

Husserl, Edmund.1973. *Zur Phänomenologie der Intersubjektivität. Texte aus dem Nachlass. Zweiter Teil: 1921-1928*. Ed. Iso Kern. Husserliana, Vol. 14. The Hague: Martinus Nijhoff.

Husserl, Edmund. 1953. *Ideen zu einer reinen Phänomenologie und Phänomenologischen Philosophie*, Vol. 2: *Phänomenologischen Untersuchungen zur Konstitution*, ed. Marly Biemel, Husserliana Vol.4, The Hague: Martinus Nijhoff.

———, 1998. *Ideas Pertaining to a Pure Phenomenology and to a Phenomenological Philosophy: Second Book.* Trans. F. Kersten. Dordrecht/Boston/ London: Kluwer Academic Publishers.

Husserl, Edmund. 1966. *Analysen zur passive Synthesis* (*1918-1926*). Ed. Margot Fleischer, Husserliana Vol. 11. The Hague: Martinus Nijhoff.

———, 2001. *Analyses Concerning Passive and Active Synthesis,* Trans. Anthony J. Steinbock, Kluwer Academic Publishers.

Ströker, Elisabeth. 1987. *Investigations in Philosophy of Space.* Trans. Algis Mickunas. Athens, OH: Ohio University Press

Rudolf Bernet, Iso Kern, and Eduard Marbach. 1993. *An Introduction to Husserlian Phenomenology.* Evanston, IL: Northwestern University Press.

De Warren, Nicholas. 2009. *Husserl and the Promise of Time, Subjectivity in Transcendental Phenomenology,* Cambridge/New York/ Melbourne/Madrid/Cape Town/Singapore/Sao Paulo/Delhi. Cambridge University Press.

Dodd, James. 1997. *Idealism and Corporeity*: *An Essay on the Problem of the Body in Husserl's Phenomenology,* Dordrecht/Boston/London: Kluwer Academic Publishers.

———, 2004. *Crisis and Reflection*: *An Essay on Husserl's Crisis of the*

European Sciences, New York, Dordrecht/Boston/London/Moscow, Kluwer Academic Publishers.

Gurwitsch, Aron. 1977. Outlines of a Theory of Essentially Occasional Expressions. In: *Readings on Edmund Husserl's Logical Investigations*, Ed. J.N. Mohanty, The Hague: Martinus Nijhoff.

Zahavi, Dan. 2002. *Husserl's Phenomenology*. Stanford: Stanford University Press.

———, 1999. *Self-Awareness and Alterity: A Phenomenological Investigation*. Evanston: Northwestern University Press.

———, 2003. Husserl's Intersubjective Transformation of Transcendental Philosophy. in: *The New Husserl: A Critical Reader*, Ed. Donn Welton, Indiana & Bloomington: Indiana University Press.

14

A Heideggerian Approach to Self and Freedom

Wenjing Cai

The purpose of the present paper is to spell out a notion of self that can be found in Heidegger's philosophy. Since contemporary self theorists as well as non-self theorists have more or less reached a consensus that self can hardly be viewed as something substantial in the sense of a Cartesian "res cogitans", the inquiry into the nature of self would then not be one into a particular type of entity called "self" which has its own properties. Rather, in contemporary discussions, the question of self becomes closely related to that of consciousness. The notion of self comes to the fore in the context of discussions regarding the relation of consciousness towards itself. Self is then often formulated in terms of the following questions: What is the structure of self-consciousness? Is there a unified core called self present in the state of consciousness? How is self intimated to itself in an original way? These are questions self theorists are mainly concerned with.

At first glance, it might seem dubitable whether Heidegger's theory can contribute to a theory of self or self-consciousness. He does not very often talk about self, and even less about consciousness. However, how one is related to oneself or how the subject or Dasein understands itself remains a central theme for Heidegger and has a crucial role not only in his analysis of Dasein's mode of existence, but also in his thoughts of being in general. Although Heidegger is never willing to call his idea a theory of consciousness, his view, as we shall see, may nevertheless shed some new lights on the issue of self.

1. "For the Sake of Oneself" (Umwillen seiner selbst)

In the lecture course *Introduction to Philosophy (Einleitung in die Philosophie)*, Heidegger says that the "for the sake of one's own" (Umwillen seiner) constitutes the selfhood of Dasein (GA 27, 324).[1] Though his formulation is somewhat unusual, what the phrase "for the sake of one's own" captures is precisely Dasein's relation to itself, or more precisely, the way self is intimated to itself. In several lecture courses around the same time, Heidegger discusses the mode of givenness of self and remarks that such primordial givenness is by no means in the sense of self-knowledge acquired through inner perception or reflection. As he notes in the lecture course *The Basic Problem of Phenomenology* (*Die Grundprobleme der Phaenomenologie)* in 1927, reflection is not the primary way of self-disclosure; rather the self at stake is "*before* all reflection" (GA 24, 226).[2] By these words Heidegger makes explicit that Dasein's selfhood is a phenomenon distinctive from and more primordial than a reflective self-understanding. The prominent question is then how one's own self is intimated in the mode of "for the sake of one's own".

Though Heidegger denies that reflection as bending back towards an inner and isolated ego can illustrate the primary selfhood or self-relation of Dasein, he nevertheless thinks it possible to apply the term "reflection" in the optical sense, namely, reflection as "to break at something, to radiate back from there, to show itself in a reflection (Widerschein) from something" (GA 24, 226). We say, for example, that the light of the sun is reflected from the moon. But if Dasein's primary self-intimation is a reflection in the sense of "Widerschein", from what then is it reflected or radiated? Things, thus answers Heidegger. It is in the things that Dasein primarily and constantly finds itself (GA 24, 226). In ordinary life, we are passionately absorbed in the world, pursuing things and becoming enchanted or frustrated by them; all these concerns about things "reflect" back our self-concern. Note, however, that according to Heidegger things in everyday life do not show up in the first place as isolated objects present at hand and standing over against us, i.e. in an epistemological relation to us *qua* subjects. We hardly merely look at things, like spectators. Rather, we ourselves are immediately involved when things in everyday life manifest themselves, not as something present at hand but as having its particular role in a teleological whole. For instance, as I notice the room gets dark, I switch on the lamp on my desk. In such comportment, the thing, i.e. the lamp, does not show up as a mere object for observation; rather, switching it on means that I understand it as something that can lighten the room and is good for my writing. The lamp, so to say, is understood in a contextual whole, which in the end points back towards myself as someone who is in need of more light for writing. In other words, the mode of being of the lamp which I turn on with no explicit thought of it reveals or reflects a concern for myself and an understanding of who I am and what I need. This is why Heidegger states that "everyone is what he pursues and cares for." (GA 24, 226)

We have to fend off a possible misunderstanding of Heidegger's thesis that one's self is always involved or revealed in how things are. One may regard Heidegger's view as a form of subjectivism, taking him to argue that we project our own interests onto things and make them reflections of our souls. This is anything but what Heidegger wants to say. His intention is rather to emphasize that the meaning-conferring act taking place in everyday life is first of all an existential or ethical matter rather than epistemological. What things are and how they manifest themselves are related to a contextual whole in which we ourselves as everyday copers are at stake. The lamp, for instance, calls upon me as someone who is busy writing an essay in the dim light to switch it on; the knife shows itself as handy and proper for cutting the meat which I prepare for the whole family. In these everyday contexts, it is not that I, as subject, face an objective thing which carries either theoretical or practical meaning in the first place; rather, the meaning of the thing unfolds in terms of my comportment and in such a way that it has to do with my existential situation or concern.

Heidegger's view is sometimes referred to as supporting the reflexivity thesis of self-consciousness. According to such a thesis, consciousness, which is directed at an object, is necessarily, in addition to its object-directedness, given or present to itself in a pre-reflective manner.[3] Notably, however, there is a significant difference between such a well-accepted thesis on consciousness's self-luminosity and Heidegger's account of Dasein's essential self-understanding. The reflexivity thesis is the view that consciousness has not only a world-directed content but also a formal aspect, namely, its self-givenness. Such a non-reflective self-awareness constitutes the first-person perspective each consciousness is characteristic of. If I am having a chocolate, the taste of the chocolate is not simply given to me, but in a first-person manner so that there is a so-called "what-it-is-likeness". No consciousness can lack such a dimension. Theorists of consciousness thus more or less reach a consensus on the fact that consciousness is self-illuminating, even though they may disagree upon whether the dimension of pre-reflective self-awareness sufficiently amounts to the existence of self. Heidegger's view nevertheless follows a different line of argument and has a distinctive orientation. What he discovers is not a mere formal, content-free aspect of consciousness, namely, its being given first-personally, no matter what the content of this consciousness is. What Heidegger attends to may also be said to be the first-person perspective of experience, but in a different sense from that of the reflexivity thesis; it designates what we might call a *first-person involvement*. For Heidegger, a third person perspective reduces Dasein to a mere spectator and things to objects, the meanings of which are neutral to the former; whereas a first person involvement pertaining to Dasein's experience entails that a thing is not merely given to me, but is given *in light of* my present concern, my practical identity, etc. To this extent, my experience is first-personal not only because I am the one who experiences whatever is in front of me but also for the reason that the things are given *as such and such* for the sake of myself. The meaning of the things are intrinsically mediated by my self-concern.

Henceforth, Heidegger reveals a more intimate relation between selfhood and worldly things that manifest themselves in one's experience. Self-understanding becomes not merely a necessary and formal dimension accompanying all object-consciousness, but rather is *one* with the thing's revelation. In other words, an understanding of oneself amounts to an understanding of the thing or letting the thing that one deals with be; they are so to say "Widerschein" to each other or two sides of the same phenomenon. What now requires a further explanation is through what the two aspects, i.e. self-understanding and world-understanding, are united, or what it means to let things be in one's self-understanding qua "for the sake of oneself".

2. Self-Understanding as Beholdenness to Things

For Heidegger, selfhood is something that is peculiar to us as human beings. In the lecture course *Basic Concepts of Metaphysics (Die Grundbegriffe der Metaphysik)*, Heidegger claims that only human beings have a world and henceforth have the character of being a self (GA 29/30, 398).[4] It thus becomes clear that for Heidegger world and self are concepts closely related to each other and cannot be viewed separately. In other words, those who have a world necessarily present themselves as "selves", and conversely, those who are "selves" must be world-forming creatures. More precisely, as was already mentioned, on Heidegger's account, the openness of a world is not merely something beside but one with the disclosure of a self as self-understanding and caring for one's own sake. How can we understand such "oneness" between self-disclosure and world-openness? An answer to this question can also shed significant light on what self and world mean for Heidegger.

At this moment, we have to particularly take notice of an aspect of Heidegger's thought, which is called by some interpreters "normative pragmatism".[5] The notion does not refer to a type of pragmatism that gives priority to practical effects, but points precisely to the fact that for Heidegger our primordial relation to the world is existential and ethical, constituted by praxis that is normatively constrained. This becomes even clearer as we attend to Heidegger's definition of our "basic comportment" (Grundverhalten) as "letting oneself be bound" (Sich-bindenlassend).

It is at the very end of the 1929/30 lecture course *Basic Concepts of Metaphysics* that Heidegger turns to such a definition of human being's basic comportment (Grundverhalten). In the second half of this lecture, Heidegger compares a human being's mode of existence with an animal's life form and concludes that they are in essence different. Whereas the life of an animal is characterized by "captivation" (Benommenheit) and "being taken" or driven (Hingenommenheit) by instincts, the mode of a human being lies in a fundamentally distinctive comportment (Verhalten)—a term Heidegger reserves only for human beings—that immediately opens a world. This openness of a world, as Heidegger formulates, means "from the very outset a free holding oneself towards whatever beings are given there in letting oneself be bound" (von Hause aus das sich-bindenlassende freie Sich-entgegenhalten zu dem, was da als Seiende gegeben ist, GA 29/30, 496). *Prima facie* Heidegger's formulation is unintelligible, since it involves two moments that seem to contradict each other, namely, the moment of letting oneself be bound and that of freedom. What does it mean to let oneself be bound? And in what way can it still be conceived of as a "free" comportment?

First of all, what is binding for us? Or to borrow a term from John Haugland, what is it that one is "beholden to" in a primordial way?[6] According to Heidegger, it is the thing as it is that binds us in terms of obligation (Verbindlichkeit). In other words, things obligate us. In what sense can a thing be said to have a binding force when we encounter it? To be sure, this obligatory force need not be of a moral type, such as the force a moral law exerts upon us. Yet, as was explicated before, a thing binds me to the extent that it has an immediate normative appeal to me; it calls upon me to treat it, i.e. to let it be in a way that accords with a contextual whole in which I am at stake. For instance, when in the class I want to explain something to the students in a clearer way, I grasp a chalk on the lectern and make a few notes on the blackboard. In this situation, the chalk and the blackboard do not show up as isolated objects in the first place; I do not take notice of their properties such as shape, colour or texture. Instead, the chalk instantly requests or invites me to use it to draw something on the blackboard, for the sake of giving a better explanation to the students, which I am responsible for. To speak in another way, the chalk manifests itself in such a way that it involves me in no time with a binding force and summons me to treat it in an appropriate way so that I can fulfil my role as a teacher.

My self-understanding thus lies in the fact that I let things be in being obligated by them. For Heidegger, being bound by the obligation, my understanding of the thing as it is and the openness of a world are basically one and the same thing. On this account, my primary relation to a worldly thing as well as to a fellow human being is far from that of a knowing subject facing an object, for in that case, a relation of obligation would be impossible and I am more like a ghost hovering in this world; rather, as was already pointed out, comportment with self-understanding necessarily entails a first-person involvement which enables me to act in response to normative appeals.

3. Self-Legislation and Freedom

However, what Heidegger claims is not merely that things bind us, but more precisely that we let ourselves be bound (Sich-bindenlassen). The binding force of the thing comes from nowhere else other than from ourselves. How could this be possible? In the lecture course *On the Essence of Human Freedom (Von Wesen der menschlichen Freiheit)* in 1930, Heidegger says the following:

> Basically the manifestness of beings in the binding character of their so- and that-being, is only possible where the comportment to beings, whether in theoretical or practical knowledge, already acknowledges this binding character. But the latter amounts to an originary self-binding, or, in *Kantian* terms, *the giving of a law to oneself*. (GA 31, 303; my italics)[7]

Here Heidegger claims that the primary "letting oneself be bound" can be understood as "giving oneself a law" or self-legislation in the Kantian sense. This is by no means an improvisation, for the second half of Heidegger's lecture is precisely devoted to a critical analysis of Kantian ethics. Although he criticizes Kant's understanding of freedom and the metaphysical preconception behind it, he nevertheless sees in the Kantian ethics something of a radical nature. In his view, Kant has pushed the traditional ideas of freedom and being to the very limit, and to a certain extent, Heidegger's lecture can be seen to be a reformulation of his own idea in the Kantian terms. Similarly, in the earlier lecture course *The Basic Problem of Phenomenology from 1927*, Heidegger expounds on Kant's notion of *personalitas moralis* and in his view Kant presents a notion of moral self-consciousness that is essential to our existence; it characterizes the fundamental self-relation of a human being. Notably, for Heidegger, the term "moral" is understood in a special sense; as he says, to understand oneself "morally" means to see oneself "as an acting being" (als handelndes Wesen; GA 24, 186); that is to say, the moral self-relation at stake is related to our essence of being persons that act or comport.

The moment of letting ourselves be bound or being self-legislative in coping with things and others refers to the moral self-consciousness Heidegger addresses. However, such a self-relation should not be understood as a second-order, reflective one; rather, as both Kant and Heidegger stress, it is an immediate "feeling" (Gefuehl) of respect (Achtung) for the law that grounds our everyday comportments. As Heidegger clarifies, the feeling here at stake is not "the one we customarily have in mind in our everyday understanding—feeling, contrasted with conceptually theoretical apprehension and self-knowledge, as indefinite, vague, a momentary presentation and the like." (GA 24, 187) That is to say, the respect or self-legislation is not an emotional state one gets into occasionally, only when one is faced with a moral decision; rather, by the term "feeling", Heidegger as well as Kant attempts to articulate a particular mode of self-consciousness or what Heidegger calls "self-feeling" (Sichfuehlen), in which one's self is immediately disclosed or understood as oneself in its willing to be bound. As long as one copes with things or others, the moral self-understanding sways in our life to the extent that one respectfully submits oneself to a law or consents to rules and norms. In such a respect that characterizes our comportments, we are not compelled by any external forces or mere inclinations to follow the norms; it is rather we ourselves that choose or will to be obligated by things, that is, to let them show up in light of certain norms, for these norms at stake concern ourselves, our own existential situation, practical identity, etc. In the previously discussed example, I will or choose to switch on the lamp for the reason that it can bring more light and again this is for the sake that I can finish a manuscript of a lecture that I have to present to my colleagues the following morning. The being of the lamp is inevitably loaded with normative significance, or in other words, it becomes what it is in a normative context, as something good for lightening the room and ultimately good for my writing. To cope with it in such a normative way is not something forced upon me, or driven by any instincts; rather, I choose to let the lamp bind me, i.e. to be responsive to its solicitation and do what I should or had better do.

However, it requires further explanation what it means to say that one wills to be bound in the self-related respect. As Heidegger makes explicit, the will here at stake is not an act of will that is parallel to other types of acts such as judgment, wish, etc. (GA 9, 163)[8] In the everyday context, one has neither an explicit idea of being bound by certain norms nor that of deliberately choosing to be bound. One simply lets the thing be in coping with it in a pre-reflective way. Heidegger calls this immediate involvement with things or "transcendence to the world" (GA 9, 163) freedom in the primordial sense, that is, freedom that goes ahead of any free wills in the cases of decision-making. It is a form of freedom that is destined to human beings in the sense of letting oneself be bound by things for the sake of one's own. Only we human beings who are intrinsically morally self-conscious can be free or not free. For creatures like us, to will freely is not to do whatever one's desire demands, but to respectfully consent to a law or norm in the first place; to will to be bound is to say that I am not forced but have a reason for what I am doing under the guidance of norms. Ultimately the primordial freedom denotes the fact that one always comports to things and others for a reason or for the sake of something, a reason that one can well express if being asked. Why do you turn on the light? Because the room is too dark and I cannot see clearly what is in the books. In those cases when a reason seems to be absent or one cannot exactly articulate it, one may always say "I just feel like doing it; I don't know why."[9] However, this does not mean that the person is not free in his/her action or he/she does the thing for no reason at all; rather, the answer he/she gives is one that indicates the relevance of norms; it is, so to say, still a normative response that only we human beings can provide. Accordingly, freedom of self-legislation entails that we as conscious, rational beings are responsive to normative questions and responsible for what we do. This responsiveness is not something that merely comes into view afterwards, but has its origin in our basic, pre-reflective comportment characterized by the primordial freedom of self-legislation. Thus any proper interpretation of the basic structure of our experience must take into account this peculiar aspect that our pre-reflective experience is so structured as to be responsive to normative questions due to our fundamental freedom.

On the one hand, the phenomenon of letting oneself be bound, or simply, of self-legislation is for Heidegger one with the phenomenon of the world's openness. The world, as Heidegger phrases, is not the sum total of the inner-worldly things, animals, human beings, etc; it is rather "a structural moment of the mode of being of Dasein" (GA 24, 237), and as human beings, we always already understand the world. Only on the grounds of such initial understanding can inner-worldly things and fellow human beings manifest themselves, not in an objective manner, but with their binding characters. Things come into being as I comport to them; or more precisely speaking, as Haugland puts, I "find" them, "showing that they make sense in some determinate way, and can consistently be told and otherwise coped with as such" (Haugland 1998, 329). On the other hand, for Heidegger, in the primordial freedom also bears the facticity of one's self; that is to say, in freely letting oneself be bound or comporting to things normatively, one also comes to be oneself as a person who cares for his own sake. In other words, self is acknowledged by Heidegger as this mode of existence of human Dasein that freely comports to things and others and hence opens a world. Freedom, world and self are indeed phenomena interconnected to each other.

Finally I want to make a few remarks on what Heidegger's view can contribute to a contemporary discussion on self. It can be seen that, for Heidegger, it is out of the question whether self exists or not, for self is defined by him as the peculiar mode of being of human Dasein and its facticity is not proved in any existent entity but indicated by our praxis or comportment. According to Heidegger, self-intimation is not merely a matter of consciousness's self-reflexivity (somehow one is aware of one's own perception), but rather that of how such self-awareness can be understood in its oneness with the openness of the world. More precisely speaking, Heidegger is particularly concerned with how one's self is united with the manifestation of what one perceives or copes with in terms of the primordial freedom of committing oneself to norms. Without conceiving of our experience as fundamentally existential and normative, one cannot make such unity or oneness intelligible. That the world constitutes itself normatively through my self-concern is for Heidegger already an indication of our selfhood, and my respect of the norms that obligate me in my encountering with things is at the same time a respect of myself as myself (GA 24, 191). On this account, the first-person perspective of our experience becomes a more concrete and real one here. It has to do not merely with an implicit awareness of what and how I experience (which is still understood in an epistemological framework), but with how the world can come into being at the very beginning in one's primordial freedom. The world is not merely given as an image, nor just teleologically; it rather manifests itself through myself as a free, ethical person, as someone who wills to commit to certain norms and takes responsibility for oneself. Thus, one can see that Heidegger's notion of self is a somewhat thick one; that is to say, it is a notion intrinsically embracing the notions of world, freedom as well as others in it. For Heidegger, none of these notions can be viewed separately, as an independent part or layer of our existence. To ask what self is would be to inquire into the peculiar mode of human existence, and this for Heidegger is something *sui generis* and its concreteness cannot be reduced.

NOTES AND REFERENCES

1. Heidegger's collected work (Gesamtausgabe) is referred to GA here. Heidegger, M., GA 27: *Einleitung in die Philosophie.* Frankfurt am Main: Vittorio Klostermann, 1996.
2. Heidegger, M., GA 24: *Die Grundprobleme der Ph□nomenologie (Summer semester 1927).* Frankfurt am Main: Vittorio Klostermann, 1975.
3. Many contemporary scholars such as Dan Zahavi and Shaun Gallagher find in the texts of traditional phenomenologists (Husserl, Heidegger, Sartre, Merleau-Ponty) such a thesis of pre-reflective self-awareness.
4. Heidegger, M., GA 29/30: *Die Grundbegriffe der Metaphysik. Welt - Endlichkeit—Einsamkeit (Winter semester 1929/30).* Frankfurt am Main: Vittorio Klostermann, 1983.
5. See, for instance, Brandom, R.B., "Dasein, the Being that Thematizes", in *Tales of the Mighty Dead*, pp. 324-347, Harvard University Press, 2002.
6. Haugland, J., "Truth and Rule-Following", in *Having Thought*, pp. 305-362, Havard University Press, 1998.
7. "Offenbarkeit von Seiendem in der Verbindlichkeit seines So- und Da seins, wird nur möglich, wo das Verhalten zu Seiendem als solchem den Grundzug hat, da es dem, was möglicherweise, ob in theoretischer oder praktischer Erkenntnis, oder sonstwie offenbar wird, im vorhinein Verbinlichkeit zugesteht. Vorg□ngiges Zugestehen von Verbindlichkeit aber ist ursprḷngliches Sichbinden, Bindung als fḷr sich verbindlich sein lassen, d.h. kantisch, sich ein Gesetz geben." Heidegger, M., GA 31: *Von Wesen der menschlichen Freiheit.* Frankfurt am Main: Vittorio Klostermann, 1982.
8. Heidegger, M., GA 9: *Wegmarken*. Frankfurt am Main: Vittorio Klostermann, 1976.
9. Only we human beings can understand a question which demands a reason and find out in certain circumstances that such a reason cannot be offered; this dimension is essentially closed to other animals.

15

The Chain of Freedom: Moral Autonomy with Cosmopolitan Intent

Hans Feger

In man "is the deepest abyss and the highest heaven"
(Schelling, *Philosophical Investigations*, 1809)

According to Kant, in order to resolve the dispute in metaphysics, a position that excludes one's own partiality is required. In a letter to Herder,[1] he writes that a "deep indifference towards my opinion or that of others" characterizes his attitude as a critical philosopher, because it is not truth that causes conflict between people, but rather their mutual falsity. This existential lack of security, which breaks out when experience and tradition no longer provide orientation and only the "*conflict* of reason with itself"[2] remains, is for Kant not only his personal point of departure, but also the methodological one for his critical philosophy as a whole.[3] Reason authorizes itself to go to court or arbitration when it first sees indifference, powerlessness, and agony not as weaknesses or "despair",[4] but rather as a point of view from which it can support valid claims, dismiss unfounded presumptions, and eventually steer reason along the "secure path of a science"[5] with impartial and disinterested indifference.

This method of resolving conflict which characterizes the position of the critical philosopher is extremely modern.[6] It is certainly not a "polemic method"[7] in the sense of a *negative* critique that uses the "language of protest" to articulate the passionate "outrage over wrongness" (Adorno), as in the worthy tradition of the Frankfurt School; nor is it a "dogmatic method" in the sense of an *affirmative* critique that defends the pluralism of opinions and positions as its greatest asset and cultivates traditions. It is neither prosecutor nor defender; rather, it officiates as a judge who, between apologia and incrimination, "lets the arguments of reason speak out against one another in total freedom" (*KdrV* B 535) and—in a sceptical manner—dissociates itself from both of them.[8] However, this position only really becomes the *critical* method in the sense of a *judicial* critique when it matures into reflexive self-critique—when it applies its own standards to the critic's position as well—and consequently does not seek the basis of the decision within the limits of a particular dispute but outside of them: in impartiality.[9] In philosophy, judicial critique is *critical transcendental philosophy*: it takes a step back to the *conditions for the possibility* of the dispute in order to settle it. Kant maintains that it is by using this transcendental process of arbitration that the dissent between fundamentally opposed positions becomes methodologically available at all.

This methodological preliminary remark is necessary (especially in a country which has a completely different legal tradition) in order to structure my thesis: that it is Kant's basic insight into the essence of human freedom (and generally into the essence of human reason as well) that its proper application also includes its thorough misuse, and that only Kant's transcendental legal process of critical ethics protects against this natural misuse of human freedom. Questions concerning the proper use of freedom—how does freedom position itself in the individual ethics of each person when he/she wants to act morally? how does it position the community in legal ethics when it merges in a liberal state through the peacemaking function of the law? or how does the community of states position itself in international law when, with cosmopolitan intent, freedom devotes itself to a utopian peace mission?—These are always questions concerning the concept of freedom which has emerged from a critical process of arbitration. And it is through this critical process of arbitration that something becomes apparent that by deliberately modifying the expression 'chain of being'[10] (the ancient belief in an immutable order in creation) —which I want to call the 'chain of freedom' (the modern belief in an immutable order in self-creation): is always part of the process which it wants to see emerging. The discourse on freedom that Kant unfolds in his writings on the history of philosophy, especially in his essay *Idea for a Universal History with Cosmopolitan Intent* (1784), is a constitutive component of the moral perspective whose key concept is the notion of freedom. This is why critical philosophy, as Kant says, has its own "chiliastic expectation",[11] and the critical philosopher is a prophet who himself "occasions and *produces* the events he predicts"[12]. However, in this paper, I not only want to present the optimistic side of this moral image of history, which should also convey the historical process of freedom itself,[13] but I also want to point out where this process is endangered. I want to examine the predictions that Kant links to his concept of freedom from three points of view. These predictions are:

1. Freedom, as Kant understands it, has the inherent tendency in its law-governed form to become universal with a *cosmopolitan intent*. The categorical imperative, as a *law of self-preservation of freedom*, is just such a law-governed form.
2. In this process of universalization, freedom extends *in stages* from the moral to the legal form, and to the political constitution, whereby one link in the chain is so interlocked with the other that a reversal destabilizes the whole process.
3. This gradational process rejoins its origin—just like a chain—in that the highest form of the political organization of freedom, the global legal system, also has repercussions on the rights of individuals.

1. The Law of Self-Preservation of Freedom

To be confronted with the abyss of freedom—with the burden of responsibility—is certainly not, as false pathos often suggests, an act of liberation from obligations nor a license 'to do as you please'; rather, it is a confrontation with the enigmatic side of modern subjectivity. Not just Kant's definition of transcendental freedom as the "self-creation" of the actor, but also his interpretation of the French Revolution as a "moral tendency of the human race"[14] clearly reveals the inner instability of human freedom. No cause antedates it, no choice precedes it; even the motivation that would be empirically or psychologically evoked, such as the will to preserve oneself, would not do justice to its absolute essence. Kant's concept of freedom that is linked to the idea of autonomy is based on a timeless, *transcendental act*. In Kant's view, an action is only free as a specific kind of causality: namely, as a spontaneous, timeless causality born out of freedom. This already reveals what critics of this concept of freedom have always objected to: namely, that Kant does not provide any theoretical proof of a transcendental freedom, since only something that is itself unrecognizable can serve him as a justifiable ground. Nevertheless, on the other hand, it is precisely this lack of provability that also constitutes the strength and the incontestability of the Kantian concept of freedom. It releases Kant 1. from the metaphysical burden of proof, but without thereby discrediting freedom or *absolute* spontaneity as a metaphysical category.[15] 2. It remains intact as a *conditio sine qua non*, since without the foundation of an absolute spontaneity, a moral law could never be obligatory for the individual,[16] and moral phenomena such as conscience, remorse, and responsibility for one's own actions would be inexplicable; and finally, 3. It is the core of the peaceable evocation of the third antimony (*KdrV* B 560-586) which produces the proof that such an absolute spontaneity can mutually exist with natural causality consistently and that, in principle, it does not have to cancel itself out. Only as a *free* being can the human being transcend himself as a natural being.

Precisely this idea of an absolute and hence unprovable, purely theoretically validated and substantiated capacity for self-creation also implicates that it still has to be integrated into a second thesis; namely, that this capacity for self-creation must once again obey its own imperative. Human freedom is not inherently effective; rather, it is effective as a self-determined and therefore self-preserving freedom in the performance of *actions*. The individual's freedom is not a lawless freedom that more or less acts on its own initiative; as an absolute capacity for self-creation, it still requires a law-governed link to its effect in order to become evident.

The categorical imperative presents such a link. Despite a prevalent misunderstanding, this is *not* a behavioural guideline which wants to express human insight into the reciprocity of sensible ways of behaving, but rather a condition that must be fulfilled in order to enable one to act morally at all. It is not to be understood in a logically consistent way[17] as a *general precept* of moral behaviour that one applies in certain cases (as it is often misunderstood in the Anglo-Saxon tradition[18]); rather, it is a law of *self-preservation of freedom* that must be fulfilled if one wants to act morally—regardless of how one does this.

Kant first explicated this second thesis with great clarity in the *Critique of Practical Reason*, which makes a clean break with the material metaphysical premisses of the concept of freedom in his early writings.[19] Since freedom—as moral law's ground of deduction—is an "unfathomable capacity", as he now calls it, consciousness of moral law itself becomes a "fact".[20] Therefore, as there is no ostensive proof, the argumentation is deployed indirectly: without the precondition that we are free, we are totally unable to be conscious of a moral law that places an *absolute* obligation on our will. The fact *that* we actually regard ourselves as free is thus indispensably tied to consciousness of the absolute obligation of moral law and is primarily mediated through this.

However, what is decisive about this justification, that is arrived at by reversing the deductive sequence and that now retrogresses from the *ratio cognoscendi* to the *ratio essendi*, is not that we thereby simply understand a precondition that would otherwise have remained unknown to us; it is rather that when we fulfil the demands of the moral imperative with its absolute obligation, only then do we first open up the inner possibility of this transcendental freedom. Only a will that is "driven to act"[21] by the moral maxim can be understood as a will through which the source of freedom *does not run dry*. This is certainly not a process of deprivation that concerns the self-determination of the acting individual alone. Indeed, Kant's entire political concept of freedom also takes this idea of moral self-determination as its starting point in such a way that one has to say that through Kant's moral imperative, one can study that which moral laws, norms or universals, as well as legal principles and strategies of political justice, must always refer back to if they are to be understood as the expression of a human will that is free. The modernity of Kant's categorical imperative consists precisely in raising questions about the intelligible core of moral codes, laws and norms, that may possibly have their source in a concealed repressive doctrine, and thus to protect against misuse. As a result of this inquiry, Kant did not expect morals to improve, but rather a moral culture to develop that leads to a law-governed peace.

If one interprets the categorical imperative as a law of self-preservation of freedom—indeed, as a security measure against the self-endangerment of human freedom and the instability of modern autonomy—then one also gains access to a problematic that Kant first revealed in detail in his later work, *Religion Within the Limits of Reason Alone* (1793). This is because the legality with which reason orders the will to link the cause and effect of freedom can also be corrupted, in fact, in such a radical sense that the legality is deliberately inverted. Kant called this disturbance in the relationship of the will with itself when it results in the inversion of the law of freedom—radical evil. The perversion of freedom is thus itself an act of freedom. Kant called it *radical* evil not because evil would be completely or totally evil, but because it has its roots (lat. radix) in what is "the persistent condition for the only value which people can give themselves"[22]—freedom. Evil, just like goodness, testifies to human autonomy and takes root in the freedom that is the prerequisite for every single action. It does not have its source in every single natural tendency that would be morally reprehensible; rather, it originates in the fundamental inclination to put natural tendencies generally in the place of moral laws and to make them into the most authoritative ground for determining action. Thus, it does not just deviate from moral law, but it deliberately contradicts moral law, whose maxims it inverts. Interpreted in this manner, evil is not an infirmity, a deficiency, or dishonesty that could be made good through reform, remorse, or penance.[23] Radical evil is not "to be sought in tendencies but in the inverted maxim and thus in freedom itself"[24]. Schelling, who metaphysically reformulates this Kantian idea of radical evil, writes in his *Freiheitsschrift* (1809): "It is in evil—the self-consuming and always self-destructive contradiction—that it aspires to become natural, precisely by destroying the bond of naturalness, and because of its high-spirited aspiration to be everything, it falls into non-existence."[25]

The evil that must also destroy itself again in the very act of its creation is therefore not the evil that is avenged by inflicting evil—as in paying someone back in their own coin according to the old principle of *lex talionis*. It depicts a contradiction that causes the source of freedom to run dry. In morally judging an evil deed, one does not therefore need to produce evidence "that it would necessarily harm others; as lawyers stipulate by definition (...). Because it harms others all the time, if not exactly another person, but rather humanity in general, by making the source of justice unusable."[26] This evil is always already gradually at work if the will contradicts itself in its absolute relation to itself; for example, if an instrumental, pragmatic or egotistic way of dealing with oneself or other people displaces free self-determination. The depersonalization of ethics is not a perversion of freedom just because it makes a thing out of a person, but because it corrupts, spoils, indeed it can eventually even invert the relationship of the will to itself as self-legislation. The categorical imperative, however, has its telos in human freedom and not in the organization of necessities.

2. The Universalization of Freedom

If one interprets the categorical imperative as a law of freedom that prohibits freedom from contradicting itself and thus—as in the case of evil—from destroying itself too, then one gains access to the legal and political dimension of the law of freedom. Even the imputability of an act, and hence of the legal capacity as well, is only established in the freedom of the act. Without this imputability, a person performing an "act" could never be "considered as the initiator of the effect."[27] Legally, when neither the will nor the maxims that evoke an act, but the action alone is considered[28], the self-determined will has to justify itself to a collective will. The law as "the epitome of the conditions under which a person's will can be united with that of others in accordance with a general law of freedom"[29] admittedly only judges "external (legal) freedom"[30] (which is also why innocence is always presumed in case of doubt[31]). But in doing so, it also always refers back to the free self-determination of the individual. For it is only on this basis that legal principles can be desired and do not just have to be followed blindly. Hence, the coercion that the law is permitted to use is also just "a *hindrance* to a *hindrance of freedom*" and therefore "will thus be consonant with freedom in accordance with universal laws."[32]

As long as the authority of the law to coerce (Kant: "the authority to use coercions"[33]) only prosecutes claims that people bring against each other, its legitimacy is guaranteed. Thus, the legitimation of coercion is at the same time a limitation of coercion.[34] As in the case of the categorical imperative, the criterion for a legal system that can also be desired—i.e. harmonizes with the freedom of the will—is whether the generalizing self-questioning of the (sovereign) legislator, in all his decision-making, conceives of himself as an end in itself. However, this reduces his legitimacy as a ruler, for during the course of this self-questioning he is no longer acting on his own authority (in the sense of the *potestas legibus soluta* to which Carl Schmidt still refers); rather, he is acting on the basis of a sovereignty that consists in precisely *renouncing absolute power.*

Still, what about imputability in politics, which is nevertheless target-oriented by preference? Kant promptly reduces politics to an "exercising of jurisprudence" and anchors it in this. The political calculation of purely instrumental politics orients itself exclusively to consequences, such as the "physical advantage" of the "expected welfare and happiness" of the state, or just orients itself to a "moral advantage" contravenes the "absolute concept of the responsibility of the law".[35] Above all else, the true politician must be conscious of the legality of his actions. But because he must also orient himself to political targets that are subject to calculation, a double role must be demanded of him—to be as cunning as a snake but with the constraining moral condition "without falsity, like a dove".[36] A political regime can therefore only be established by someone who takes responsibility for its limits, who therefore guarantees what it does *not* decree – which is why "true politics", just like the law, "cannot take a step without having paid tribute to ethics beforehand".[37] And although Kant is anything but a moral preacher, he categorically warns: "Woe betide him who accepts policies that do not regard the laws of justice as sacred".[38] The conflict between ethics and politics that is pre-programmed here can only be resolved through the constant updating of positive law, because this alone is the inalienable initial condition for a legal practice that progressively evolves towards increasing humanitarianism. Here too, yet another link in the chain dovetails into the next one: politics refers to the law and this refers back to ethics; all the links are so interconnected with ethics that they simply can not be separated from it without having to renounce themselves.

The development from a primitive to a modern, tolerant society that is able to opt out of the principle of revenge and retribution is consequently not a question of legal empiricism either. The "pragmatist" for whom "ethics is pure theory"[39]—who assumes a separation between law and ethics—is for Kant "like the wooden head in Phaedrus' fable, [which] may have a fine appearance, but will unfortunately contain no brain!"[40] The conquest of the moral natural state is not a question of improving ethics or of moral correctness. Instead of conquering the moral natural state, a moral calculation would only strengthen it, indeed, promote a *depersonalization of ethics*, just as it is accompanied nowadays by an *elimination of ethics from the law*. The "good principle's state of constant battle that resides in every human being through evil"[41] can only be conquered by a community which does not enforce the law, but rather acknowledges the laws of virtue, free of all coercion. A legislation that follows a normative rule or a behavioural code is never able to internally promote the moral legislation of ethics.[42]

And so, it is not an ever increasing quantity of morality in its attitude,[43] but an "increasing number of actions governed by duty, whatever the particular motive behind these actions may be. In other words, the profit will result from man's good *deeds* as they grow ever more numerous and successful, i.e. from the external phenomena of man's moral nature."[44] The ethics of both political and legal structures are in principle of the same kind as those to which individuals orient themselves.[45] They are "the epitome of the conditions under which a person's will can be united with that of others in compliance with a general law of freedom,"[46] thus, they obtain their authority from moral law.

One could object here that it is demanding too much of a moral principle, as it ought to be pursued in legal and political freedom, to be the only source of legitimation. Norms that have been handed down, i.e. religious or collectively binding norms, must come to join it. But precisely in this instance, Kant's governmental philosophy is wonderfully clear. The relevance of the liberal, constitutional state[47] with respect to state power does not consist in subduing these, but in *constituting* them. Here, the law takes on the role of political power. This positive law knows no subjects over whom it rules, nor a political sovereign. Neither can its claim to legitimacy be derived from religious, traditional or patriotic roots (nor from what is American or not). Rather, it obtains its source of legitimation from *the only thing that can relate to itself*: the autonomous subject. In turn, each and every subject is all that representatives of religious or traditional doctrines may coerce into reflecting upon their own respective limits. To argue that the legal system cannot ultimately legitimize its own claims to legitimacy, because it originates in the democratic legal process, scales down the problematic and does not retrace legitimacy back to legality.[48] Then, the autonomous citizen is only squeezed into the role of an election assistant, but not taken seriously in terms of his freedom.

A further objection concerns the insecurity of whether compliance with the moral principle actually brings with it enough motivations for it to become anchored both legally and politically. The problem is that the motivation for *respect for the law* can only be derived from the awareness of the validity inherent in the law alone. Therefore, Kant regards it as extremely necessary to insert the motivational function of the idea of a moral image into his philosophy of history.[49] This legitimizes itself by teaching the interests of the individual to stop egoistically exploiting and to become oriented towards the common good. Other motives, as they are traditionally mediated by religion (that the republican ethos wants to reactivate today), are to be rejected by the secular constitutional state and be replaced by images of history and historical utopias that portray a moral progress of history. Such utopias differ from religious or ideological models precisely in that the individual can respond to them with moral designs for living and a cultural commitment instead of just obeying and adapting to them. The foundations of democracy are also based on this distinction. For only the constitutional state that not only grants its citizens negative rights—in the bad sense of tacit permission—but also wants their active participation in public life and encourages it, thus proves to be a democratic one.

Only the chain of freedom that links together a *democratic* process in which civil rights are *actively* exercised leads to a solidarity whose obligation is also desired and which does not just exhaust itself in patriotic lip-service. On the other hand, *imposed* solidarity is *enforced* democracy which leads to neither socialization, nor legal responsibility, nor to a political culture that knows how to appreciate the achievements of a peaceful regime. Separatism, ghettoization, ethnic differences and rhetorics of particularism[50] are the consequences. Only the solidarity that—without being legally enforced—is freely desired prevents the liberal constitutional state from eroding into a conglomerate of isolated and selfish "monads who only point their subjective rights at each other like weapons."[51] Indeed, it is precisely because of this participation of the individual as part of humanity that Kant rejects a utilitarian understanding of the state that is founded on the principle of happiness. "The best form of government is not the one under which it is most comfortable to live (eudaemonia), but the one under which the rights of the citizen are most secure."[52]

3. The Transformation to Cosmopolitan Civil Rights

The universalization of freedom graduating from the national to the international legal system—thus, the transition from classical international law to what Kant calls the "cosmopolitan condition"—is the final link in the chain of freedom. To the same extent that national sovereignty declines, international regulations or a transnational legal system become necessary.[53] In the tradition of Kant's cosmopolitanism, an international system of collective security can only be established through the peacemaking effect of a legal condition that is multilateral; otherwise, it would only remain limited to the international protective measures of an imperial liberalism (or a hegemonic unilateralism[54] in the tradition of John Stuart Mill's liberal nationalism).

Such an international legal system should not just simply be understood as an extension of the national legal system—in the sense of an expansion of its sphere of influence. If one understands the transnational legal system to be just an extension of the national one, then one easily overlooks that it only comes into existence by feeding back into each respective national legal system, which certainly can not just be grafted on to it. This genesis of an international legal system has its origin in national law and this, in turn, in individual law—but as it develops, it has also repercussions on the continued existence of national, indeed even individual laws, out of whose transformations it eventually acquires legitimacy. At this point, the chain of freedom comes to an end.

Kant's idea becomes plausible if one rises to the challenge that the current idea of so-called 'democratization from the outside' entails.[55] The democratization of systems of rule that ought to contribute towards global security and stability is no longer aspired to through the classical policies of defence or balance of power (Metternich), but through the policy of peace that makes partners (and not just those who are conquered) out of enemies, by integrating them into a democratic system of mutual cooperation. This democratization from the outside is a process which turns the evolving chain of freedom upside down: the influence does not spread from bottom up, but from top down; it does not affect the individual first, but the political system that can decentralize, break down its hierarchies and, at worst, destabilize it. From the point of view of international law, the protection of state sovereignty and the necessity of intervention in domestic affairs are incompatible with each other: democracy and republicanism become polarized.[56] But this destabilization and social polarization[57] is nevertheless necessary during a phase of system transformation, because they stimulate the process of democracy which grinds to a halt because of state hierarchies and power structures. The effect which promotes democracy consists, on the one hand, in taking away the external threat from a system of rule, and with it the pressure exerted on its borders, whereby this pressure can be integrated into an interactive space of power distribution; on the other hand, it consists in developing the internal strengths of democratization and freedom and in enhancing these from the national to the international level—by making out of the legal citizen of a particular state, a legal person of a "common cosmopolitan entity".[58] Kant explicitly addresses both these aspects when he makes the "perfect civil constitution (...) dependent on the problem of a law-governed relations among states"[59]—and not the other way round.

It is just as unlikely that an island of democracy—such as that which ought to emerge in the Near East—can exist as a bastion of democracy that sees itself as a kind of universal monarchy of freedom in the line of succession to the Roman Empire. Not one single utopian world state, but rather the multiplicity of sovereign states that are united in a "large future federation of states"[60] can become a reality through a *peaceful* process of mutual cooperation. For Kant, this future "federation of states" is (only) a "negative surrogate"[61] for the idea of a world republic, because to him plurality is of a higher order than conformity. But neither is it just a loose collection of states that, in case of doubt, can revoke the federal association in favour of the national state, because otherwise its freedom would be endangered. What matters to Kant is the *individual citizen* and his transformation from a national citizen into a citizen of the world. For only as a citizen of the world does he first achieve *the* degree of institutional protection to which the universal claim of the categorical imperative has already entitled him.

Kant's idea of a cosmopolitan civil state is directly derived from the moral principle with which all rational subjects must comply if they want to regard themselves as free. This maxim also restricts the sovereignty of states if they expand to become a cosmopolitan civil state. The sovereign states which unite themselves in the federal state structure of a cosmopolitan civil state "buy the authorization for their national citizens to be world citizens at the cost of mediating their own status."[62]

So is it a duty of democratic states to establish an international legal system?[63] With reference to Kant's moral principle, one must definitely answer 'yes' to this question: the dissent between national jurisdiction and an international legal system can only be resolved in principle by referring back to the moral core of human rights that must be maintained even if these are *contrary* to the constraints of one's own culture.

There is a particular problem here that raises the question of which authority is to be attributed with the required neutrality, when it comes to assessing moral principles or abstract legal principles within the terms of a political act that commits itself to a cosmopolitan intent. In Kant's opinion, this conflict, which already recurs constantly between law and politics, can only be resolved in favour of the formulation of moral demands and objectives when the *public*—that is, publicity and the media—take on the function of a critical corrective. In Kant's later philosophy, the public is given the status of an informal institution which should keep the scope for action open. This should prevent politics from escaping into the idealism of the law, as well as prevent the law from being corrupted by political calculation. The forum of the world public demands a dimension of thought that involves anybody's standpoint[64] —that is, a dimension that lives up to the maxim of generalization that we should think in the categorical imperative.

But at the same time we must be warned about an idealistic overestimation here. When Kant says in his "transcendental formula ratified under public law"[65] that only those political maxims may be followed which need publicity in order to fulfil their aim—he does not mean that an automaticity could be implemented. The pluralistic consensus is only a possibility of an understanding that provides perspective and which is only entitled to the role of a critical inspection and corrective authority. A nascent world public is easily tempted to consider itself to be a cosmopolitan society already, because through it—as Kant says—"the violation of rights in *one* place on the earth is felt throughout the world."[66] However, as an individual, one can never represent the point of universality;[67] just like the "positive idea of a world republic", it has to be replaced by a "negative surrogate".[68]

This brings the argumentation back to the metaphysical core of the Kantian concept of freedom upon which the entire chain of freedom is based: the *real* position of universality is the position of freedom that *is at the root of* all our thoughts and actions—a position that always ought to be, but never becomes real, which always should be, but never become real. and although this is never really the case, it always should be. It is not a position that can be coerced; neither has it the function of a 'super-self' to which one must be subordinated. Thus, an ethical neutrality or indifference towards this position of freedom is just as morally unthinkable as the possibility of refusing to accept it. The laborious process of establishing human freedom, which the gradual legalization of human rights entails, is *always* accompanied by shortcomings and the suspicion that the world cannot be morally better anyway. But this is not an objection that can be raised against freedom.

The moral imperative is a promise that is not subject to temporal conditions. Along with it, the only thing that can be proclaimed is what follows in its wake. From an existential philosophical point of view, one has to say: we have *already* decided and we must always—more or less adequately—abide by this decision. Kant deliberately throws us back into the crisis of modernity when he considers the discovery of freedom itself as a crisis. The *moral* decision alone—in its totally indispensable necessity—is the only self-aware relation to this location where a timeless act takes place; it accomplishes the paradox of supreme free choice, which consists in adopting what one has been chosen for. In this respect, Schelling, who developed the Kantian metaphysics of freedom further, says: "Only thus is a beginning possible—a beginning that never ceases to be a beginning, a truly endless beginning. For it is also essential that the beginning must not know itself. Once an act has been done, it has been done forever. The decision that ought to somehow make a truly new beginning must not re-enter one's consciousness—not be recalled—which would effectively mean cancelling it. Whoever reserves for himself the option of reviewing a decision never makes a beginning."[69]

NOTES AND REFERENCES

1. Letter of May 9, 1768 (Kant *Acad.-Ed.* X, 74; all translations are mine unless indicated otherwise).
2. Kant *KdpV* V, 107.
3. Cf. my essay *Antimelacholische Kritik. Kants Theorie des Erhabenen und die Verengung des Vernunftgebrauchs zum unausbleiblichen Erfolg.* In: Kant-Studien 87 (1996), pp. 42-68.
4. Kant remained true to this methodological approach right up to his last writings: "Diese Antinomie der Vernunft setzt sie nicht allein in einen Zweifel des Mitrauens gegen die eine sowohl als die andre dieser ihrer Behauptungen, welches doch noch die Hoffnung eines so oder anders entscheidenden Urtheiles ḷbrig l¤t, sondern in eine Verzweiflung der Vernunft an sich selbst, allen Anspruch auf Gewiheit aufzugeben, welches man den Zustand des dogmatischen Scepticismus nennen kann. / Aber dieser Kampf der Vernunft mit sich selbst hat das Besondre an sich, da diese sich ihn als einen Zweikampf denkt, in welchem sie, wenn sie den Angriff thut, sicher ist, den Gegner zu schlagen, so fern sie aber sich vertheidigen soll, ebenso gewi, geschlagen zu werden. Mit andern Worten: sie kann sich nicht so sehr darauf verlassen, ihre Behauptung zu beweisen, als vielmehr die des Gegners zu widerlegen, welches gar nicht sicher ist, indem wohl alle Beide falsch urtheilen möchten, oder auch, da wohl Beide Recht haben möchten, wenn sie nur ḷber den Sinn der Frage allererst einverstanden w¤ren" (Kant *Welches sind die wirklichen Fortschritte* (1796), 3. Manuscript, edited by F. Th. Rink, 1804, XX, 327).
5. Kant *KdrV* B XIV.
6. Otfried Höffe placed this methodological feature of critical transcendental philosophy—that it creates legal peace—back at

the center of critical philosophy. "Philosophisch aufschlureicher ist ein Kritikalphabet, das das Gleichrgewicht nicht einer List der Vernunft lberl¤t, die auf dem Markt der öffentlichen Diskurse beiden Seiten zu ihrem (relativen) Recht und dem Ganzen zur Balance verhilft. Systematisch lberzeugender ist eine Kritik, die das Gleichgewicht zum Thema macht und aus sich heraus beides leistet, je nachdem die Emanzipation oder aber die Affirmation. In dieser sowohl inhaltlichen als auch intentional und methodisch neutralen, eben judikativen Kritik, liegt nicht, was Habermas beflrchtet: ein zu hoher Anspruch. Als Richterin entzieht sich die Philosophie der Suggestion einer einfachen Alternative 'Emanzipation oder Affirmation' und presentiert sich als eine 'dritte Option'." (Otfried Höffe: *Kategorische Rechtsprinzipien. Ein Kontrapunkt der Moderne.* Frankfurt am Main 1995, in particular pp. 33-50).

7. In order to bring about peace in the dispute in metaphysics, according to Kant—as he explicates in the *Doctrine of Method* in the *Critique of Pure Reason*—the *dogmatic* method is not necessary, because it "deceives philosophy" (*KdrV* B 765, 2. edition), nor is the *polemic* method, which is only a "dogmatic unification of the same thing" (*KdpV* B 767), but neither is "scepticism", which only wants to "establish (...) a doctrine of doubt" (*Refl.* 5037, XVIII, 69); rather, the *critical* or "sceptical method" (*KdrV* B 451), which alone remains, is "on a sure footing (...) dadurch da sie in einem solchen auf beiden Seiten redlich gemeinten und mit Verstande geflhrten Streite den Punkt des Miverst¤ndnisses zu entdecken sucht, um, wie weise Gesetzgeber thun, aus der Verlegenheit der Richter bei Rechtsh¤ndeln flr sich selbst Belehrung von dem Mangelhaften und nicht genau Bestimmten in ihren Gesetzen zu ziehen" (B 451 ff.).
8. Kant writes about the sceptical method, which he clearly differentiates from scepticism in his autobiographical reflections, in this sense: "Ich versuchte es gantz ernstlich, Satze zu beweisen und ihr Gegentheil, nicht um eine Zweifellehre zu errichten, sondern weil ich eine illusion des Verstandes vermuthete, zu entdecken, worin sie steke" (Kant *Acad.-Ed.* XVIII, 69).
9. Kant differentiates scepticism in his work even as early as *Reflection 3706*: "Das heisst nicht philosophiren, wenn man lediglich darzuthun sucht, da etwas wie ein Wahn, eine T¤uschung des Verstandes sey, sondern man mu auch einsehen lernen, wie eine solche t¤uschung moglich w¤r[e]" (Kant *Acad.-Ed.* XVII, 242).
10. Cf. Spinoza, *Ethics*, all possibilities are actualities: 43. 7 (I. 16 cor.1),

56. 2 (I. 33 sch. 2), 56. 8 (I. 35), 62. 5 (App. to Part I), 66. 9 (II. 7 cor); Leibniz, *Discourse* ṣ 3; Descartes, *Meditations* 110.4.

11. Kant *Idea for a Universal History with Cosmopolitan Intent* A 404 (= 8th Sentence).
12. Kant *Contest of the Faculties* A 132 (transl. after ed. Reiss, p. 177).
13. To give an example: Kant's theorem of "unsocial sociability", that he introduces in sentence 4 of his essay *Idea for a Universal History with Cosmopolitan Intent*, creates a potential for conflict whose peculiarity consists in interpreting even unethical behaviour as expedient for historical process, but without legitimizing this unethical behaviour as such. Kant interprets this kind of fictionalization of history as a motive for its own authentification of the idea of freedom.
14. Kant *Contest of the Faculties* A 142.
15. In the early reflections of the 1770s, Kant does not explicitly exclude the metaphysical dimension as well from this conception of freedom. He still writes in the Poelitz-postscript of his lectures on metaphysics: "Das Ich beweiset aber, dass ich selbst handele; *ich* bin ein Prinzip und kein Principatum (...). Dadurch dass das Subjekt libertatem absolutam hat, weil es sich bewut ist, beweiset es, da es nicht subjetcum patiens, sondern agens sei (...)" (Kant *Vorlesungen ḷber die Metaphysik.* Ed. v. Poelitz. Erfurt 1821; Reprint 1964, p. 206).
16. Kant first stresses the anti-metaphysical characteristic of his deduction in the *Deduction* of moral law in the *Groundwork* (1785) in stating that "die Frage also, wie ein kategorischer Imperativ möglich sei, (...) so weit beantwortet werden [kann], als man die einzige Voraussetzung angeben kann, unter der er allein möglich ist, n¤mlich die Idee der Freiheit, (...) aber wie diese Voraussetzung selbst möglich sei, l¤t sich durch keine menschliche Vernunft jemals einsehen" (IV, 461).
17. In the *Critique of Practical Reason*, Kant explicitly avoids talking about consequences that result from determining the will. The only place where he does this, V 24, only serves to reject *blissful happinesss* as a possible consequence of absolutely determining the will.
18. This doctrine of the transcendental act characterizes the "stumbling block for all *empiricists*," writes Kant in the *Critique of Practical Reason* B 13.
19. Cf. Klaus Dḷsing: Spontaneit¤t und Freiheit in Kants praktischer Philosophie. In: Klaus Dḷsing., Subjektivit¤t und Freiheit. Stuttgart/Bad-Canstatt: fromann-holzboog 2002, pp. 211-236.

20. Kant *KdpV* V, 42; cf. also V, 31.
21. Kant *KdpV* V, 42; A 72.
22. Kant *KdpV* V, 86.
23. Cf. Kant *Contest of Faculties* VII, 58.
24. Kant *Religion Within the Limits of Reason Alone* VI, 57.
25. Schelling *Philosophical Inverstigations* VII, 390 ff.
26. Kant *On a Supposed Right to Tell Lies from Benevolent Motives* (1797) VIII, 426.
27. Kant *Metaphysics of Morals* VI, 233.
28. Kant *Metaphysics of Morals* VI, 225, 230.
29. Kant *Metaphysics of Morals* VI, 230.
30. Kant *Perpetual Peace* VIII, 350.
31. Since "what is right in accordance with external laws" is "just (iustum)" (Kant *Metaphysik der Sitten* VI, 224), the precondition for "a respectable (iusti) person" is an "authority" that lies "inherently in the principle of innate freedom" (Kant ibid., VI, 238).
32. Kant *Metaphysics of Morals* VI, 231.
33. Kant *Letters* (to Heinrich Jung-Stilling – 1789, Nr. 347).
34. "Nicht schlechthin ist das Bestehen öffentlicher Gewalten gerecht, sondern nur sekund¤r und subsidi¤r zu einer – im groen und ganzen – gerechten Rechtsordnung" (Otfried Höffe: *Gerechtigkeit als Tausch? Zum politischen Projekt der Moderne.* Baden-Baden: Nomos 1991, p. 34).
35. Kant *Perpetual Peace* VIII, 379: "The god of morality does not yield to Jupiter, the custodian of violence, for even Jupiter is still subject to fate. In short, reason is not sufficiently englightened to discover the whole series of predetermining causes which would allow it to predict accurately the happy or unhappy consequences of human activities as dictated by the mechanism of nature; it can only hope that the result will meet with its wishes, But reason at all times shows us clearly enough what we have to do in order to remain in the paths of duty, as the result of wisdom require, and thus shows us the way towards our ultimate goal" (Kant *Perpetual Peace VIII*, 370, transl. after ed. Reiss).
36. Kant *Perpetual Peace* VIII, 370; B 72.
37. Kant *Perpetual Peace* VIII, 380.
38. Kant *Metaphysics of Morals* XIII, 345.
39. Kant *Perpetual Peace* VIII, 371.
40. Kant *Metaphysics of Morals* ș B. VI, 230.
41. Kant *Religion Within the Limits of Reason Alone* VI, 97.
42. The only legislator for whom the laws that govern virtue are at

the same time those that govern justice, i.e. "all *true obligations* (...) must be understood as his commandments", is God as the moral ruler of the world.

43. The opposite is also valid: "Gewissenlosigkeit ist nicht Mangel des Gewissens, sondern Hang sich an dessen Urtheil nicht zu kehren" (Kant *Metaphysics of Morals* VI, 401).
44. Kant *Contest of Faculties* VII, 91.
45. Cf. Kant *Metaphysics of Morals* VI, 218 ff. Ethics and legality differ only with regard to their driving force or motivation (Kant: "Nötigung"); for a legal act, an "external (legal) freedom" (Kant VIII, 350), can admittedly be in agreement with the maxims of a moral legislation, but it does not have to happen out of obligation.
46. Kant *Metaphysics of Morals* VI, 230.
47. For Kant, the ideal form of government is—according to an ancient linguistic use of the word—the republican. He rejects the democratic form with the argument that—as the counterpart to the monarchic—it only leads to despotism headed by the people [Volksdespotismus]. But the government ought to (in the modern understanding of a representative democracy) unite "the wills of all the people" (*What is Enlightment* VIII, 40) within itself through a "representative system" (*Perpetual Peace* VIII, 353). For Kant, the state is "a society of people over which nobody other than itself has command or at its disposal" (*Perpetual Peace* VIII, 344). Thus, the decision to wage war can only be a legitimate decision if "citizens decide about it for themselves" (*Perpetual Peace* VIII, 351), and therefore it "requires (...) the "approval of the citizens" (ibid.). This idea of government is very similar to the modern constitutional state. "A government that would be founded on the principle of goodwill against the people, like a father against his children" is for Kant " the biggest despotism imaginable" (*On the Common Saying* VIII, 290 ff.).
48. Cf. Wolfgang Böckenförde: *Die Entstehung des Staates als Vorgang der S¤kularisation* (1967). In: W. Böckenförde, Recht, Staat, Freiheit. Frankfurt am Main: Suhrkamp 1991, p. 91 ff.
49. See my essay: *The Moral Image of History. Kant's Theory of a Historical Sign.* Paper presented at the Beijing International Symposium on Kant's Moral Philosophy in Contemporary Perspectives. Peking University, May 2004.
50. "Eine Rhetorik des Partikularismus verhindert die Artikulation der universalistischen Restmotive, auf die gerade derjenige sich heute zu stltzen hat, dem die Verteidigung des kulturellen Pluralismus entschieden am Herzen liegt" (Axel Honneth in

Merkur No. 512, November 1991).

51. Jḷrgen Habermas: *Zur Diskussion mit Kardinal Ratzinger*. In: Information Philosophie. Oktober 2004, No. 4, pp. 7-15, here p. 10.
52. Kant *Postscript* XXIII, 257.
53. On the other hand, whoever has doubts about the mandatory nature of a global human rights system or at least a transnational code of ethics, falls back on the values that one's national state provides as orientation and on one's cultural-political conception of oneself, if one is still so liberal within one's national borders. The sceptic who contests a global legal system uses an argument that Thomas Hobbes has already proposed: only that state that, like a dragon (Leviathan), wages war externally against all other states can internally maintain an artificially organized order which guarantees the freedom of the individual at most. Macchiavelli has already proposed the tenet that it is only possible to manage a form of order that preserves freedom by adopting policies of maximum deterrence. These positions cannot provide a reason for this scepticism with regard to a global law-governed peace. The war of nations has, like the natural state among people, the status of a self-evident principle. Given this precondition, the domestic ethics of a national state cannot be extended to the intergovernmental level. Kant concludes: the principles that hold good for the peaceful coexistence of people are extendable; they also hold good for the peaceful coexistence of nations. There are not two different codes of ethics, as Hume asserts—one that applies to relations between people, and another to relations between nations—on the contrary, both are in principle the same. The scepticism with regard to a globalizing code of ethics, that exists in the conceptions of Hobbes and Macchiavelli, is transformed by Kant into its opposite: only a code of ethics whose principles hold good beyond the borders of the community and the state are also good for the coexistence of people (cf. in detail the typology of this scepticism proposed by Wolfgang Kersting in a "kosmopolitischen Kognitivismus", "geltungstheoretischen Kontextualismus" and the scepticism of the "Sonderethikthese" (Wolfgang Kersting: *Recht, Gerechtigkeit und demokratische Tugend. Abhandlungen zur praktischen Philosophie der Gegenwart.* Frankfurt am Main 1997, pp. 243-256).
54. Just like it has been raised to the level of a political doctrine in the USA since 1991 (cf. Stefan Fröhlich in the *Frankfurter Allgemeinen Zeitung*, 10. April 2003).
55. Cf. Ernst-Otto Czepiel: *Demokratisierung von_auen*. In: Merkur. Deutsche Zeitschrift fḷr europ¤isches Denken. Issue 4, Year 58,

June 2004, pp. 467-479.

56. One can see a lack of clarity in Kant's conception here. On the one hand, the universal legal principles target a cosmopolitan solution; on the other hand, they conflict with the verdict of the legal autonomy and sovereignty of the state which achieves the status of an empirical premiss from the cosmopolitan aspect of the solution (cf. M. Lutz-Bachmann, J. Bohmann (eds.): *Frieden durch Recht. Kants Friedensidee und das Problem einer neuen Weltordnung.* Frankfurt am Main 1996). This problematic can only really be resolved genetically: the lawful sovereignty of an individual state is the precondition for a sovereign international law that, in the course of its concrete definition, can and must in turn limit the legal sovereignty of the individual state in favour of the legal relations between states (cf. W. Kersting: *Philosophische Friedenstheorie und internationale Friedensordnung.* In: ibid., Recht, Gerechtigkeit und demokratische Tugend. Abhandlungen zur praktischen Philosophie der Gegenwart. Frankfurt am Main 1997. Kersting resolves the problematic by graduating the different forms of sovereignty (p. 332 ff.)). A difficulty here is raised by the question of whether, as with human rights, there also have to be national rights (in the sense of basic rights) that must remain inalienable and, therefore, may not be tampered with by the united will of the nations either. Ottfried Höffe writes in this way about a "human right of states" (Otfried Höffe (ed.): *Immanuel Kant: Zum ewigen Frieden.* Berlin: Akademie Verlag, 1995, p. 116f.). Moreover, the problem contains potential for conflict with regard to how the sovereignty of a state can be limited in favour of the welfare of all states, if at the same time this state is interested in extending its power so that it can exercise the role of a supervisory power on a global level. This conflict, which is currently being fought out during the process of uniting Europe, will also become increasingly more important in the relations between Europe and the USA, because it requires that criteria for an intervention policy be demanded of the USA.
57. The political left, which is universalistic, neutral, emancipated and ideologically critical, and the political right, which is anti-universalistic, religious, patriotic and particular, will thus both become responsive as the two sides of a *single* position between the particular and the universal claim to legitimacy.
58. Kant *On the Common Saying* VIII, 311.
59. Kant *Idea for a Universal History with Cosmopolitan Intent* VIII, 24.
60. Kant *Idea for a Universal History with Cosmopolitan Intent* VIII, 128.

61. Ibid.
62. Jḷrgen Habermas: *Der gespaltene Westen*. Frankfurt am Main 2004, p. 123.
63. The vision of Hardt and Negeri (M. Hardt/A. Negri: *Empire*. Harvard: Harvard University Press 2002), that an empire of globally effective economic and cultural logic with no capital could arise, only becomes an acceptable vision if this decentralization of power is accompanied by an elimination of the state from law-governed relations whose internationalization, nevertheless, also has repercussions on the positive right of the national laws. For in this way, the Kantian vision—the vision of an understanding of the law whose principles retain their validity beyond the borders of the state also generally holding good for the coexistence of people—would be realized. The test of internationalization therefore has the same function as the generalizing maxim of the categorical imperative.
64. "Eine Weltöffentlichkeit setzt genau jene Form unbegrenzter Kommunikation voraus, die Kants Ideal des gemeinen Menschenverstandes verlangt" (James Bohman: *Die ffentlichkeit des Weltbḷrgers: śber Kants Çnegatives Surrogat'*. In: M. Lutz-Bachmann et al., Frieden durch Recht. Ibid., p. 95.
65. Kant *Perpetual Peace* VIII, 381.
66. Kant *Perpetual Peace* VIII, 360.
67. The "post-political, multicultural universe of tolerance of all differences, from which nobody is excluded", is not a *real* tolerance of the "negotiated coexistence of different groups"; rather, it joins forces "with its radical opposite, with the thoroughly contingent outbreaks of [right-wing] violence" (Slavoj Zizek: *Ein Pledoyer fḷr Intoleranz*. Vienna 2001, 2nd edition, p. 42f.). Slavoj Zizek has criticized the half-baked multiculturalism of radical liberalism as a hidden form of capitalistic colonialism—a position that deals with *every* local culture from a kind of empty global standpoint in the same way that the colonialist treats his colonial subjects. (ibid., p. 70).
68. Kant *Perpetual Peace* VIII, 360.
69. F.W.J. Schelling: *Die Weltalter. Fragmente.* In the original versions from 1811 and 1813, ed. Manfred Schroeter, Munich: Biederstein (reprint 1979), p. 102. The central idea of Schelling's theology of freedom is that man's identification with God is only confirmed in and by God's radical self-reliance—a position that makes precisely the *negative theology* into a modern and open theology that surpasses the frontiers dividing religions.

List of Contributors

Bijoy H. Boruah is retired Professor of Philosophy at the Department of Humanities and Social Sciences, Indian Institute of Technology, Delhi. Earlier, from 1986 till 2010, he was teaching at Indian Institute of Technology, Kanpur. He was a Fellow of Indian Institute of Advanced Study in 1997 and Fulbright Senior Fellow at the University of Texas at Austin in 2000-2001. He has published widely in the areas of philosophical aesthetics, philosophy of mind, ethics and value theory, and metaphysics of the self.

Wenjing Cai is Associate Professor at the School of Humanity, Shanghai Jiao Tong University. Her research interests include issues of reflection, subjectivity and methodology in the tradition of phenomenology and contemporary philosophy. She has published in journals such as *Husserl Studies*, *Human Studies*, and *Journal of the British Society for Phenomenology*.

David Carr is Charles Howard Candler Professor Emeritus at Emory University (Atlanta) and Adjunct Professor of Philosophy at the New School for Social Research, New York City. His areas of research are 20th century phenomenology, especially Husserl; theory of historical narrative; and philosophy of history. He is the author of *Phenomenology and the Problem of History* (1974, reissued in 2009); *Time, Narrative and History* (1986); *Interpreting Husserl* (1987); *The Paradox of Subjectivity* (1999); and *Experience and History* (2014)

Amita Chatterjee is Professor Emeritus at Jadavpur University, Kolkata and was the Editor-in-Chief of the *Journal of Indian Council of Philosophical Research* till 2017. She is the Second Vice President of the Division of Logic, Methodology,

Philosophy, History of Science and Technology (DLMPST) of International Council of Sciences. She was National Fellow (2012-2014), Indian Council of Philosophical Research, New Delhi, Professor of Philosophy and Co-ordinator of the Centre for Cognitive Science, Jadavpur University. She was the first Vice-Chancellor of Presidency University, Kolkata. Widely published, her areas of research include logic (Indian and Western), fusion philosophy, philosophies of logic, language, mind and cognitive science. As part of her academic engagements, she has researched and taught at universities in the U.K., Europe, U.S.A. and across India.

Tal Correm is a Postdoctoral Faculty Fellow in Liberal Studies at New York University. Her research focuses on the intersection of political philosophy and ethics, specifically with relation to political violence in democratic transition. She explores issues in constitutional theory, reconciliation, and transitional justice. Other areas of interest include comparative philosophy, especially the dialogue between phenomenology and Indian philosophy, aesthetics, and continental philosophy.

Christian Coseru is Professor of Philosophy at the College of Charleston and Editor of the Springer Series in Cross-cultural Philosophy of Traditions and Cultures. He works primarily on philosophy of mind, phenomenology, and cross-cultural philosophy, especially Indian and Buddhist philosophy in dialogue with Western philosophy and cognitive science. He is the author of *Perceiving Reality: Consciousness, Intentionality, Cognition in Buddhist Philosophy* (OUP, 2012) and *Moments of Consciousness* (forthcoming with Oxford University Press).

Hans Feger is Adjunct Professor for Philosophy at Free University Berlin. He specializes in German idealism, existentialism, moral philosophy and aesthetics in an intercultural context. His recent publications are: Die Macht der Einbildungskraft in der ṇsthetik Kants und Schillers (1995, Japanese translation 1996); Poetische Vernunft. Moral und ṇsthetik im Deutschen Idealismus (2007); Handbuch fḷr Literatur und Philosophie (2012). He has published numerous books as editor and many articles on practical philosophy, German literature, moral theory and aesthetics. He coordinates the

German-Asian Graduate Group of Humanities at Free University Berlin and is the international editor of the *Yearbook for Eastern and Western Philosophy*.

Jonardon Ganeri is a philosopher whose work draws on a variety of philosophical traditions to construct new positions in the philosophy of mind, metaphysics and epistemology. He is the author of *Attention, Not Self*; *The Self*; *The Concealed Art of the Soul*; *The Lost Age of Reason*; and *Semantic Powers*, all published by Oxford University Press. He joined the Fellowship of the British Academy in 2015, and won the Infosys Prize in the Humanities the same year. *Open Minds* magazine named him of its 50 global "open minds" for 2016.

Siby K. George is Professor of Philosophy at the Department of Humanities and Social Sciences, Indian Institute of Technology, Bombay. His area of interest is contemporary European philosophy. He writes on themes such as development, technology, pain and dying, political ethics, education and subjectivity from a phenomenological vantage point, specifically emphasizing Indian and nonwestern contexts. He is author of *Heidegger and Development in the Global South* (Springer, 2015), and one of the editors of *Cultural Ontology of the Self in Pain* (Springer, 2016).

Matthew MacKenzie is Professor of Philosophy at Colorado State University, USA. He specializes in Buddhist philosophy, classical Indian philosophy, and the philosophy of mind. His primary research is at the intersection of Buddhist philosophy and contemporary philosophy of mind, with a special focus on consciousness, self-consciousness, embodiment, and the self. His articles have appeared in *Philosophy East and West*, *Phenomenology and the Cognitive Sciences*, *Asian Philosophy*, and *Journal of Consciousness Studies*, among other journals. He has contributed chapters to several volumes including *The Oxford Handbook of Virtue*, *The Bloomsbury Handbook of Indian Epistemology and Metaphysics*, and *Self, No Self? Perspectives from Analytical, Phenomenological, and Indian Traditions*.

T.V. Madhu is Professor of Philosophy, University of Calicut, Kerala. He specializes in philosophy of the body, self and the other and recent issues in Continental philosophy. He has published widely in various issues in Continental philosophy; edited a special issue of Indian Philosophical Quarterly (IPQ) entitled *Theorizing the Body;* and has authored two books in Malayalam on Neo-Marxist thought and on the question of self and the other.

Nishad Patnaik is a visiting Assistant Professor of Philosophy at the Centre for Exact Humanities, International Institute of Information Technology, Hyderabad. His research interests include German idealism, phenomenology, Marx and critical theory, and ethics.

Ramesh Chandra Pradhan is retired Professor in the Department of Philosophy, University of Hyderabad. He has been engaged in teaching and research for the last forty years or so. Widely published in the major areas of contemporary analytic philosophy, he specializes in analytic philosophy, philosophy of language and mind, and Wittgenstein. Of late he has developed interest in metaphysics of self and consciousness.

C.A. Tomy is Professor of Philosophy in the Department of Humanities and Social Sciences, Indian Institute of Technology, Delhi. Prior to joining IIT Delhi, he taught at IIT Kanpur and Goa University. His research and teaching interests are in the areas of philosophy of mind, epistemology and history of early and late modern philosophy.

Ajay Verma is Associate Professor of Philosophy at Jawaharlal Nehru University, New Delhi. His areas of interest include continental philosophy, Indian philosophy, comparative philosophy and Ambedkar studies. He has authored and edited books in these areas. He has also published several articles and research papers in national and international journals.